Getting the Donkey Out of the Ditch

Getting the Donkey Out of the Ditch

THE DEMOCRATIC PARTY IN SEARCH OF ITSELF

Caroline Arden

Contributions in Political Science
Number 224

Greenwood Press
New York • Westport, Connecticut • London

Soc
JK
2317
1988

Library of Congress Cataloging-in-Publication Data

Arden, Caroline.
  Getting the donkey out of the ditch : the Democratic Party in
search of itself / Caroline Arden.
    p.   cm.—(Contributions in political science, ISSN 0147–1066
; no. 224)
  Bibliography: p.
  Includes index.
  ISBN 0–313–25838–4 (lib. bdg. : alk. paper)
  1. Democratic Party (U.S.)   2. United States—Politics and
government—1945–   I. Title.   II. Series.
JK2317   1988
324.2736—dc 19   88-10253

British Library Cataloguing in Publication Data is available.

Library of Congress Catalog Card Number: 88–10253
ISBN: 0–313–25838–4
ISSN: 0147–1066

First published in 1988

Greenwood Press, Inc.
88 Post Road West, Westport, Connecticut   06881

Printed in the United States of America

∞

The paper used in this book complies with the
Permanent Paper Standard issued by the National
Information Standards Organization (Z39.48–1984).

10   9   8   7   6   5   4   3   2   1

Acknowledgments

The author and publisher are grateful to the following for granting permission to quote from their works or statements:

Bringing Back the Parties by David E. Price. Copyright 1984, Congressional Quarterly Inc. Used by permission of the publisher.

The Congressional Party: A Case Study by David B. Truman. Copyright 1959, David B. Truman. Used by permission of the author.

Consequences of Party Reform by Nelson W. Polsby. Copyright 1983, Nelson W. Polsby. Used by permission of the author.

"The Democrats" by Elizabeth Drew in *The New Yorker*, 22 March 1983. Reprinted by permission.

Parties and Politics in America by Clinton Rossiter. Copyright 1960, Cornell University Press, Ithaca, New York. Used by permission of the publisher.

Party Committees and National Politics by Hugh A. Bone. Copyright 1958, University of Washington Press, Seattle, Washington. Used by permission of the publisher.

Party Government by E. E. Schattschneider. Copyright 1942, Holt, Rinehart & Winston, New York. Used by permission of the publisher.

Party Organizations and American Politics by Cornelius P. Crotter, James L. Gibson, John F. Bibby, and Robert J. Huckshorn. Copyright 1984, Praeger, New York. Used by permission of the publisher.

Party Renewal in America: Theory and Practice, Gerald M. Pomper, editor. Copyright 1981, Praeger, New York. Used by permission of the publisher.

"Political Journal" by Eliazbeth Drew. In *The New Yorker*, 28 March 1983. Reprinted by permission.

Political Reform and the American Experiment by William J. Crotty. Copyright 1977, Thomas Y. Crowell Co., New York. Used by permission of the publisher.

"Politics and Money, Part I" by Elizabeth Drew. In *The New Yorker*, 6 December 1982. Reprinted by permission.

The Politics of Congress by David J. Vogler. Copyright 1974, Allyn and Bacon, Newton, Massachusetts. Used by permission of the publisher.

Politics Without Power: The National Party Committees by Cornelius P. Cotter and Bernard C. Hennessy. Copyright 1964, Cornelius P. Cotter and Bernard C. Hennessy. Used by permission of the authors.

The Real Majority by Richard M. Scammon and Ben J. Wattenberg. Copyright 1970, Richard M. Scammon and Ben J. Wattenberg. Reprinted by permission of the Putnam Publishing Group and Harold Matson Co., Inc.

Republican Politics: The 1964 Campaign and Its Aftermath for the Party, Bernard Cosman and Robert J. Huckshorn, editors. Copyright 1968, Henry Holt & Co., New York. Used by permission of the publisher.

Sam Dawson, interview granted June 1982.

Sherry A. McGowan, interview granted June 1982.

Richard A. Pinaire, interview granted June 1982.

Jessie M. Ratley, interview granted June 1982.

Contents

Preface

The research for this study began on November 5, 1980, the day after the 1980 presidential election, as a stunned Democratic Party counted its losses. The presidency was lost by a popular vote of 41.0 percent, to the Republican's 50.8 percent; Senate control was lost, with a gain of twelve seats for the Republicans; and the House was shaken with a total loss of thirty-three Democratic seats. The 1980 election marked the first Republican control of either house of Congress since 1954. The research ended in 1987, covering the continued efforts of the Democrats to regain their party identity and their political power.

This is a case study of a major political party under extreme stress, showing in detail what that party actually *did* in the two years immediately following its humiliating defeat in 1980. Those events, and party actions of the ensuing five-year period (1982–87) that contribute to an understanding of the consequences of the reactions to that extreme stress, are noted in the Conclusion. Throughout the observation period, the Party was viewed as a dynamic political organism, capable of acting willfully.

The working hypothesis for this study was that the Democratic Party was under the most severe stress it had experienced in the twentieth century and that this stress was made severe not only by a palpable loss of an election, and the perceived (if not real) threat of a major party realignment, but also by the fact of the Democrat's long-term status as a majority party. The Democratic party system reacted to this stress in a highly random manner, and its search activity, though vigorous, was not productive or constructive. The study shows that in the two years following the 1980 election, the Democratic Party did not perform a fundamental or effective restoration of a unifying center. It seems that the Party, more from want of will than from want of power, was unable to use the information available to it. The Party never identified or assigned a locus of power, no "brain" or centralized switching system that could sort out the information and stimuli received by the various individuals and segments of the Party. They had literally lost their collective head and were not able to find the stability and identity they so frantically sought. One of the primary reasons for this failure to effect a recovery was the fact that the actors within the party system, both individually and in organizational or congressional groups, reacted to the problem limited by their own narrow perspectives and proprietary attitudes. The Democratic Party was also handicapped by its own recent history as a majority party and by its volatile organizational structure. The fact that the Party had become a mass party, governed not only by unintended consequences but also by amateurs, exacerbated the Party's stress and increased random, nonproductive behavior.

In conducting the study it was important to define the Democratic Party in terms of not only what it did, but also who did what and where. There were three clearly discernible separate, interacting, quasi-independent entities in the organic whole: (1) the organized national party, found in the Democratic National Committee; (2) the Congressional Party, a majority in the House and a confused minority in the Senate; and (3) the "extra-legal" party, made up of those groups that have a formal organization and control over membership and that attach themselves to the Democratic Party in a more or less continuous way. These extra-legal organizations tend to be intellectually ideological in nature, although many blend activism and even party fund-raising goals with their ideology. These are not necessarily "pressure groups," in that they do not coalesce around a single issue or a single occupational or ethnic group.

The rationale for this study stems from the belief that a healthy, competitive, "responsible" party system is a requisite of democratic politics in a modern state; therefore, it is important to monitor the vital signs and the therapy employed by a party when it is stricken. The hyperactivity of the wounded Democratic Party, with its symbolic donkey in the ditch, offers unique case evidence of how a party, under the stressful circumstances of losing its long-held majority status, behaved in its attempts to recover its former health and vigor.

Getting
the Donkey
Out of
the Ditch

1

The History of Reform, 1960s to 1980s

One measure of a revolution is the volume of commentary concerning causes and consequences that it generates. By that measure alone, the rapid changes since 1968 in the process of nominating candidates for President and the associated alterations in the party system merit being called "revolutionary." Participants in the "reform" movement, along with scholars and journalists, have produced a substantial literature on what has happened, why it has happened, and what the consequences have resulted for the political activists, the party system and the Republic.[1]

In order to understand many of the concerns and actions of the Democratic Party in its time of extreme stress in the early 1980s, it is necessary to know something of the history of the reforms put in place by the Party following another stressful time in the late 1960s and early 1970s. Turmoil was never a stranger to the Democratic Party. Chaos has frequently brought forth the best and the worst from the Party. What follows is a brief outline of the various commissions and committees put together by the National Party which changed the entire Party character in the twelve years prior to the startling 1980 defeat. No critical commentary on these reforms is given, for that has been done by others in definitive degree, as evidenced in the opening quotation by David Truman. This summary points to the nature of the commissions, their participants, their accomplishments, and the events that instigated their creation. Nelson Polsby argues that

changing the rules of politics changes the incentives for political actors; that changing the incentives leads to changes in political behavior; and that changing behavior changes political institutions and their significance in politics.[2]

It is not my purpose to defend or refute Polsby's thesis, but there is clear evidence that the Democratic Party *was* changed by the reforms and that much of what the Party was able to do after the reforms was affected and, in many cases, was limited by the Party's recent history.

A Demand for Equal Rights in the Early '60s

It is generally thought that the reforms of the Democratic Party were spawned in the chaos of the 1968 convention. However, their inception really began in the wake of the 1964 convention that nominated Lyndon Johnson. At that convention there were a number of challenges to the seating of delegates brought by problack forces from the South. William Crotty gives us this account of the activity:

> The most newsworthy of these unanticipated (and from the na-
> tional party's point of view, unwelcome) challenges involved the
> Mississippi Freedom Democratic Party, in particular. The recitation
> of racial abuses at the midpoint in an era of newfound civil rights
> awareness stimulated a good deal of publicity.[3]

Although some token representation was given to black delegates at that time, it was not enough to quell the rising discontent. In fact, the "tokenism" served merely to exacerbate the frustration felt by the black members of the Party, and the convention established the Special Equal Rights Committee. This group was first chaired by Gov. David Lawrence of Pennsylvania. At his untimely death in November 1966, the committee was taken over by Gov. Richard Hughes of New Jersey. The work of this committee would set the stage for the McGovern-Fraser Commission which followed four years later. The Special Equal Rights Committee produced what it called "six basic elements." These elements included a demand that all public meetings of the Democratic Party in each state be open to all members of the party, regardless of race, color, creed, or national origin; that no test for membership and no loyalty oath to the party be required or used to force acquiescence upon any party member to condone or support discrimination on any of these groups; that all meetings be widely publicized, and held in accessible places, large enough to accommodate all interested persons; that the Democratic Party at all levels support the broadest possible registration without discrim-ination; that the rules for selecting Party officers and representatives be widely publicized and the publications of all procedures be done in such a fashion that all members of the Party would have an opportunity to participate in such selection and elections; and that the Party in each state publicize and distribute the "legal and practical qualifications for all officers and representatives, so that all prospective candidates would have full opportunity to compete for office."[4] The Special Equal Rights Committee went further than just suggesting reform elements. As Crotty has noted, "The Special Committee circulated its six basic elements to the state parties during the summer of 1967 and informed them that they *must* enforce the rule or face disbarment from the next national gathering."[5] Crotty interprets this move on the part of the Special Committee as a "bold one," observing that "within a national party system notorious for its chaotic decentralization and lack of central direction, the seeds of revolution were being quietly sown."[6] The first resounding volleys of that revolution were heard and felt in Chicago in the August heat of 1968.

The McGovern–Fraser Commission and the O'Hara Commission

Much of what happened at the Chicago Democratic Convention in August 1968 was merely a microcosm of the broader unruly social and political upheaval of the entire nation at that time.[7] Just prior to the convention, an *ad hoc* committee, led by Gov. Harold Hughes of Iowa, formed to put the machinery in place to follow up on the recommendations of the other Hughes committee and to continue earlier work. This *ad hoc* group recommended the formation of two new committees to carry out further study and reform, and on the last night of the Chicago convention the delegates mandated the formation of one commission to study and improve upon delegate selection and one to codify the convention's laws and streamline its procedures: the Commission on Party Structure and Delegate Selection (otherwise known as the McGovern-Fraser Commission) and the Commission on Rules (the O'Hara Commission).

Although these two commissions were born simultaneously, there was little sibling relationship except for some jurisdictional rivalry. The O'Hara Commission made recommendations that would serve to spread power more evenly among delegations and would limit some of the arbitrary power of the National Party leaders, such as the convention chairman and the National Party chairman. Crotty sees the O'Hara Commission's greatest contribution in its recommendation calling for formal arbitration procedures in cases when credentials might be challenged. He notes that the reform "was little appreciated when first installed," but he points out that it served the Party well in the 1972 convention when there was a bitter fight over the seating of the handpicked delegation of Mayor Daley of Chicago.[8] Implicit in the charge to the O'Hara

Commission was the development of a party charter. However, the O'Hara group and the McGovern-Fraser Commission each saw such a charter within the scope of its own work. They skirmished over jurisdiction, but neither produced a finished document. David Price gives this account:

> The two commissions eventually cooperated in producing a draft charter on the eve of the 1972 convention. But the issues were too complex, the document too controversial, and the party's divisions too deep to permit the convention to deal with the proposal. Instead, a new commission was authorized to develop a party charter and bring it to the midterm convention in 1974.[9]

The new directive to hold a midterm convention in 1974 was one of the reform programs put in place by the 1972 convention as the delegates adopted the reports of the O'Hara and McGovern-Fraser commissions.

With its appointment in February 1969, the McGovern-Fraser Commission "began quickly and never stopped running."[10] George McGovern was chosen as chairman of the commission, and Harold Hughes of Iowa, the man whose committee had set the whole thing in motion, was chosen as vice-chairman. McGovern lost no time in appointing Robert W. Nelson, "a party professional with an extensive background in campaign management and government work as staff director."[11] Beginning on March 1, 1969, the twenty-eight-member commission began to hold a series of seventeen public hearings throughout the country. These meetings, held during the summer, produced testimony on abuses of party procedures in almost every state. The Democrats were washing their dirty linen in public, but for once they received only favorable review from the press for their efforts. They were able to show the public that the Democrats were willing to clean their own house, and support for the commission's efforts grew apace.

By September of 1969 the commission was ready to draft a set of proposals for "structuring a set of broad guidelines against which to measure each state's national convention delegate selection methods."[12] In November the commission adopted its set of eighteen guidelines and sent them out to the states for study and comment. The changes recommended were viewed as momentous by many and radical by some. They enlarged upon the work of the Special Equal Rights Committee and mandated representation of blacks, women, and young people, calling upon the states to take "affirmative steps" in ensuring representation in "reasonable relationship to the group's presence in the population of the state." Despite the commission's avowal that such was not its intent, it was from this recommendation that much of the controversy of "quotas" would arise and continue to haunt the Party for years to come. The commission included in its guidelines requirements for the states to adopt written rules for delegate selection and to remove mandatory assessments of delegates and to set filing fees at no more than ten dollars. The state parties were required to give timely public notice of all party meetings, primaries, and caucuses. Noteworthy among its recommendations was the elimination of the unit rule that allowed for winner-take-all primaries. Proxy voting was forbidden in delegate selection caucuses, and state committees were required to have a quorum of at least 40 percent or more of registered party members. The commission limited the number of delegates to be chosen directly by party committees to 10 percent of the state's delegation and recommended that committee selection by the state committee by eliminated entirely. Striking another blow at the party "professionals," the commission prohibited the *ex officio* designation of delegates to caucuses or conventions at any level. When the new guidelines were sent to the states in late November 1969 they were accompanied by two notices. One gave an individualized assessment of the state's existing regulations vis-à-vis the guidelines and indicated where improvement should be made in order for the state to comply. The second notice gave the state parties the firm warning that the guidelines, once adopted by the 1972 convention, would become mandatory.

The eighteen months from January 1970 until the 1972 convention in July were given over to implementing the guidelines. When McGovern resigned as chair of the commission to pursue the nomination for the presidency, Congressman Donald M. Fraser of Minnesota took over the leadership of the commission. When the 1972 convention convened, forty state parties and the District of Columbia were found to be in "full compliance" with the guidelines, and ten were in "substantial compliance."[13] Given the remarkable state acceptance of the McGovern-Fraser Commission guidelines, the Democratic Party had become what might be considered the political paradox of the century. It was now a "nationalized" party of amateurs. It had ceased to have its old character of a loose federation of state parties, governed by cadres of old-boy professionals. The ease with which the member states in the old "states rights" party acquiesced caused astonishment in many and dismay in some. Such obedience was not typical of Democratic Party behavior. However, Gary Wekkin has found that "cooperation is more common than conflict" and that "sometimes state parties even comply with rules that are anathema to them. Southern state parties have complied, however reluctantly, with affirmative action requirements since 1968."[14]

The Mikulski Commission of 1972

Although the states complied, they did not do it quite so meekly as the commission's assessment of compliance might lead us to believe.

McGovern's nomination, brought about by a convention that included more "amateurs" than ever before or since in the Party's history, and the disastrous campaign and loss by McGovern in 1972 brought strong reaction to the guidelines.[15] In anticipation, or perhaps just to hedge its bets, the 1972 convention had called for yet another commission on delegate selection to be assembled. This time the thankless job of reforming the reforms went to Barbara Mikulski, at that time a member of the city council in Baltimore, Maryland. The AFL-CIO, party regulars from the states, and members of the Coalition for a Democratic Majority were in the vanguard fighting to have the guidelines rescinded. However, the fiesty Mikulski took the charge to her Commission on Delegate Selection and Party Structure seriously.

The 1972 convention had called for the commission to attack the troublesome question of "quotas." The Mikulski Commission stated strongly that quotas were absolutely prohibited, except in state delegations, which must be composed half of women and half of men. However, states were to practice "affirmative action" and set up plans for a broad participation of racial and ethnic minorities and young people. Another change put in place by the Mikulski group was to place the burden of proof on the National Party that a state was not in compliance, rather than on the state to prove its compliance, as required under the McGovern-Fraser guidelines. To implement this decision, a Compliance Review Commission was recommended which would serve as a clearing house for state plans and also as a sort of preliminary Credentials Committee. This Compliance Review Commission was put in place early in 1974, under the direction of Robert Wagner, former mayor of New York, thus moving the Party more and more toward the center and national institutionalization. The Mikulski Commission also set a minimum limit of 10 percent of elected delegates to represent a candidate if he/she were to claim any delegate seats at the convention. The Democratic National Committee ultimately raised that minimum to 15 percent. Crotty terms this change "the most significant innovation of the Mikulski Commission."[16] Significant as this rule might have been, it did permit some exceptions for those states that held direct election of delegates. Illinois, Pennsylvania, New York, Ohio, and New Jersey had such primaries, which became known as "loop-hole" primaries because they permitted a way out for states not wanting to adopt the proportional representation guidelines. In effect, the "loop-hole" primaries could amount to the old winner-take-all primary. Price notes, "This was because voters favoring a given presidential candidate were likely to vote for all (or as many as possible) of the delegate candidates pledged to that preference."[17] It was this "loop-hole" primary, along with "quotas," which would continue to haunt the Democratic reform movement.

Probably the most stringent and controlling Mikulski rules dealt with a requirement that "any delegate mandated to vote for a presidential candidate be selected in a manner which assures that he or she is a bonafide supporter of the candidate," and furthermore, "a presidential candidate shall have the right to approve any candidate for national convention delegate identified with that person's candidacy."[18] Although this rule was carte blanche for slate making, the perogative had been taken away from the state party and given to candidate organizations. As Price points out, this rule served to nullify the openness of candidate selection that the McGovern-Fraser group had sought:

> There was nothing in the rules to prevent a candidate from approving only one candidate for each delegate slot to which he or she was entitled. The commission did not seem to appreciate the paradox: the fidelity of the convention to rank-and-file preference was being sought through a mechanism that effectively would deny the rank-and-file of any choice as to who represented them as delegates.[19]

There were other less momentous changes made by the Mikulski Commission, many dealing with a loosening of the more stringent of the McGovern-Fraser guidelines. Party officers and elected officials were still forbidden *ex officio* status, but they were to be extended convention privileges. However, these privileges did not include the right to vote on the convention floor unless the official had been duly elected as a delegate. Mikulski opened the door just a bit wider for party regulars than had McGovern-Fraser. The limit on delegates to be appointed by party committees was raised from 10 percent to 25 percent. Yet, no state could select more than 25 percent of its delegates at large. Proxy voting was again allowed if individuals actually came to a meeting and then chose to leave, but no one person could hold more than three proxy votes. The Mikulski Commission was at work not quite two years; upon presenting its report to the Democratic National Committee (DNC) in 1973, it went out of existence.

The Party Charter

There remained the question of drafting a party charter, called for by the 1968 convention. A hastily prepared draft charter by the joint Fraser and O'Hara commissions late in 1972 was presented to the Democratic National Committee on the last night of the July convention. The draft charter was not accepted, but the membership did set up the Charter Commission to be chaired by former North Carolina Gov. Terry Sanford. This group worked simultaneously with the Mikulski Commission. Whereas Mikulski and her task force had very specific problems to attack, the Sanford group, made up largely of party centrists, had an ambiguous assignment. Beginning with a large public meeting in May 1973, the Charter Commission listened to statements and testimony that called for party unity and compromise, yet the meeting was opposed by the organized labor forces of the Party, by party regulars, and even by former allies such as O'Hara who opposed further attempts at reform.[20] The Charter Commission was large, with some 164 members, as compared with the 28-member McGovern-Fraser Commission. Fraser was a member of the Charter group, and brought with him much of the experience and ideas that he had gleaned from his own commission's work in preparing the hapless draft charter of 1972. With Fraser's experience and Sanford's skilled administration and determined leadership, the Charter Commission produced in a year and a half a document of "almost totally unexpected contributions [which] would amaze even the most ardent of the early proreform advocates."[21] According to Robert Huckshorn, the charter adopted by the Democrats in 1974 produced "one of the most far-reaching changes" in American party history. He summarizes the accomplishments in this way:

> This document created new units of party government, such as the judicial council, the finance council, and the education and training council. The result of these changes was to establish at the national level a governing structure composed of legislative, executive and judicial branches. The center of control is the national party. The state party organizations, in effect, relinquished some of the traditional sovereignty that they possessed in the past.[22]

The Charter Commission adopted an unofficial draft of the new charter in March 1974, and in mid-August put the final touches on the document for the midterm conference in December. Among the topics carried over from the March meeting were (1) a mandatory rather than optional midterm conference; (2) the establishment of the judicial council which would codify and apply party law "in such a manner as to avoid divisive intraparty fights and prolonged court battles";[23] and (3) a provision on the tenure of the national chairman. A good bit of controversy and discussion occurred on the latter point. The majority on the Charter Commission wanted a set term of four years for the National Party executive, to be elected immediately after the national nominating convention. This would have given the quadrennial presidential nominee a controlling voice in the selection. Others on the commission favored choosing the chairman early in the year *following* a presidential election in order to find a chairman more responsive to total party needs rather than just those of a particular candidate. During the months between March and the August meeting, members of the AFL-CIO leadership worked diligently to stack the commission with individuals sympathetic to the cause of labor. There were some resignations of commission members during that time, and others would not be able to attend the August meeting. Crotty describes the ensuing battle this way:

> First, and with little effort, the conservative forces quickly voted down the liberal alternatives on the charter issues before the commission. Then the right wing indulged in a bad case of overkill. They attempted to void the fragile compromise on affirmative action that had been adopted by the Mikulski Commission and, in turn, the Democratic National Committee and the Sanford Commission as a substitute for the quota concept. The conservatives did not want affirmative action to apply to all party affairs (only to delegate selection) and they wanted to replace the words *insure representation* (of minorities) with *encourage participation.* . . . Party conservatives initiated another attack. They proposed that prohibitions on the unit rule and winner-take-all primaries . . . be stripped from the charter and left to party bylaws. . . . The opening of these issues to debate proved a strategic mistake and caused a backlash that would eventually cost the conservatives dearly.[24]

It is important to remember here that a number of other political events were going on between March and August of 1974. Richard Nixon resigned the presidency on August 9, 1974, scarcely a week before the interim meeting of the Charter Commission. Sanford had been encouraged to put off the final adoption of the charter until the midterm conference, *after* the November 1974 elections. By the time the midterm convention convened in Kansas City in December, the Watergate backlash had resulted in the landslide congressional election that gave the Democrats a gain of forty-nine seats in the House and four in the Senate.[25] Flush with victory and vindication, the Democratic governors gave a boost to the proposals of the Mikulski Commission by endorsing them wholeheartedly. Crotty sees the governors' action as pivotal in the outcome of the adoption of the Sanford charter:

> In reality, they [the governors] symbolized a turn in party affairs that gained momentum through their actions and would sweep the basically centrist gathering in Kansas City. . . . More remarkably, consensus was to be achieved through the adoption of a progressive party constitution more reformist than any would have dared to predict. . . . The Democratic Party had indeed set itself on a new course.[26]

The charter gave the Party a strong national direction while broadening the democratic participation of both its state and federal segments. The

charter also provided the once *ad hoc*, catch-as-catch-can party with new
continuity. With the adoption of the charter, the Democrats had the tool
that could give them the power to control the internal centripetal forces
of party. All they needed was the will to make it work.

The Winograd Commission

Not quite a year after the adoption of the charter, National Party
Chairman Robert Strauss appointed still another commission—the Commission on the Role and Future of Presidential Primaries, to be chaired
by Morely Winograd, state party chairman from Michigan. Inherent in
the liberalized rules for delegate selection set in place by the McGovern-
Fraser and Mikulski commissions was a tendency for delegates to be
chosen by primary elections rather than by party caucus or convention.
The primary was the surest way in which to allow for full participation
by a wider group of party members, and it gave some insurance that
delegations so chosen would not be challenged for seating at the national
convention. The primary not only allowed for more participation by
Democrats but also allowed, in some states, for participation by Republicans and independents. The proliferation of primaries is a prime example of one of the "unanticipated consequences" of Democratic party
reform. Polsby cites an argument that there was little cause and effect
between the reform guidelines and the proliferation of primaries, but
the evidence is not conclusive:

> It has been denied that the proliferation of primaries in the delegate
> selection process—from 17 Democratic and 16 Republican in 1968,
> before the guidelines were promulgated, to 23 Democratic and 22
> Republican in 1972, the next presidential year—was inspired by
> McGovern-Fraser Commission reforms. Two former staff members
> of the commission—conceivably in a mood to defend their work
> from well-meant erosion or from political attack—have generated
> a short list of other possible motives for switching to primary elec-
> tions. These include a desire on the part of state party leaders to
> attract coverage of the national television networks for the purposes
> of drawing attention to state or regional problems.[27]

By 1980 thirty-one states held Democratic primaries; Republicans held
thirty-three.[28]

Commission on Presidential Nomination and Party
Structure—Winograd II

The 1976 Democratic Convention that nominated Jimmy Carter for
the presidency extended the work of the Winograd Commission and

changed the name to the Commission on Presidential Nomination and Party Structure. The delegates also voted to amend the charter and to reinstate the dreaded quotas by requiring affirmative action programs which would contain "specific goals and timetables."[29] The 1976 convention also passed a resolution directing its new commission to interpret the charter's "fair reflection" language calling for delegates to be allotted to a candidate in a manner fairly reflecting the expressed presidential preference of the primary voters. In other words, the "loophole" that would allow for a winner-take-all primary was closed.

The ink was hardly dry on the Mikulski document and the charter before the Democrats were tinkering again. The Winograd Commission incorporated both of these resolutions in its final report. The Winograd group also raised the threshold of the percentage of delegates needed before a candidate could claim any share of the delegate seats. Mikulski had suggested at least 10 percent; this was raised to 15 percent by the DNC. Winograd called for at least 25 percent. The fact that there was a Democratic president in the White House had much to do with this decision. The Winograd Commission had the dubious pleasure of being the first of the reform commissions to operate under a Democratic president. As an incumbent bent on running for a second term, Carter could benefit from the higher threshold, although this would not have benefitted him in his campaign for the 1976 nomination. Price states: "The White House augmented the Winograd Commission with members supportive of the president and strongly influenced its deliberations."[30] However, the DNC rejected the higher threshold and compromised with a proposal "that set the district-level threshold in primary states at 100 percent divided by the number of delegates to be chosen in the district (but no more than 25 percent)."[31] Much of the Winograd document appeared to have been written by the author of the Internal Revenue Code. Finally the Compliance Review Commission got into the act and instructed the Winograd Commission to include language that would prevent "winner-take-all" elections at the district level. The convolutions continued and the rules thickened. Price quotes Donald Fraser, an old hand at reform, as saying: "I think it was clear that a majority of the Winograd Commission would have liked to do something about the proliferation of primaries, but then President Carter was elected and a large number of members were added to the commission. The work of the commission was diverted to rewriting rules in order to protect the incumbent."[32]

To its credit, the Winograd group did attempt to shorten the primary season. They decided to set a "window" period during which primaries could be held. This was in the hope that a reduction in time might reduce the number of states that would choose the primary route. The commission set the "window" period to extend from the second Tuesday in March to the second Tuesday in June as the period in which all primaries and first-stage caucuses should be held. The DNC whittled away at this ruling of the commission by exempting two primary states, New Hampshire and Massachusetts, and three caucus states, Maine, Iowa, and Minnesota. The boldest and perhaps the most efficacious move the Winograd Commission made was to rule against open primaries. Although Mikulski had required state parties to take direct action in correcting state statutes that would allow for open primaries, this had not had much effect. Michigan and Wisconsin had made no move to change from the open primary wherein any registered voter could vote. In fact, the Wisconsin open primary was a landmark in the drive for enfranchisement of the Progressive Era under the leadership of Gov. Robert La Follette. Open primaries might be good for democracy but they were not good for latter-day Democrats, when Republican and independents could vote for the weakest of the candidates, hoping he or she would get the nomination and be more beatable in the general election. The Winograd Commission made absolute the requirement that only registered Democrats could vote in a Democratic primary. It was this rule that caused the open warfare between the Wisconsin State Democratic Party and the Democratic National Committee, finally reaching the Supreme Court in 1980. The Court ruled that a national party had the right to enforce a closed primary and to seat only delegates elected in such manner.

The Winograd Commission made a small step toward returning the party regulars in the form of elected officials to the delegations. Each state was given additional at-large seats in the amount of 10 percent of its base delegation. However, the commission rejected a move to have these delegates attend the convention uncommitted to a particular candidate. It also refined one of the Mikulski regulations which had the potential for slate making by a presidential candidate. The Winograd Commission extended the number of approved delegates from one to three while allowing the candidate to veto any prospective delegate who might announce to run in the candidate's name. A measure taken by the Winograd group that drew little notice at the time called for delegates to vote for the candidate they were elected to support at least on the first ballot at the national convention. It was this rule that was vociferously debated at the 1980 convention when Ted Kennedy contested the nomination of Jimmy Carter and called for an "open convention." The "faithless delegate" arose as a specter to haunt the reformers for some time to come.

The Winograd Commission tampered and tinkered. For each small timid step forward, it seemed to stumble two steps backward. Price quotes Austin Ranney's assessment: "The main triumph of the Winograd Commission was keeping the party from being weakened further."[33]

Summary

There is no doubt that many of the reforms put in place by the Democrats during the years 1964–1979 were needed and, for the most part, well taken. Many decisions of the McGovern-Fraser Commission were probably inspired by the model for a "responsible party," which is democratic, responsive, has internal cohesion, and offers compromise among interests. The Democrats did change the entire character of their party with their reforms. They became a national, mass party. They provided the mechanisms that would allow the Party to govern itself on a continuous basis when, in an effort to prevent fragmentation and diffusion of power, they centralized their governance in the National Party. They opened the door to new blood which, though bringing a new vitality to the Party, also brought enthusiastic inexperience. On balance, what they did was good, but like so many other progressive movements, they just did not know when to quit. Reform has become a way of life for the Democrats . . . almost being an end in itself, rather than a means to an end. As one observer has stated, "Reform is the Democrats' disease."[34]

Notes

1. David B. Truman, "Party Reform, Party Atrophy, and Constitutional Change: Some Reflections," *Political Science Quarterly* 99 (Winter 1984–85): 637.

2. Nelson W. Polsby, *Consequences of Party Reform* (New York: Oxford University Press, 1983), 5.

3. William J. Crotty, *Political Reform and the American Experiment* (New York: Thomas Y. Crowell Co., 1977), 238.

4. Commission on Party Structure and Delegate Selection, *Mandate for Reform* (Washington, D.C.: Democratic National Committee, 1970), 39.

5. Crotty, 240.

6. Ibid.

7. A brilliant account of this turbulent time is to be found in Lewis Chester, Godfrey Hodgson, and Bruce Page, *An American Melodrama: The Presidential Campaign of 1968* (New York: Viking Press, 1969).

8. Crotty, 240.

9. David E. Price, *Bringing Back the Parties* (Washington, D.C.: Congressional Quarterly Press, 1984), 150.

10. Crotty, 243.

11. Ibid.

12. Ibid.

13. Ibid., 245.

14. Gary D. Wekkin, "National-State Party Relations: The Democrats' New Federal Structure," *Political Science Quarterly* 99 (Spring 1984): 53.

15. Price, 29; Jeffery L. Pressman and Dennis G. Sullivan, "Convention Reform and Conventional Wisdom: An Empirical Assessment of Democratic Party

Reforms," in Demetrios Caraley, ed., *American Political Institutions in the 1970s* (New York: Columbia University Press, 1976), 107.

16. Crotty, 247.

17. Price, 151.

18. Commission on Delegate Selection and Party Structure, *Democrats All* (Washington, D.C.: Democratic National Committee, 1973), 17.

19. Price, 152.

20. Crotty, 248.

21. Ibid.

22. Robert J. Huckshorn, *Political Parties in America* (North Scituate, Mass.: Duxbury Press, 1980), 387.

23. Crotty, 249.

24. Ibid., 250.

25. John F. Bibby, Thomas E. Mann, and Norman J. Ornstein, *Vital Statistics on Congress, 1980* (Washington, D.C.: American Enterprise Institute for Public Policy Research, 1980), 8.

26. Crotty, 251, 252.

27. Polsby, *Consequences*, 57.

28. Ibid., 64.

29. Price, 153.

30. Ibid.

31. Ibid.

32. Ibid., 154.

33. Ibid., 155.

34. Norman J. Ornstein, "The Democrats' Disease: Reform," *Washington Post*, 1 July 1984, C5.

2

The Search for Stability and Leadership

A major function of the national committee is to survive.[1]

This chapter examines how the Party went about its search nationally for internal stability, how it chose an executive to guide the Party, how it chose to sustain itself in an unaccustomed out-of-power role, and how it sought to enhance its means of support not only for the Party but also for its candidates. This chapter describes the Party's somewhat futile attempts to articulate the Party's mission.

It is important to identify what the National Party is, or at least what the conventional wisdom thinks it ought to be, by noting the peculiar characteristics of the Democratic National Party and by accounting for how it got that way. By describing the conventional types of national party chairmen, an attempt is made to assess why the Democrats made the choices that they did. The efforts of each new party chairman are evaluated in terms of how well he accomplished his own goals. The Party's various efforts are identified as meaningful and productive or as taken in a random manner.

Recognizing a National Party

Precisely what *is* a National Party? How will we know one if we see it? The question is not asked facetiously, nor is it an opening gambit to launch into a survey of the definitions of *party* to be found in the voluminous literature of political science. Cornelius Cotter and Bernard Hennessy have already warned us:

> Unlike most of the other governmental units and agencies which social scientists set themselves to describe or explain, the national

party committees have little identifiable and definable being. They
are not embedded in law. They do not display those patterned and
regular interactions among persons and roles which sociologists
find in groups such as the family, organizations like the YMCA,
or associations like the AFL-CIO. The national party committees
are, in some ways, "non-things."[2]

Although Duane Lockard has dismissed as "too absurd to be considered" Edmund Burke's definition of British parties as "groups of like-
minded men,"[3] we find something very close to that in Cotter and
Hennessy:

> . . . the national committees themselves are large groups of peo-
> ple variously selected, representing different amounts and kinds
> of political interests, who come together now and then to vote on
> matters of undifferentiated triviality or importance, about which
> they are largely uninformed and in which they are often uninter-
> ested.[4]

These authors soften what they say admittedly may seem like a "smart-
aleck" description by stating, "The committees, as committees, are important mainly for what they will acquiesce in, rather than what they
will propose or decide."[5] It is precisely this acquiescence as well as the
relatively continuous, standing existence of the National Committee that
gives us our working definition of the National Party. Although it may
be highly volatile, ebbing and advancing in power and influence, the
National Committee is always "there"—therefore, it is.

The Democratic National Committee was organized in 1848 at the
Democratic Convention in Baltimore,[6] and according to Cotter and Hennessy, the National Committee, collectively with the Senate Campaign
Committee and the House Campaign Committee, continues to this day
to "comprise the permanent 'standing' national party apparatus."[7] However, we must not confuse nor equate "standing" with "stable." Stability
is rare in any American political party. For the Democratic Party the
very search for stability embodies the Party's tragic flaw—wherein is
often found its greatest strength and appeal. As the Party continually
seeks to maintain a balance among its many diverse constituencies all
may at some time feel desirable, but none will feel completely satisfied.
Frequently the more intensely the Democratic Party seeks to strike a
"stable" balance, the more frantic and random the search becomes. This
sort of fractured and fragmented search can lead, and most often *has*
led, to the Party's disarray.

Even the use of the words *permanent* and *standing* as modifiers of the
national committees is somewhat misleading. The national committees of

both of the major parties are, as Bone has termed them, "creatures of the national conventions and subordinate to their control and direction."[8] The committees do not have a duly adopted constitution and set of bylaws as do other organized interest groups and associations, nor are they "embedded in the law."[9] The Democratic Party did attempt, and to a degree achieve, a semblance of a "constitution" when the National Committee adopted the "Democratic Charter" on December 7, 1974. This document was the product of the Sanford Charter Commission; it outlined, among other things, the duties of the National Party, but it continued to "recognize the National convention as the supreme governing body of the party."[10] Crotty sees this document as an instrument whereby

> more authority would gravitate to the national party while at the same time the procedures of both the state and, more specifically, the federal party would be democratized. To the extent that an essentially lifeless and unresponsive organization could be made more accountable to and representative of its grassroot membership, the reforms would be a success.[11]

E. E. Schattschneider sees the lack of "public" governance as no deterrent to the parties' existence or to their responsiveness to the *voters*.

> The parties do not need laws to make them sensitive to the wishes of the voters any more than we need laws compelling merchants to please their customers. The sovereignty of the consumer in the economic system consists in his freedom to trade in a competitive market. . . . Democracy is not to be found *in* the parties but *between* the parties.[12]

Prior to the Democratic Charter, both major parties tended to depend on manuals which set down some of the rules adopted over the years at national conventions. Bone commented on this previous lack of internal formal governance and continuity: "Both [parties'] compilations [of rules and procedures] are surprisingly brief and set forth the methods of selecting the committeemen, terms of office [four years], filling of vacancies, officers of the national committee, time of the first meeting of a newly chosen committee, and related matters."[13]

Membership and Governance of the Democratic National Committee

During the period covered by this study, 1980–82, the Democratic National Committee was composed of some 366 members, representing all fifty states, the District of Columbia, Latin America, Guam, Virgin Islands, Democrats Abroad, Members-at-Large, Congressional Representatives, Democratic Governors' Conference, Conference of Democratic Mayors, Young Democrats of America, National Democratic County Officials, State Legislative Leaders Caucus, and the National Federation of Democratic Women. From this representation the governing officers of the committee were chosen, composed of a chairman, three vice-chairmen, a secretary, a treasurer, and a national finance chairman. Each state delegation had a state chair and a state vice chair.[14] So we can see from this listing that there were some sixty-three groups and sub-groups represented on the Democratic Committee of 1982.

There was also an Executive Committee of the Democratic Party which was made up of the governing officers plus thirty-one others drawn from the general membership of the committee. This representation was drawn from the Congressional Representatives, Democratic Governors' Conference, Conference of Democratic Mayors, Association of State Democratic Chairs, Young Democrats of America, National Federation of Democratic Women, Members-at-Large, and four regional caucuses from the states representing the Eastern, Midwestern, Southern, and Western Regions.[15] The presence of an executive committee is a relatively new phenomenon in the Party's organization. In an effort to bring about some sense of stabilizing authority, an executive committee of eleven "was set up on October 31, 1951, . . . as a part of a Truman-inspired effort to prepare for the convention and campaign of 1952."[16] Some fifteen years after its creation, Cotter and Hennessy found little evidence to indicate that the executive committee was used much by the chairman—it was rarely called together and was "not often called separately."

> Here, as in all such arrangements, the requirements of geographical representation almost ensure that the membership of the Executive Committee will have neither the physical closeness which allows consultation among mere acquaintances nor the personal friendships which move individuals to consult by letter and phone over long distances.[17]

Here again we see that the Party, in trying to be open to and representative of its various constituencies, becomes cumbersome to the point of being unworkable. Samuel Eldersveld has observed that the party is "inevitably a conflict system," as it represents and exploits "multiple interests for the achievement of direct control over the power apparatus of the society."[18] In the process of promulgating many of the well-meaning reforms of the 1970s, intended to *broaden* participation in the governance of the Party, the Democrats have, ironically, achieved their goal at the cost of internal stability and over-all party effectiveness and credibility. In the reforms set forth by the McGovern-Fraser Commission in 1970, power and control was shifted from the state and local party to the centralized national party. "Democracy" was forced on the party membership, and the results have been a dilution of governance by a stratarchy, where the power is diffused throughout different layers of the Party.[19] As Nelson Polsby summarizes the consequences of the McGovern-Fraser Commission requirements, "Thus, formerly more or less independent state party organizations were put on notice that they would be expected to follow requirements of the national party as outlined by the McGovern Commission . . . the conclusions of this Commission in due course became binding upon the parties of the several states."[20] Eldersveld admonishes against centralized control of a party in his defense of a stratarchical arrangement of power:

> The very heterogeneity of membership, and the subcoalitional system, make centralized control not only difficult but unwise. In the process of adaptation, then, the party develops its own hierarchical pattern of stratified devolution of responsibility for the settlement of conflicts, rather than jeopardize the viability of the total organization by carrying such conflicts to the top command levels of the party.[21]

The same criticism lodged against the executive committee can only be magnified when one considers the size of the entire National Committee. It would be an interesting and informative study to inquire of individual members of the National Committee if they see themselves as really representing an identifiable constituency and if they make any effort to poll constituents and vote accordingly on National Committee matters. My guess here is that Robert Michels's "iron law of oligarchy" is at work, where the elite or insiders have the effective control of the party and the mass membership of partisans have little to say about party governance.[22] Although Thomas Dye and L. Harmon Zeigler stated the contrary—"The evidence suggests that American parties, within the activists' cadre, are not a perfect fit for Michels' model, for party activists are neither as homogeneous nor as numerically small as his model requires"[23]—I hold that this thesis is worthy of further research and could prove useful to the Democratic Party in its search for cohesion and stability. Of course, it might also be argued that the Democratic National Committee is governed by the "iron law of anarchy," as many of the findings in the current study will show.

Multiple Interests and Party Conflict

Absence of highly structured rules and regulations has been both beneficial and deleterious to the Democratic National Party. Too often, even when "it ain't broke" they tend to want to fix it. The Democrats have had an especial penchant for tinkering with their machinery since the turbulent days of the 1968 convention and election, which led to the landmark party-reform document *Mandate for Reform*, issued by the Commission on Party Structure and Delegate Selection, familiarly known as the McGovern-Fraser Commission of the Democratic Party.[24]

Too stringent restrictions of a party constitution would render it difficult if not impossible for the party to maintain any degree of flexibility or responsiveness to change. Of course, it might be argued that just that sort of discipline is what the Democratic Party needs. In its attempts to be all things to all members and constituencies, it has sometimes become a fragmented, blithering cacophony of voices, responding to all and responsive to none. But, as Cotter and Hennessy have said, "committees . . . are important mainly for what they will acquiesce in." The committee of the *whole* may acquiesce, but the *individual* committee members do not appear to do so either quietly or readily.

The Darwinian thesis of "survival of the fittest" is inherent in the American political system, being only a more modern statement of James Madison's ideas about faction seen in *The Federalist 10* and, indeed, an extension of the basis of the American government's system of "checks and balances." Dean Acheson saw this prospect in the Democratic Party of his own time, as he wrote in his eloquent appraisal of the Party, *A Democrat Looks at His Party*:

> Policies and programs within the party must be developed in which no single interest is permitted to dominate the others. Labor, organized and unorganized, skilled and unskilled; white-collar workers, farmers, professional people; persons dependent on savings or pensions; intellectuals; people in search of housing or some minimum medical care; as well as businessmen—all these criss-crossing groups have interests and points of view which insistently demand attention and which in themselves form a rudimentary system of checks and balances.[25]

Here we see, succinctly stated, not only an analysis of the composition of the Party but also a diagnosis of possible sources of decay and a prescription of how the Democratic Party might maintain its "responsible" homeostasis and health: no single interest should be permitted to dominate.

Competition in the "Responsible Party" System

In its classic report "Toward a More Responsible Two-Party System," the American Political Science Association asserted, "In a two party system, when both parties are weakened or confused by internal divisions or ineffective organization it is the nation that suffers."[26] Yet other observers, such as scholar Austin Ranney, see both intraparty competition and competition between the major parties as providing a healthy volatility which keeps the party and its participants honest and responsive.[27] Eldersveld views the party "inevitably" as a "conflict system," adding, "above all, and this is the unique structural characteristic of the party in this regard, conflict within the party must be tolerated."[28] Competition and conflict, whether held to be useful, tolerable, or destructive, are indeed a fact of political life in the American system. Richard Rubin has pointed to the pervasiveness of this phenomenon of party instability, and states that the Democratic Party appears to have a particularly difficult time of maintaining party harmony:

> While the development of internal conflict has permeated the entire party system, interestingly and most importantly the scope of mass instability was not found to be equally shared by both parties, since substantial increases in both the number of contested primaries and in the rates of rank and file turnout were lodged primarily in the Democratic Party.[29]

If the major function of the National Committee is to survive, as Cotter and Hennessy have stated, and if the Democrats seem to have the greatest difficulty in maintaining party stability, then it would follow that the resolution of conflict is of greatest importance to the Democratic National Committee and especially to the national committee chairman. John Stewart remarked on this very fact in his classic call to arms for the Democratic Party, *One Last Chance*, when he wrote of the Party during one of its more turbulent periods, "the job of Democratic National Chairman Robert Strauss is not hard to define: to persuade everyone to keep their knives under the table, at least at public meetings. . . ."[30] Bone also cites the role of mediator or "negotiator between dissident elements of the party" as an increasingly important function of the national chairman, although in "earlier decades [around the turn of the century], the chairman was generally the leader of the victorious group in a factional struggle." However, Bone points to evidence that indicates that the role of the national party chairman "over the years . . . has become much more than a fiscal agent and harmonizer. . . . Modern chairmen see themselves as public relations men for the dominant faction of the party," serving in the manner of *"personae gratae* to the presidential nominees of their respective parties and are virtually named by them."[31] In the case of the Democrats, great agility and perspicacity are called for in determining exactly which faction is dominant at any given time, especially when the presidency is lost and the party becomes known as being "out-of-power," as it was in November 1980.

John Bibby and Robert Huckshorn point out that the function of the out-of-power National Committee, being the only "established mechanism available to coordinate the activities of the party and set the tone for its rehabilitation," will tend to emphasize party organization rather than ideology or policy and will seek a party chairman who is nonideological and gifted at building unity and consensus from the many factions and splintered interests that are left in the wake of defeat.[32] These authors also state very strongly the importance of the National Committee to the health and vitality of the out-of-power party:

> Lacking the resources and benefits that go along with winning the White House and often badly split internally, the out party desperately needs a national party organization to direct its intended recapture of major offices. Hence, the national committee of the out party is normally of more significance than that of the in party.[33]

The Tenuous Tenure of the Party Chairman

All of these factors and aspects of the National Committee and its chairman, cited by the political scholars, were present and observable a little over a week after November 4, 1980. One of the first things the Democrats did was to seek a new party chairman. Bone sees the fact of the high turnover in national chairmen as one of the major "maladies" of the national parties, observing:

> Few large national private-interest groups would regard such frequent changes in top leadership as desirable. Party chairmen gain competence and wide acquaintances only to be replaced with new chairmen who must do the job all over again. While turnover may reflect political reality and the party's sensitivity to change, it tends to be upsetting in the national office.[34]

Commenting on the Democrat's condition, political analyst Adam Clymer of the *New York Times* wrote, "The effort to rebuild the Democratic party on the rubble of its crushing electoral defeat last Tuesday has begun with an intense focus on the future of John C. White, the party's national chairman." Clymer went on to point out that White wanted to stay on for a time with the Party in order to unify the remaining fragmented forces which had not been totally demolished. One of Senator Kennedy's aides said that the idea of White remaining was "not acceptable." (At this particular time Kennedy was viewed as a very strong contender for the 1984 presidential nomination, and indeed remained so until he removed himself from contention on December 1, 1982.) White had been a strong supporter of Carter in the primaries. His man lost and White would have to go.[35] The situation for a national party chairman of an out-party will be greatly influenced by the amount of importance and prestige the defeated presidential candidate maintains within party circles.[36] To say that Carter was unpopular both in and out of the Democratic Party is to state the obvious. He was to the end an outsider, never close to the Party regulars. And he made it clear that he would not attempt to make any further claim on the Party or its policies. Carter halfheartedly attempted to support the beleaguered White when, in a press conference on November 12, he said that White should be considered for another term in the post along with other candidates. As for the defeated president, he said he "would return to Plains, Ga., next Jan. 20 to write his memoirs and 'live the life of a former president.' "[37]

Long before the Carters started to pack for their departure from Washington, candidates for White's job began to appear, announcing their prescriptions for the Party recovery. As Ross Baker wrote in the *New York Times*, "The struggle over control of the Democratic National Committee is like the battle over the Iranian city of Khurramshahr: armies locked in desperate struggle over a ruin."[38] Clymer reported that "there is general agreement that the party's chairman should be a good spokesman, skilled in fund-raising, interested in helping Congressional and state candidates and neutral between Mr. Kennedy and Vice President Mondale. But there is little consensus on who fits the bill."[39]

There were several men who thought they could "fit" the bill, including White. White called a meeting of the Democratic National Committee's Executive Committee on December 9, 1980. Prior to that meeting he had repeated his desire to continue as chairman. He also announced that the election of a chairman would be held in February of 1981. Among the others who were very much interested in the chairmanship were Joseph F. Crangle and Patrick J. Cunningham, both former New York State Democratic chairmen. Gov. Bill Clinton of Arkansas had been mentioned as a likely candidate as had Charles E. Curry, a committeeman from Kansas. Also heeding the call to put together the Party's pieces was Charles T. Manatt, the Democrat's chairman of their National Finance Council. Manatt had been an able fund-raiser for the party, and although he acknowledged that he held a good bit of interest in heading the Committee as chairman someday, he said in November that he was "loyal to Mr. White."[40] Loyalty from Manatt notwithstanding, White announced his withdrawal from the race late in November. House Speaker O'Neill was not sorry to see him go. O'Neill was quoted as saying that White had been "the worst ever" with his excessive attention to the reelection of the president and the neglect of the congressional races. "They gave everything to Carter," the Speaker complained.[41]

If, as Speaker O'Neill charged, White did direct his energies and the Party's resources to the election of the presidential nominee rather than to the congressional races, he was not acting without precedent. Indeed, "the Democratic National Committee was organized in 1848 as an outgrowth of a 'central committee' appointed in 1844 to 'promote the election of Polk and Dallas.' "[42] Bone points also to the lack of a base or real "place in the state party organization, and national committeemen often do not participate in party decisions at the local level."[43]

The Republicans saw the inherent inequity and loss of party cohesion in just such attitudes and made a concerted effort in their own 1964 rebuilding process for the national chairman to establish a "satisfactory relationship with his own party's congressional leaders."[44] The relationship of the Congressional Party leadership and that of the National Party and its chairman is a critical element in the stability of any party, but especially so for an out-party. It will be a recurrent theme throughout this study.

The Democrats' Search for Party Leadership

The recognized task at hand for the Democrats in the early days after the November defeat was to get someone in place at the National Party headquarters who could provide "leadership." There were some differences in just exactly what the various individuals and groups had in mind, and the particular abilities of the candidates for White's post were not clear, at least to Speaker O'Neill. He invited all potential candidates for the chairmanship to address the House Democratic Caucus "to say what they would do if elected." He added that the House Democrats were telling the state party chairmen that a "rebirth of the national party" was what the House members wanted.[45] A few days later the Democratic governors were calling for much the same cause and commitment.[46] It would appear from this early focus by the various segments of the Party that the Democrats really did understand the need to work as a cohesive party. Furthermore, they gave some evidence of viewing the national party chairman as the individual who could carry forth those unification efforts. But as political scholars and even amateur political observers can testify, what politicians say and what they do are not always compatible, much less contiguous.

The personality of a national chairman is probably the most important asset he has in seeking the leadership of an out-party. Bibby and Huckshorn state it succinctly:

In assessing a new party leader, one must go beyond the political conditions that led to his election. His personality, style of leadership, and background are all important to an understanding of the leadership role he plays.[47]

Cotter and Hennessy see very much the same elements at work:

If the chairman has not come to the position at the sufferance of the defeated candidate, but subsequently by election of the committee itself, his influence will depend very largely on that which he brings with him to the committee from his state and national activities and that which he can amass through adroit playing out of his position as chairman.[48]

February 27, 1981, had been set as the date for the National Committee to meet in Washington and to select, for better or worse, a new national chairman. As the time neared for the election, all but two of the contenders for the chair had dropped out. Governor Clinton had said he was never much interested anyway, Charles E. Curry of Kansas decided to make a bid for the Party's treasurer, and on February 19 Patrick Cunningham withdrew from the race. The only ones that remained were Manatt and Crangle. (It was fortunate for the Party that Cunningham withdrew and was not elected. He was indicted in early July 1981 on "federal charges of conspiracy, tax evasion, perjury and obstruction of justice."[49] Although he entered a plea of not guilty, he was found to be so on July 17. He was convicted of tax evasion and conspiring to cover the crime. He was automatically disbarred from the New York State bar as a result of the felony conviction.[50]) Manatt was elected unanimously when Crangle withdrew on the day of the February 27 meeting.

Enter Charles T. Manatt

What special qualifications, abilities, and especially, personality did Manatt bring to the National Party? One critic of the choice of Manatt, who requested not to have the quotation attributed to him, said "Manatt bought that job." Certainly there was circumstantial evidence that that might well be the case, but no member of the committee who was questioned would substantiate the charge. Cotter and Hennessy state that "in the early years [around the turn of the century] a wealthy man might buy the chairmanship of either party."[51] Even if the charge that Manatt "bought" his way to the chairmanship is true, it would seem to indicate that he had a commitment to the Party and was willing to invest in that commitment. Dye and Zeigler have observed, "In essence, power in American parties tends to rest in the hands of those who have the time and the money to make it a full-time, or nearly full-time, occupation."[52]

Manatt, a self-made multimillionaire who came off an Iowa farm to work his way up through the Party and through law school at George Washington University spent about $75,000 on his campaign for the chairmanship. He gave further evidence of his determination and largess when he announced at a news conference following his election that he intended to take no salary from the committee, or only a small one if it were deemed legally necessary. He said he would continue to be paid by his Los Angeles law firm, Manatt, Phelps, Rothenberg and Tunney.

Promising to renew the Party, Manatt declared, "I want to send a message to the American people. The Democratic Party is alive. The Democratic Party is well. The Democratic Party is ready."[53] Here we see Manatt in the role of "hell-raiser," as described by Cotter and Hennessy:

> Part of the accepted style of the national chairman is to be continuously, openly, and unremittingly partisan. When he speaks to the party faithful, he can be the very embodiment of the slogan "My party, right or wrong." . . . His job is often to be a partisan's partisan: to oversimplify, to moralize, to attract the sympathies and the emotions (if not the intellectual assent) of the voters for his party and the candidates for his party.[54]

Manatt was characterized by political columnist Richard D. Lyons as a "superb manipulator, a Methodist Sammy Glick who is always on the make."[55] Apparently the Democratic Committee saw in Manatt, who had formerly held the post of the Party's finance chairman, a shrewd financier, a manager who would bring strong organizational skills to the national headquarters of the Party and one who would seize every opportunity to put himself and the Party forward. He was, in effect, the very textbook model of a modern major party chairman. The Party needed strong administrative leadership.

The out-party must depend upon the party chairman and the National Committee for daily continuity as well as for the goods and services that only the organization can provide. The Party charter and the various reform commissions had institutionalized the Party, giving strong control at the national level. Such a federalized structure needs a strong and able chief executive, one who can see that the mail gets out and the bills get paid, not to mention that there should be money in the bank to pay them. The risk the National Committee ran here, as would any board of directors in the private sector choosing a chief executive officer, was whether the man could translate personal ambition for the limelight into ambition for putting the organization in the forefront.

The Manatt Management Style

It has been pointed out that the national chairman can be either an organizer or a spokesman for the party. It would be difficult to find both qualities in the same individual, and probably not even desirable for the Democrats in early 1981. The fact that the Democrats did not opt for a spokesman can probably be explained by the additional fact that they could not agree on precisely what should be said. Ideas and subsequent policy had been elusive for the Party in recent years, and would prove to be so for some time to come.

Manatt came to his candidacy for the chairmanship with some liabilities which would prove to hamper him throughout his tenure. To begin with, he was a Washington outsider. Although he had served as a party officer, and had been educated in Washington, he had little experience in dealing with party members in the Congress. He was not well known in the private salons of sociopolitical Washington, and was viewed by some as an upstart. Although the Party in general had become highly democratic in its membership, with its conventions frequently influenced by amateurs, there remained an intellectual and powerful elite which had had its fill of being snubbed by the Carter White House and its Georgia "Mafia." This exiled elite coterie was probably very wary of the ambitious and assertive Manatt—"the Methodist Sammy Glick." Soothing fractious factions and bringing about unity and cohesion are vital roles which the out-party chairman must play skillfully.

Probably the best quality Manatt had going for him, as far as the rank and file committee members were concerned, was that he had no ties to any of the visible presidential contenders. Another factor in his favor was his California residency and business ties. His California experience also gave him a good idea of state political concerns, especially as they were affected by the closing of the "loop-hole" primaries by actions of the Winograd Commission. Manatt's work with the Young Democrats in Iowa was also good training for heightened awareness of state party power and integrity. His tenacity and penchant for hard work were a mixed blessing. He would need to be tough, but toughness does not lend itself to flexibility. Manatt was a no-nonsense business man, which was certainly something the Party needed. But the Democrats are often given to nonsense, and Manatt was not a particularly patient man.

Manatt made it clear throughout his campaign for the chairmanship, and again in his acceptance speech when he was chosen, that he would be a tough-minded and indefatigable organizer and office manager. Cotter and Hennessy have stated, "The chairman of the national committee is not only a leader of a kind of a party legislature, but also is the head of a small bureaucracy." These scholars also list the major roles that a party chairman may assume: "image-maker, hell-raiser, fund-raiser, campaign manager, and administrator."[56] Bibby and Huckshorn cite two types of leadership patterns that are "possible in the national chairmanship of an out-party: that of the 'speaking' or issue-oriented chairman or that of the 'office,' or organization-oriented chairman."[57] Manatt was not disposed to being "issue-oriented." He was a good speaker, but was certainly not going to assume the role of spokesman.

In his acceptance speech after his election to the chairmanship, Manatt declared: "The Democratic Party has been out-conceptualized, out-organized, out-televised, out-coordinated, out-financed and out-worked."[58] He went on to outline his solutions for the Party's distress:

1. Development of a new American agenda of political ideas to be assembled by a party policy council; 2. instituting a vigorous direct mail fund-raising campaign concentrating on small contributors; 3. working with state and local Democratic parties to recruit candidates, register voters and train campaign workers.[59]

Apparently Manatt had chosen to be the organization man, and was probably chosen by the National Committee for that reason. He would definitely leave the shaping of policy to a party council and would not personally become involved in raising issues . . . but he would raise a lot of money and maybe a little hell.

Not all of the Party faithful were as confident that a manager was what the Party needed. Joseph L. Rauh, Jr., who had held a number of offices in the Democratic Party, wrote an open letter to Manatt, published in the *Washington Post* four days after Manatt's election. Rauh despaired that too many Democratic leaders were urging Manatt to be a "nuts and bolts chairman concentrating on organization and finances and staying as far as possible from issues and ideology."[60] Some days later, Robert Squier, a Democratic campaign consultant who admitted to having the bias of a technician, chided Rauh and offered gratuitous advice to Manatt. Squier saw a chance for Manatt to reverse the tradition of giving all the Party's support to the presidential candidate and to "build a party structure that can give technical support to all of our candidates for public office . . . he [Manatt] looks like the kind of man who knows where the tools are and is willing to pick them up and use them to build this party."[61]

Clymer, who had followed the fall of White and the rise of Manatt rather closely, observed:

The election of Mr. Manatt, a Los Angeles lawyer, banker and party fund-raiser does not indicate whether the Democrats are, like the earlier victims of landslides, to rebound, to languish or to vanish. What it does signify is an intention to maintain the franchise they have tended so carelessly of late—to operate as a national political institution in the era of computers, direct mail, and polling, to which the oldest political party in the world has not yet adjusted. . . . But his energy cannot obscure the fact that the Democrats took a thrashing on Nov. 4, and that since then they have done little or nothing to regain the political initiative. By several long-term measures the Democrats' problems are serious.[62]

Summary

Although Charles Manatt lacked some of the political social graces, he brought strong organizational and managerial skills to the disarrayed Democrats. In its search for both stability and leadership, the Democratic Party, for the most part, was well served in its choice of Charles Manatt as National Chairman in 1981. It is true, as Elizabeth Drew observed, "the Democrats had been drowning in democracy," due to their extensive reforms and affirmative action rules in delegate selection to National Party conventions and in the enlargement of the Democratic National Committee. However, the charter adopted by the National Committee in 1974 gave Manatt one of the tools he needed to "institutionalize" the Party, as he had promised to do at the time of his selection.

Notes

1. Cornelius P. Cotter and Bernard C. Hennessy, *Politics Without Power; The National Party Committees* (New York: Atherton Press, 1964), 8.

2. Ibid., 10–11.

3. Duane Lockard, *The Perverted Priorities of American Politics* (New York: The Macmillan Co., 1971), 72. Burke wrote, "Party is a body of men united for promoting by their joint endeavors the national interest upon some particular principle in which they are all agreed" (*Edmund Burke: Selected Writings and Speeches*, ed. Peter J. Stanlis [Garden City, N.Y.: Doubleday & Co., 1963], 143).

4. Cotter and Hennessy, 3.

5. Ibid.

6. Hugh A. Bone, *Party Committees and National Politics* (Seattle: University of Washington Press, 1958), 5.

7. Cotter and Hennessy, 10.

8. Bone, 6.

9. Cotter and Hennessy, 11.

10. Democratic Charter Commission, *Charter for the Democratic Party of the United States* (Washington, D.C.: DNC, 1974), in William J. Crotty, *Political Reform and the American Experiment* (New York: Thomas Y. Crowell, 1977), 253.

11. Crotty, 252.

12. E. E. Schattschneider, *Party Government* (New York: Holt Rinehart & Winston, 1942), 60.

13. Bone, 5.

14. Democratic National Committee, *Official Proceedings of the 1982 Democratic National Party Conference* (Washington, D.C.: DNC, June 25–27, 1982), 249–53.

15. Ibid., 245–55.

16. Cotter and Hennessy, 38.

17. Ibid.

18. Samuel J. Eldersveld, *Political Parties: A Behavioral Analysis* (Chicago: Rand McNally & Co.), 6.

19. See the description by Harold Lasswell and Abraham Kaplan, *Power and Society* (New Haven: Yale University Press, 1950), 219–20.

20. Nelson W. Polsby, *Consequences of Party Reform* (New York: Oxford University Press, 1983), 34–36.

21. Eldersveld, 6.

22. Robert Michels, "The Iron Law of Oligarchy," in C. Wright Mills, ed., *Images of Man: The Classical Tradition in Sociological Thinking* (New York: George Braziller, 1960), 233–61.

23. Thomas R. Dye and L. Harmon Zeigler, *The Irony of Democracy: An Uncommon Introduction to American Politics* (Belmont, Calif.: Wadsworth Publishing Co., 1970), 183.

24. Commission on Party Structure and Delegate Selection to the Democratic National Committee, *Mandate for Reform* (Washington, D.C.: DNC, April 1970). For a discussion of this report, see Polsby, *Consequences*, 34–36. See also Byron Shafer, "The Party Reformed: Reform Politics in the Democratic Party, 1968–1972," (Ph.D. dissertation, University of California, Berkeley, 1979), 8–64.

25. Dean Acheson, *A Democrat Looks at His Party* (New York: Harper & Brothers, 1955), 30–31.

26. Committee on Political Parties of the American Political Science Association, "We Need a Stronger, More Responsible Two-Party System," in Neal Riemer, ed., *Problems of American Government* (New York: McGraw-Hill Book Co., 1952), 153. This landmark document first appeared in *American Political Science Review* 44 (September 1950).

27. Austin Ranney, *The Doctrine of Responsible Party Government* (Urbana: University of Illinois Press, 1954).

28. Eldersveld, 6–7.

29. Richard L. Rubin, *Party Dynamics: The Democratic Coalition and the Politics of Change* (New York: Oxford University Press, 1976), 175.

30. John G. Stewart, *One Last Chance: The Democratic Party, 1974–76* (New York: Praeger Publishers, 1974), 186.

31. Bone, 10, 7.

32. John F. Bibby and Robert J. Huckshorn, "Out-Party Strategy: Republican National Committee Rebuilding Politics, 1964–66," in Bernard Cosman and Robert J. Huckshorn, eds., *Republican Politics: the 1964 Campaign and Its Aftermath for the Party* (New York: Frederick A. Praeger, 1968), 231–32.

33. Ibid., 207.

34. Bone, 11.

35. Adam Clymer, "Democrats Seek Party Chairman in Bid for Unity," *New York Times*, 12 November 1980, 1.

36. Bibby and Huckshorn, 96.

37. Terrance Smith, "Carter Forseeing Only Limited Role in Rebuilding Party," *New York Times*, 13 November 1980, 1.

38. Ross K. Baker, "Democrats '84 Play," *New York Times*, 14 November 1980, 31.

39. Clymer, 12 November 1980.

40. Ibid.

41. Adam Clymer, "Two Democratic Leaders Seek Aid for Local Candidates," *New York Times*, 22 November 1980, 8.

42. Bone, 4.

43. Ibid., 12.

44. Bibby and Huckshorn, 216.

45. Clymer, 22 November 1980.

46. *New York Times*, 9 December 1980, sec. 2, p. 18.

47. Bibby and Huckshorn, 213.

48. Cotter and Hennessy, 96–97.

49. *New York Times*, 2 July 1981, sec. 2, p. 1.

50. *New York Times*, 19 June 1981, 27.

51. Cotter and Hennessy, 64.

52. Dye and Zeigler, 183.

53. Adam Clymer, "Democrats Select Manatt as Chairman," *New York Times*, 28 February 1981, 7.

54. Cotter and Hennessy, 70.

55. Richard D. Lyons, "New Leader for the Democrats," *New York Times*, 28 February 1981, 7.

56. Cotter and Hennessy, 5, 67.

57. Bibby and Huckshorn, 232.

58. Clymer, 28 February 1981.

59. Ibid.

60. Joseph L. Rauh, Jr., "Dear Charles Manatt . . . ," *Washington Post*, 3 March 1981, A13.

61. Robert D. Squier, "Dear Joseph Rauh (Copy to Charles Manatt) . . . ," *Washington Post*, 5 March 1981, A19.

62. Adam Clymer, "What Next? Democrats Seek a Way to Rebound," *New York Times*, 1 March 1981, sec. 4, p. 2.

3

The Search for a New Mission

> For the party out of power, the chairman is the one person who has day-to-day responsibility for drumming up the party's fortunes on a national basis. To him people will unavoidably look for policy guidance as well as for the major formula of electoral victory.[1]

In the first weeks following his election, Manatt proceeded rapidly to put the resources in place to implement an ambitious five-part program which was to occupy him for much of the first eighteen months of this chairmanship. This program had the following objectives: (1) to convene a party policy council; (2) to set up a "vigorous" direct mail fund-raising campaign; (3) to plan and organize a midterm conference; (4) to organize and conduct a series of regional National Training Academies to train party workers in campaign strategies; and (5) to appoint and support a commission that would review the presidential nomination process and make recommendations to the National Committee. Each of these endeavors will be treated separately, although activity was going on simultaneously involving all of them during the months from March 1981 through June 1982.

Less than a month after his election, Manatt had assembled a staff for the Democratic National Committee headquarters of professionals which included Eugene Eidenberg, a fellow at Harvard's Kennedy School of Government, as committee director, Ann F. Lewis as political director, and Ronald H. Brown as chief counsel. (Manatt had raided two congressional offices in recruiting this senior staff. Lewis had been administrative assistant to Rep. Barbara Mikulski of Maryland and Brown had served as general counsel and staff director for Sen. Edward Kennedy.)[2]

Although he had not mentioned it specifically in his inaugural stem-winder, Manatt had campaigned on a promise to move directly to implement the charge, authorized by the 1980 Democratic National Convention, to reorganize and streamline the presidential nomination process while bringing elected officials further into the decision-making arena. This kind of reform was certainly no novelty to the Democrats, as shown earlier.

The events of the 1980 convention—especially regarding the "unit" vote and delegates bound to vote on the first ballot for the candidate whom they had supported in the primaries (the controversy aroused by the "unit" vote came to be known under the catch phrase as the drive for an "open convention" prior to and during the 1980 convention)—led to the authorization by the 1980 convention for a study to address these practices as well as other considerations of delegate selection methods.[3]

There was much in the Democrats' past history that led to their perception that reform was needed once more. The National Party guidelines adopted as a result of the McGovern-Fraser *Mandate for Reform* in 1970 and the 1974 Sanford Charter Commission report had caused the state party organizations and elected party leaders to play a diminished role in the governance and direction of the National Party. Another important element of these reports was the abolishment of "unit voting" by state delegations, which was reinstated at the 1980 convention through the vigorous efforts of the Carter campaign forces. As was pointed out in chapter 1, there were many unanticipated consequences of the Democratic Party's attempts at reform, a subject covered extensively in the literature of political science.[4] Polsby draws this significant conclusion:

> Developments like these have given rise to the displacement of state party leaders and leaders of interest groups associated with them in the presidential nomination process—the demise, so to speak of presidential nominations as repertory theater.[5]

Rebuilding the Party Structure

Manatt was very much aware of the drain on the Party's coffers, not to mention the attention span of the American people, that had been wrought by the proliferation of primaries, the long, drawn-out nomination process, and the winner-take-all, locked-in nominating convention process. The necessity of reorganizing and streamlining the nomination processs was obvious. But it seemed imperative to Manatt to return elected officials, such as governors and members of Congress with proven political skills and identifiable constituencies, to the top levels of decision making. Manatt, the opportunistic pragmatist, the organization man who knew "where the tools" were, set about once more to tinker with the Party machinery . . . the reforms would have to be reformed.

Manatt began to do this by appointing the members of yet another commission. This would be the Commission on Presidential Nomination, chaired by an elected official, Gov. James B. Hunt of North Carolina. Former Chairman John White had announced the formation of this commission and had appointed Hunt as its chairman just prior to his leave taking as national chairman. Manatt inherited the concept of the commission and Hunt, but it would be up to him to work with Hunt and the National Committee in setting the priorities for the commission's work and for appointing the sixty-nine other members. By July 2, 1981, Manatt had the commission in place and presented it with its charge to undertake a "complete review of the Presidential Nomination Process for the purpose of making specific recommendations to the Democratic National Committee."[6] Hunt shared the responsibility for the commission with co-chairs Douglas A. Fraser,[7] president of the United Auto Workers, and Dorothy Zug, vice-chair of the Pennsylvania State Democratic Party. In announcing the formation of the commission and its sixty-nine members, Manatt said that the "main goal" would be to shorten the "seemingly endless" preconvention season.[8]

The Party got a boost in enforcing its reforms early in March 1981. The U.S. Supreme Court ruled in the case of *Democratic Party of U.S. v. La Follette* that the Party was not bound to seat delegates who had been chosen in the "open primary" in Wisconsin. The National Democratic Party, in adopting recommendations of the Mikulski Commission, had banned "cross-over" primaries, which allow any registered voter to vote in any primary without declaring party affiliation. (It is ironic that this La Follette amendment, so hailed in the Progressive years as "giving government back to the people," should have been the cause for the Democrats' case.) Columnist George Will, certainly no lover of Democrats, agreed with the National Party's action when he wrote: "The National Democratic Party rightly believes that party responsibility is enhanced by excluding from decision-making 'those whose affiliation is . . . slight, tenuous or fleeting.' "[9] However, Polsby predicts that if the Democrats persist in exercising their right to refuse to seat delegates elected in an open primary, they will "undoubtedly suffer marginal losses in popularity in the state. This sort of reform provides a pristine example of an excellent principle pointlessly—indeed fatuously—pursued. It gives a bad name to reform."[10]

In May 1981, a month or so before the appointment of the Hunt Commission was announced, Haynes Johnson, a columnist from the *Washington Post*, toured the country talking to Democrats, labor leaders,

independents, and "just plain folks"—a technique perfected by Johnson
in taking the national pulse. In a report of his odyssey he outlined the
problems and tasks before the Democrats in their resurrection process.
Johnson also offered a clear and direct prescription for the Party's rehabilitation. He saw three areas as vital, "and none of them easy."

> They must rebuild and regenerate the party structure that has fallen
> into such disrepair over the long years of lulling success; and they
> must bridge the widening gaps of sectionalism that further threaten
> to tear apart the party.
> They must find common ground—and a common theme—that will
> unite them for the different political realities of the closing years
> of this century.
> Above all, they must pay greatest attention to the changing national
> demographics that spell a population shift of profound political
> and economic consequences.[11]

The Hunt Commission

It was the task of rebuilding and regenerating the party structure that
fell to Gov. Jim Hunt and his commission. Six months after their formation in July 1981, the commission adopted their report on February
5, 1982. The full Democratic National Committee adopted the report on
March 26, 1982. Hunt and his fellow members of the commission were
careful to maintain a participatory structure throughout the hearings
and deliberations that accompanied the preparation of the report. With
an eye to regionalism, Hunt called for public hearings in four locations,
representing the Midwest at Des Moines, the South at Chattanooga, the
West at Los Angeles, and the East at Washington, D.C. All of these
meetings took place between September 24 and November 5, 1981, with
more than 140 "Democrats representing a broad cross-section of the
party" presenting testimony. The commissioners found that although
there was disagreement, the "level of interest" was extraordinary. The
commission as a whole averred that it "felt keenly its responsibility to
keep faith with these Democrats, to write rules that are fair to all groups
within the party and that contribute to the task of party-building in
which we all have a vital stake."[12]

In the letter of transmittal of the report, Governor Hunt wrote:

> We have carried out the thorough review of the nomination process
> with which you charged the Commission last July 2. At the same
> time, we have recognized the need to work as efficiently as pos-
> sible, so that we could turn our attention to the challenges facing
> our Party and our country in this election year. The Commission

has worked harmoniously and has handled its disagreements in a spirit of good will and compromise. Foremost in our minds has been the need to write rules that will help our Party organize, campaign, and govern effectively. For reasons spelled out in the report, I believe our proposal will contribute measurably to such a strengthening of our Party at this critical historical time.[13]

The final report of the commission listed twenty rules, along with Proposed Delegate Selection Rules for state parties, as well as what was termed "Six Basic Elements" that set anti-discrimination standards. The language of these rules and standards tends to be legalistic and somewhat convoluted. The introduction to the commission report is couched in comforting, cajoling cadence, tending more to lull than to control or command. However, the authors of the report subtly let the faithful know that things were not as they should be but that they could be set to rights with the proper faith and regimen. There is a nostalgic backward glance at things as they used to be, before the "democratization" of the Party, particularly at the joy of one-on-one politics, of "working" a room or of "pressing the flesh," so effectively enjoyed by Lyndon Johnson and Sam Rayburn. The report also contains a call to the "tradition" of the "responsible party" as a mediator:

> Party politics—the politics of personal contact, deliberative judgment, coalition and compromise—have too often been replaced by remote-control campaigns, single-issue crusades and faceless government. The traditional role of party—as a mediating institution between citizens and government, as a guide to consistent and rational electoral choice, as a bond pulling the elements of government together, for the achievement of positive purposes—no longer seems secure. Yet we believe this is a role worth preserving and strengthening, for it is not clear that we have anything promising to replace it.
>
> Our Commission believes the future is potentially bright for our party system, but we are not inclined to take its durability for granted. Accordingly, strengthening the party is a cohesive force in government and within the electorate has been a primary concern as we have recast the rules governing our nomination process.[14]

The Introduction goes on to state that the adversities of 1980 should be put to sweet use, building strength at the local precinct level, mobilizing voters, and articulating "our convictions and aspirations with a new clarity." Although this is a noble and lofty goal, the commissioners could not get through the writing of the rules and standards with any sort of consistent clarity, new or old. The work of the commission and its subsequent report is very obviously the work of a committee. The whole is not worthy of, nor equal to, the sum of the parts. Clarity and literary style notwithstanding, the commission did get the job done. They set new rules, they tightened old ones, and they did not hesitate to say where things had gone wrong in the past:

> There are features of our presidential nomination system that have weakened the party. Primaries have proliferated, removing decision-making power from party caucuses and conventions. Our national convention has been in danger of becoming what one critic has called a "rubber stamp electoral college." To an alarming extent our party's public officials have not participated in and thus have felt a limited responsibility for our recent national conventions. Some of these developments, of course, are beyond the reach of any rules a single commission could write. But it is within our power to influence trends, and we have done our work with this end in view.[15]

"Influence" was about all the commission members could hope to do, and they used the very best in persuasive techniques in the language, employing transitive verbs such as *urge, persuade, recommend, provide incentives*, and *suggest*. There were no *thou shalts* and few *requireds*. The twenty rules sought to (1) bring elected and party officials more effectively into the nomination process; (2) shorten the primary/caucus season; (3) reaffirm the Party's commitments to affirmative action and equal division of delegates by sex; (4) return a measure of decision-making discretion to the national convention; (5) give the states additional options under the fair reflection guidelines; and (6) retain the ban on primaries in which non-Democrats can vote, which were contained in the 1980 rules.[16] The "fair reflection guidelines" here refers to permitting the states to operate under the proportional representation allowed by the 1980 rules or to choose either to award a "bonus" delegate to the winner in each district or to elect district-level delegates directly.

Polsby, in his *Consequences of Party Reform*, argues that

> changing the rules of politics changes the incentives for political actors; that changing the incentives leads to changes in political behavior; and that changing behavior changes political institutions and their significance in politics.[17]

Although the Hunt Commission did not want to change the Party as an institution, except to strengthen its somewhat fragile structure, it did address two of the incentives identified by Polsby. These incentives were, in Polsby's words,

> centralization of control over the certification of delegates, arising from the uncertainties introduced by the McGovern Commission guidelines [and] the separation of state conventions from delegate selection procedures owing to the risks of contamination of state conventions by candidate enthusiasts.[18]

One of the commission's main goals was to "return a measure of decisionmaking discretion to the national convention." The commission also set explicit rules for the design of the State Delegate Selection and Affirmative Action plans. The deadline for the submission of these plans to the Compliance Review Commission was April 15, 1983. Any decision by the Compliance Review Commission as to compliance or the lack of it would "be final and binding." The commission did not discourage delegate selection at party conventions, at least for the "professionals" or party regulars, stating that "a state's party and elected official delegates may be chosen by a state convention, a committee consisting of all district-level delegates, or a state Democratic Committee laid out in rule 8C."[19]

Seventy-five percent of each state's base delegation were to be "elected at the congressional district level or lower." These delegates could be selected by "caucuses, conventions, committees," or "primary."[20] The "runaway" convention was of far less concern to the Hunt Commission than the "open primary."

> The Commission reaffirms the 1980 rules (2A-C) banning the use of the "open primary"—a primary in which voters are not required to publicly declare their party preference and to have the preference publicly recorded—to select or allocate delegates to the national convention. . . . A new rule 2F would provide that no person could participate in the presidential nomination process who participated in the nomination process of another party.[21]

The commission urged state parties in states without statutes that would allow such a restriction on cross-over voting to "adopt and implement an alternative Party-run delegate selection system which complies with this rule"[22] and further to take "positive steps in a timely fashion" to draft "corrective legislation" and to "educate the public on the need for such legislation" as well as "encouraging consideration of the legislation by the appropriate legislative committee and bodies."[23] James Ceaser sees this centralization of control by the National Party as "one of the most important institutional changes of the reform era."[24]

Bringing Back the Party Professionals

A major concern of the Hunt Commission was to bring more uncommitted delegates and especially party officers and elected Democrats into the nomination process. The various commissions formed after each election loss since 1968 had tampered with the candidate selection process, always in the interest of opening up the Party and abolishing what might be termed "elitist" abuses, such as "secret caucuses, unpublicized procedures, closed slate-making, [and] racial exclusion."[25] The Democratic Party had long touted its character as the "party of the common man," and in recent years it had sought to be the party not only of everybody, but everybody and his brother. By opening up the selection of convention delegates, the Party had left its essential business in the hands of amateurs. Elizabeth Drew cites an assessment of the problem by a Democratic senator:

> We have to find a new equilibrium. The people who attend the caucuses or get selected as delegates are not the people who've been traditionally involved. You have a group of people who have been solicited, cultivated, one on one. The allegiance has been obtained on a basis that has very little to do with substance, program philosophy. . . . These people at the Convention are like mayflies: they live twenty-four hours, have their day in the sun, go to the Convention, and bring back their souvenir programs. But they are not genuine custodians and stewards of the Party trust.[26]

Hunt and his fellows on the commission saw it was time to get some control back into the hands of the professionals and the regulars. Number One in their "Summary of Recommendations" was to "bring elected and party officials more effectively into the nomination process." They planned to do this by allocating some 550 slots to the states for the inclusion of such officials who would come to the convention as *unpledged* delegates. "Some of these would be named by the House and Senate Democratic Caucuses—up to 3/5 of their respective numbers—and the balance named by the state parties, giving priority of consideration to governors and large-city mayors."[27] The extension of unpledged delegates to at least 25 percent of the convention seats would also help eliminate the "danger of the convention becoming a 'rubber stamp electoral college.' "

Another important concern of the commission was, in fact, its "primary" concern. Although the commissioners acknowledged the positive contributions of primaries to the delegate selection process, they thought them not really worth the candle: "Their proliferation has made for more protracted, more expensive, more divisive, and more media-dominated campaigns."[28] The assumptions expressed here have been confirmed and are well documented in the recent studies of political reform.[29]

Closing the Primary "Window"

Expense and divisiveness were two things the Democrats could do without. The commission also saw that primaries "threaten to eclipse the organized party."[30] The question of "timing" was uppermost in the commissioners' collective mind when they drafted the guidelines for holding primaries. They sought to shorten and condense the period for holding primaries in order to avoid or at least control the "expense and divisiveness of a prolonged campaign and the unfairness of a system which gives disproportionate influence to a few early states."[31] The desire here was not only to shorten the costly process but also to prevent what is known as "front loading," whereby a single candidate could gain a large number of delegates and momentum in the early primaries, thus limiting the chances of less visible candidates. The rules set in 1980, which established a "window" for holding primaries and first-tier caucuses no earlier than the second Tuesday in March and no later than the second Tuesday in June, were to pertain to the 1984 primaries. The commission did grant specific and very limited exemptions to Iowa, which could hold its caucuses no more than fifteen days before the second Tuesday in March, and to New Hampshire, which could hold its primary no earlier than the first Tuesday in March. The earlier date given to Iowa allowed *caucuses*, which do not attract nearly the candidate activity or the media coverage as does an early primary. In the light of their stated goals, the commissioners' rationale for these exemptions is somewhat specious, but no doubt it was politic:

> We regard it essential to shorten the primary/caucus season . . . at the same time we see some value in a few early contests where lesser-known candidates can have a greater impact and face-to-face politics still predominates. We also appreciate the importance of the early caucuses to Democratic party building in Iowa and the 30-year history of New Hampshire's early primary.[32]

Tradition and "special need" appear to be the criteria for allowing these exceptions, implying that those two states were deserving of special privilege. These exemptions were to be the source of much party argument and divisiveness, sorely testing Manatt's skills as a manager and a mediator.

New England Primary Rivalry

Vermont tradition ran head on into New Hampshire tradition in early January 1983. Vermont holds its annual Town Meeting Day, when all local governmental officials are elected, on the first Tuesday in March.The Vermont Democrats chose to hold their nonbinding party primary on Town Meeting Day. This would have put the date for Vermont on March 6, 1984, outside the "window" period but on the same date granted to New Hampshire by the special exemption. New England rivalry between the two threatened to upset the carefully laid plans of the Hunt Commission. The New Hampshire Democrats would not relinquish their right to be the first primary in the nation, even if it meant the risk of forfeiting their twenty-five delegates to the national convention. They chose instead to hold their primary a week earlier, on February 28. Tradition and Yankee stubbornness are indigenous to New England, as evidenced in the remarks of New Hampshire House (Democratic) Minority Leader Chris Spirou: "We'll find a way for New Hampshire to maintain the first-in-the-nation primary even if we have to hold it on the Fourth of July of the previous year." Vermont House (Democratic) Majority Leader Stephen A. Morse declared just as vehemently, "Town Meeting Day will not change until the earth blows up."[33]

In 1976, when talk of regional primaries was in the wind, New Hampshire had passed a state law that its primary should be held a week before any other in the country. Of course, the commission report had clearly ordered that a state finding itself with a conflict between its state law and that of the commission rules shall "take provable positive steps to achieve legislative changes to bring the state law into compliance."[34] This rule notwithstanding, New Hampshire's party chairman, Richard E. Boyer, who planned to discuss the issue with Manatt, said, "No one's going to make us come after somebody else."[35] At the same time, DNC Political Director Ann Lewis said, "In the past, the rules have been haggled like an Oriental rug bazaar. But Chuck Manatt is not a rug peddler. He's a banker, and he thinks the rules are meant to be followed."[36] The haggling continued, despite Manatt's firm stand and with the states risking a loss of their delegates after a review by the Compliance Review Committee. In August 1983 David Broder commented: "The Democrats have done it again. For the fourth time in the last 15 years, they have revised their primary and caucus calendar and rewritten their delegate selection rules in bewildering ways."[37] Even as late as August of 1983, only six months away from the opening of the "window," the primary calendar was still unsettled.

Fighting Discrimination and Fragmentation

Just after the Hunt Commission was appointed and prior to the regional hearings, political columnist Mark Shields admonished the commission not to tamper with the primary dates in trying to shorten the campaign. He pointed out that the commission had "very little ability to influence the duration of the presidential campaigns" and should spend its efforts in repeal of the 1969 guideline that demanded "reasonable relationship" representation of women and minorities in delegations, chosen "in reasonable relationship to their presence in the population."[38] The commission did heed the latter part of the advice, although it still held much the same intent as "reasonable relationship" in its perennial "Six Basic Elements" intended to guard against discrimination. The commissioners stated that the Basic Elements "reflect the action of the 1980 convention in incorporating 'sexual orientation' (along with race, sex, age, color, national origin, religion, ethnic identity, and economic status) among the forbidden bases for discrimination."[39] Several new aspects dealing with affirmative action were added to the 1980 "basic elements," including designating "affirmative action target groups" to include women, blacks, Hispanics, native Americans and Asian-Pacifics, the last group being an addition. Another change was the requirement that each state's delegate selection plan should "provide for equal division between men and women"; the commission report also called for each affirmative action plan to have "provisions to help defray the expenses of those delegates who would otherwise be unable to participate in the national convention."[40]

Here we see at work what Rep. Morris Udall terms "touching all the erogenous zones in the body politic." Expanding on Udall's wit, Mark Shields warned the Democrats against what he termed "boutique politics":

> While deploring the rise of single-issue politics, the Democrats appear determined to encourage the further fragmentation and atomization of the electorate. Hyphenated Democrats will apparently predominate at the 1984 convention, just as they did in 1980, when the only time plain old one-size-fits-all Democrats were even acknowledged was when one of the caucus spokespersons would underline the threat of accompanying that caucus's non-negotiable demands with "Let's see how *the Democrats* do without *us* in November." The 1984 Democratic Convention looks like it could be another cultural and ideological trade show.[41]

Whereas "mandatory quotas" were forbidden by the Hunt Commission, the state plans were "to set specific goals and timetables to encourage the participation of target groups to a degree commensurate with *their presense in the Democratic electorate.* [Italics added]"[42] Despite the danger of giving more power and control to amateurs and running the risk of further fragmentation, the commissioners declared: "Our Party's affirmative action efforts are among the proudest achievements of reform."[43] Ranney points out the dangers to the stability of the Party inherent in such "affirmative action" provisions:

> The national party organs now override the state parties and even state laws in laying down rules governing the selection of delegates. Most delegates owe their seats not to the favor of any state or local "boss" but to their identification with a national presidential aspirant ("favorite sons" are outlawed) who did well in their state's caucuses and convention or primary—and perhaps also to their sex, ethnic identity, or age group. Their commitments are mainly to their candidate or the demographic group, certainly not to the party.[44]

Results of the Hunt Commission's Efforts

So, the Hunt Commission had changed a few, had reformed a few of its former reforms, and had reinvited the professionals to come home to help the affirmative action amateurs. It had given the states clear directives on when and how to hold the delegate selection primaries or caucuses and had relaxed the binding constriction on delegates, depending on "good conscience" and the right of candidate approval to see that the will of the state's Democratic electorate should be done on the convention floor. The efficacy of the commission report and its rule changes depended on how well the Democrats in the states adhered to the recommendations and how effective Manatt and his staff could be in the art of persuasion. If the situation in the New England states in August 1983 is any guide, then we may have found the exception to Polsby's thesis that changing the rules changes behavior. It does not necessarily apply to Democrats. Regardless of the change of rules, regardless of the change of incentives, even punitive ones like the loss of delegates (*or* elections), they go right on behaving like Democrats. It has been assessed by Richard Moe, former Vice-President Mondale's chief of staff, that "it is in the nature of the Democrats to fight like cats and dogs."[45] Certainly, if that is the case, and there is little reason to doubt it, then this behavior needs to be changed if the Democrats are to survive in order to "build." However, if Polsby's thesis is applicable here, then perhaps the incentives built into the Hunt Commission reforms were not sufficiently enticing to bring about the desired change in destructive behavior. The report makes it plain that its "decision to refrain from more intrusive measures does not signal a lack of concern." It offers rules and it offers rationale, but its incentives are vague, either in the form of punishment or reward. It asks that delegates perform their work "in good conscience," assuming that each will hold the same value of what constitutes "good." The commissioners boldly state that they have no "ideal" system to recommend to all states but that they are opening up a "range of possibilities . . . from which the state may choose in light of their own preferences and traditions."[46]

It has been stated by more than one sympathetic critic of the Democrats' affairs that "the Democratic Party is governed by the law of unintended consequences."[47] Apparently the Hunt Commission's recommendations had not escaped the rule of that law. Even with all the commission's good intentions to eliminate the problems of past years, there were some who thought that their work was not only futile, but probably detrimental to the Democratic cause. Drew reported a year after the National Committee adopted the commission report:

> The pollster Patrick Caddell and others have warned that in its attempt to solve one problem the Democratic Party may have created another: it may have moved the party perilously close to what is in effect a national primary, which is a singularly poor idea, because it does not permit extended consideration and reconsideration of the candidates, and could become a one-shot media event. . . . Thomas Mann, the executive director of the American Political Science Association, who served as a technical adviser to the Hunt Commission . . . says, "If our system has any advantage, it is that it affords us time to give the candidates scrutiny. These changes [by the commission] take us in the wrong direction." Actually nobody knows what the effect of the changes will be; what happens will depend heavily on the nature of the contest itself, the way the candidates affect each other, and how the public relates to them.[48]

It seems to me that what Drew has described here appears to be what political campaigns are supposed to do, the other inadequacies of the Hunt Commission notwithstanding. The fact that "nobody knows," that elections are not a foregone conclusion, was what the Hunt Commission was aiming for. It is only the surprise element, the possibility of the dark horse or at least of a good horse race, that captures the interest and attention of the American voter. A little excitement could go a long way toward eliminating voter apathy. Although the Democrats decried the lack of "new ideas" as they began to pick up the pieces of the Party, feeling that they needed a fresh philosophy to capture the independent voter and to recapture the affections of the disaffected, they might now have the chance to capture the attention and imagination of the broader electorate.

Americans will be attracted more to a good race at the convention and a good race in November than they will be to intellect and ideology.

The American voter will watch it if it moves, but finds it difficult to focus attention on it if it only sits and thinks.

All in all the Hunt Commission's diagnosis of the Party's ills was very good, and its prescriptions for cure were, for the most part, more than mere placebos. The problem lay with the Party participants who refused to take their medicine as prescribed while Manatt seemed powerless to force it down their throats.

Working With State and Local Parties

In his campaign for the chairmanship of the Party, Manatt had promised to give special attention to "working with state and local Democratic parties to recruit candidates, register voters and train campaign workers." Speaker of the House O'Neill had severely criticized Manatt's predecessor, John White, for "giving everything to Carter." Manatt knew that attention must be paid. The state parties had had good reason for feeling alienated as the continuing reforms moved more and more power to the National Party and fewer and fewer state party leaders had a say in the National Party's organization and agenda. Manatt appeared to be sensitive to state party needs and sentiment. He also gave evidence of knowing how important the state parties and partisans could be in the overall recovery effort. One of the methods by which Manatt planned to accomplish this phase of the Party's rebuilding was to revive the regional training sessions which the Democrats had not held since the 1974 campaign, "when the Watergate scandal brought forth scores of congressional candidates who needed training."[49] The Republican Party had begun such activities in 1965 when Ray Bliss, as national chairman, introduced the workshop format to the National Party program. Bliss had successfully conducted workshop sessions for state legislators and party leaders when he was state chairman of the Ohio Republican Party.[50] Bill Brock, who succeeded Bliss as Republican national chairman, expanded the training concept to provide a "program of assistance to [the] party organization [which] has been unprecedented in the history of American parties."[51] Charles Longley has pointed to the essential difference between the reform and revitalization of the Republican and Democratic parties as it is exemplified by this attitude toward the educational responsibilities of the parties:

> The Democratic Party responded to systemic changes by emphasizing the necessity for intraparty democracy as a precondition for electoral effectiveness. The Republican Party has chosen to strengthen its national organization through the provision of expanded services.[52]

An "unintended consequence" of the emphasis on intraparty democratization by the Democrats was that by bringing more "amateurs" into
participation in the delegate selection process, the National Party lost
the allegiance and talent of many of its experienced partisans and campaign workers at the state and local levels. Centralization of control by
the National Committee at the expense of state parties cost the Party in
terms of experienced and *interested* workers and supporters—those who
are the "genuine custodians and stewards of the Party trust" referred
to by the unidentified senator in his interview with Drew.[53] In effect,
the Democrats, through their reform efforts and centralization, had become what Ranney described as a "mass party," in contrast to the Republicans who had become a "cadre party."[54]

One of the functions that any party, and especially a "mass" party,
can—and for the sake of its health should—perform is the education
and training not only of future leaders but also of party workers. Manatt
himself was a product of such early training, having come up through
the Party by way of the Future Farmers of America and the Young
Democrats.[55] The opportunity for the type of partisan education which
comes from apprenticeship—working in and for the Party over an extended period of time and sharing in the incentives and rewards of party
activity—had diminished as the Democrats opened their arms to the
unskilled political masses. Gerald Pomper describes the importance of
a coterie of workers who have been politically socialized:

> Yet, political parties are more than collections of voters. They are
> communities in themselves, which function to promote broader
> involvement in the larger community. They provide training, an
> awareness of others' needs and interests, and a personal under-
> standing of democratic manners. Parties promote intimacy among
> members, respect for the opinions of their constituents, and pos-
> sible future leadership for the nation . . . like members of other
> small groups, partisans get to learn one another's strengths and
> weaknesses in great depth.[56]

One attempt to bring more "socialization" to the greater mass of the
Party's membership was the formation in 1981 of the Commission on
Low and Moderate Income Participation, chaired by Rep. Mickey Leland
of Texas. When Leland gave his report of the activities of this commission
to the 1982 midterm party conference in Philadelphia, he thanked his
colleagues on the committee for "their dedication and determination to
open the doors of the Democratic Party even wider." Included in the
plans of this commission were programs for including low- and middle-
income individuals in the regional training sessions and for a voter

registration drive which called for "assertive targeting of low and moderate income communities."[57]

Whether Manatt was cognizant of the philosophical aspect of the educational imperative or was merely copying a successful Republican technique is not known. In any event, he proceeded with his plans for the five National Training Academies which were to be under the direction of Ann Lewis, the Party's political advisor. These training sessions were to be held throughout the country during late 1981 and the early months of 1982. Sessions were scheduled for Iowa, Washington, D.C., New Hampshire, Tennessee, and California. Manatt insisted that the first of the training sessions should be held in his native state of Iowa. There may have been more method in that insistence than just home state loyalty. This Hunt Commission was hard at work during this time, setting rules and guidelines to shorten the presidential selection process by narrowing the time in which party caucuses and primaries might be held. Perhaps Manatt thought that a little "political socialization" and education in Iowa and New Hampshire would make those states more amenable to strict adherence to the "window" period. If this was the strategy, it met with what one might call qualified success.

In terms of success, Manatt reported that the Des Moines session was "spectacularly successful."[58] During the last weekend in September 1981, some 250 people from thirty-seven states gathered in Des Moines for three days of intensive training in fund-raising, targeting campaigns, organizing support from unions and interest groups, learning research techniques, fighting the New Right, and using television and the other media in a campaign. Participants got all of this for a $95 tuition fee. They were taught by veteran campaigners and professional Democratic Party consultants, most of whom received only travel expenses in return for their labor. The total cost to the Party for this session was $20,000, which at $80 per participant had to be considered cost effective. Ann Lewis, commenting on the training session and those to come after said, "We can't match the Republicans on their contributions, but we can give our people the tips they need to make the most of the resources they have."[59]

In addition to the five regional training sessions, the Democratic National Training Academy held a similar workshop for delegates to the National Party Conference in Philadelphia on June 25, 1982. A "graduate school" was held in Washington, D.C., July 28–30, 1982, billed as "Campaign Countdown—90 Days to Go," which "would focus solely on the 90 day period before November 2d and what can be done to ensure victory in this critical election." The tuition for this graduate school, open only to those who had participated in one of the previous workshops, was $125.[60] The Training Academy made videotape versions of the various workshop sessions available to party workers at a cost of

$60 per cassette. These videotapes covered management, planning and budget; voter contact; targeting; fund-raising; communication and media; and direct mail. The Academy staff also published a series of campaign manuals, covering much the same materials, at $15 per set.

The National Committee made other efforts at educational assistance in a series of ten workshops put on by the DNC's State Party Building Program entitled "The State Party Works." This program was designed to bring "DNC personnel and professional consultants from Matt Reese and Associates into each state party to help develop specific programs in the areas of fundraising, communications and organization."[61] Another service provided to assist in electing Democrats in Congressional, state, and local races in the 1982 midterm election was the staff referral service set up by Ann Lewis's office "to assist [candidates] by providing them with a list of staffers from previous campaigns who would be willing to take full time staff jobs."[62] Certainly the National Committee was making a concerted effort to bring services to the state and local level. As with any educational program, results are rarely immediately assessable. If we judge only on how the Democrats fared in the midterm elections, then we could say the program was only moderately successful. However, if we measure success only by the "party model keyed to contesting elections . . . where party strength is measured in terms of funds raised, candidates fielded, services rendered, vote garnered and elections won,"[63] we will not be taking the full measure of the Democrats' success in the search for a method to build a cohesive National Party and especially in the reconciliation of disaffected party leaders. There is strong evidence that the educational program presented by the National Training Academy and the Political Division of the DNC was well conceived and efficiently executed. Only extensive research over a period of time, observing the future participation and successful involvement of the training session participants, would yield any valid measure of the true efficacy of the educational program begun in 1981.

Finances and Fund-Raising

Money is one of those resources identified by Nelson Polsby and Aaron Wildavsky that "can be easily converted into other resources."[64] All of the most carefully planned methods for party recovery and the most appealing political ideology ever to come out of a candidate's mouth or a think tank's printing press will languish and "waste its sweetness on the desert air" if there is no money to implement the plans or promote the cause. There can be no doubt in anyone's mind that funding was a major concern for the Democrats in the days after the Carter defeat. The Party had entered the 1980 election in debt, and the Carter campaign and subsequent loss was costly in every sense of the word. Carter was not a popular candidate and grew even less so as the election time approached. Funds were not coming into Democratic coffers. John White, as chairman, had not made use of the direct-mail appeal to the small contributor but had relied on larger group and corporate gifts as had his predecessor, Bob Strauss. During the 1980 presidential campaign the Democrats raised less money for their man than did any of the other campaigns, including that of John Anderson, the independent.[65] In the 1980 campaign, all Republican committees engaged in raising campaign funds outdid all such Democratic committees by a ratio of 7 to 1, or $128 million to $19 million, a gap that seems even larger than the ratio when one considers the dollar amount—$109 million.[66]

> The disparity between the parties is even worse—from the Democratic standpoint—in terms of party financial assistance to candidates, the bottom line in campaign fund raising. The gap between the parties nearly doubled in this vital area, growing from a $6 million difference in 1978—$7 million to $1 million—to an $8 million difference in 1980—$10.3 million to $2.2 million—to a $15.4 million difference in 1982—$18.8 million to $3.4 million.[67]

From these figures we see that although Manatt and his staff made some gains in raising funds, they were playing a losing game of "catch-up." The Democratic Study Group report points this out when it observes: "The growing money gap between the parties is due to the phenomenal effectiveness of the Republican fund-raising machine rather than to failure on the part of the Democratic fund raisers."[68] The writers of this report lament if the gap can ever be "significantly reduced," pointing out that the Republicans have nearly 4 million contributors whereas the Democrats have only 300,000. Although the Democratic Party at the time of the 1980 election could claim more people who said they had allegiance to the Party,[69] apparently the Republicans had more who were willing to put their money where their votes were. One could surmise here that this is because Republicans have more money to put, but this is apparently not the case. "In 1980, the average contribution to the Democrats was $500. The average contribution to Republicans by contrast was $35, largely because of the GOP direct mails appeals to small givers."[70] The characteristic differences between the Republican "cadre" party and the Democratic "mass" party were evident even in the funding area, as Drew observed:

> Just as the search for money has caused divisions among the Democrats, it has served as a unifying force among the Republicans. The Democrats are by nature a less cohesive group than the Re-

publicans, but the factor of money reinforces each party's natural inclinations.[71]

Manatt came to the chairmanship from his post as finance chairman with strong skills, although his efforts under White's administration were not spectacular. Money was Manatt's business, and he proposed to put the Democrats' financial affairs on a more business-like basis. If we compare the Democrats to themselves, rather than to the more affluent and cohesive Republicans, we find that Manatt's record for the first two years of his term shows a 45 percent increase in funds raised in the 1981—82 cycle.[72] This increase is significant in terms of measuring the new chairman's effectiveness when one considers that these contributions came to the losers. In soliciting funds in the year after the loss of the election, one letter to party members took a very sentimental approach, appealing to the sense of affection for the underdog. Defeated Sen. John Culver of Iowa sent out a letter on Democratic Study Group letterhead which began: "Dear Friend, We Democrats took a drubbing last November.... President Carter had lost support.... No one thought we could lose the Senate. But we did."[73] Manatt was more upbeat in his appeal in a newsletter that came out from the DNC early in November 1981. In *Insider's Report*, it was announced that Manatt had written the following to all National Committee members:

We Democrats are being tested as in no other time in our history. The Administration is making a disciplined effort to radically change the nature of how our society deals with its problems ... the consequences of those changes are not yet fully felt by most Americans, but it is clear to many of us that there will be a reaction in the not-so-distant future ... it is our collective responsibility to be prepared intellectually, organizationally, and politically when that reaction sets in.[74]

This same issue of the *Report* commented that direct mail appeals seemed "to confirm recent commentaries on television and in the political columns that the still-young Reagan Administration has some very serious weaknesses." There was no indication that any *money* from Democratic supporters had confirmed that belief. Most of the direct mail appeals during this period, such as one dealing with economic matters, were sent in the form of questionnaires, asking for opinions on issues generally of interest to Democrats. These were accompanied by forms on which pledges or direct contributions could be registered, but the letters themselves made only a subtle appeal for money. A direct appeal for contributions accompanying a letter concerned with the Reagan administration's proposal to limit social security benefits became one of the few controversial pieces of direct mail issued by the DNC. The letter, a brain-child of the Virginia firm of Craver, Matthews, Smith and Company, which had been hired "to wage the same kind of direct mail campaign that brought thousands of $25 contributions to the Republicans,"[75] went out in September 1981. This letter was sent in an envelope similar to those used by the U.S. government to mail social security checks and was marked next to the address window: "Important. Social Security Notice Enclosed." It carried a message from Sen. Claude Pepper admonishing the reader that social security benefits were in jeopardy under the Reagan entitlement cuts. Senator Pepper urged the recipient of the letter to help save those benefits by sending "whatever you can afford to the campaign to save Social Security." Initially 50,000 letters were sent out to a test list. The response was so good that 1.5 million more copies went out about a month later.[76] Ultimately, according to a *New York Times* report, some 3.5 million copies were sent, attracting $600,000 in contributions.[77] Although this represented only about a fifteen-cent gross return on each letter mailed, not even enough to carry the mailing and return postage, the letter was effective in stirring up the Republican administration. John Svahn, the social security commissioner, said that postal fraud laws may have been violated, and called the letter a "blatantly misleading gim-mick."[78] The return had also given the Democratic National Party head-quarters some valuable new names for its mailing list.

Before Manatt's tenure as chairman, the main fund-raising events were telethons, promoted by Bob Strauss, and gala dinners or social functions going for $1000 a plate. At that time there were some 320,000 donors to those telethons whose names were on file. George McGovern had ac-quired a mailing list of some 600,000 names. Such lists are the lifeblood of direct mail appeals. The Democrats had let that blood drain away. When Manatt began his direct mail campaign in July 1981 only 25,000 names were on file as potential donors. "It is sad to think what might have been," grieved Roger Carver, of the direct mail consulting firm hired by Manatt. "The Democratic party didn't go after those names for years and years. If we had continued with it, we'd have been even with the Republicans today."[79] By the end of 1981 the Carver firm had raised $2.2 million by direct mail solicitation. Carver had ambitious hopes for raising $6.8 million from new and old donors in 1982. It turned out that his estimate was high by $6.4 million . . . a sizeable misjudgment. How-ever, by March 1982 there were 125,000 names in the Democrats' files. This was a definite improvement, although the Democrats were defi-nitely not "even with the Republicans." In 1981 the Republicans raised $33.5 from 1.5 million donors.[80] There were slight improvements for the Democratic ledger in 1982, with the Democratic National Committee receipts rising from the 1980 level of $15.1 million to $15.5, but the Republican National Committee receipts rose from $76.2 in 1980 to $79.8

million in 1982.[81] Manatt may not have bridged the gap, but at least he was showing some financial improvement. Probably his greatest contribution was in his willingness to innovate.

As with the education programs, the real results of Manatt's efforts in setting up a direct mail system may not be known for some time. It will be according to how well the files, now somewhat restored, will be maintained and used in the future. It would also be important for the National Party staff to study the demographic nature of their files as well as to study the rate of repeat donors and, perhaps, to measure the correlation of voter turnout to donors in specific geographic areas—in other words, mount a full-scale market study of those who cared enough to send money. There is no indication in any of the reports made public by the National Party that research of this kind was going on or was planned for on the national level.

In the early fall of 1981 Manatt's staff assisted in putting together one of the traditional type of fund-raisers in the form of a testimonial dinner at $1000 a plate. The testimonial was to be to the "Return of the Democratic Party." Held in Washington, the dinner was to celebrate the "first day of the Reagan Revolution." The celebrants came from all segments and factions of the party. "Tip" O'Neill from the House, Robert Byrd from the Senate, Henry Maier, mayor of Milwaukee, Morris Udall, former presidential candidate and court jester, and Glenn Watts of the Communication Workers of America were among the guests in an old-fashioned barbecue-bread-breaking-love-fest which netted $950,000 for the Party treasury. Manatt gave a party, and everybody who was anybody came. The band played "Happy Days are Here Again" and people almost believed it.[82]

In presenting this account of fund-raising activities by the National Committee, I have made no attempt to describe or address the issue or activities surrounding political action committee contributions, "fat cat" donors, or "soft money" from unions or groups. A thorough study of these appears in Elizabeth Drew's provocative series first published in the *New Yorker* magazine, cited earlier in this work. Fund-raising by the various Congressional party groups and the components of the "extra-legal" party will be discussed in subsequent chapters covering those subjects.

The Party Policy Council and the Search for Ideology

When Manatt announced in his maiden speech as party chairman that he would convene a party policy council to develop a "new American agenda of political ideas," he did a very daring thing. Not since 1956, when the Party was under the direction of Paul Butler, had such a group been convened. Butler had attempted to assemble a Democratic advisory

council following the Eisenhower landslide "to create an advisory committee to develop a legislative program for the party."[83] Butler's efforts
met with only modest success.

> Early in December Chairman Paul Butler named twenty members
> to the group, including the seven principal elective leaders in both
> houses. . . . Despite some press reports that Butler's invitations
> were merely a formality and that acceptance had been assured
> before the list was announced, within ten days all seven of these
> leaders declined to serve . . . interpretations of Mr. Butler's some-
> what comic embarrassment almost inevitably talked about "liber-
> als" against "conservatives" in the party and about challenges to
> the Congressional leaders.
> Although party factions and the status of the Congressional leaders
> obviously were relevant, . . . the legislative leaders, Messers. John-
> son and Rayburn and their associates would have been ill advised
> to enter the group . . . for if its [the Policy Council's] decisions were
> made public, as the proposals of the subsequently reconstituted
> committee have been, the leaders of the Congressional party would
> have assumed a position of command that they may have by im-
> plication and after maneuver and negotiation but that they can
> rarely announce in open forum. . . . Given the mediate character of
> the legislative party and its attendant factionalism, commitment of
> the party by the elective leaders normally must follow internal
> negotiation, not precede it, and, if negotiation fails, the leaders
> will be better off in most cases if they are not too frequently and
> openly identified with the losing side.[84]

With this sort of case evidence in its history, it was indeed either a daring
or a foolhardy course Manatt had set when he determined to reconvene
a policy council.

In his inaugural address Manatt had listed the convening of the policy
council first in his five-part program. Whether this placement was in-
tentional, to give the highest priority to such a group, or a mere accident
is not known. From what we know of Manatt, he probably placed at
first on purpose. He had said that he would have no part in making
policy, that he would leave this important function up to the policy
council. Manatt was obviously making it abundantly clear that he was
not attempting to preempt the policy-making function of the Party, important as that role might be. With all of the public self-examination
going on with the Democrats, who found themselves bereft of "ideas,"
and the subsequent press commentary concerning their paucity of policy, it is reasonable to think that Manatt held high hopes for the policy
council. In setting it up, he committed a blunder, which indicated his

weakness at Congressional relations and showed either his ignorance or his disregard of the Butler experience. Price credits Manatt with understanding that he must " 'do something' about policy" but observed that "he did not have any well formed notion of how to proceed, and he quickly received an education in the perils awaiting such efforts."[85] Price gives this account of Manatt's early experience in trying to get the council organized:

> Manatt brought in an associate from California, Harold Kwalwasser, to put the policy operation together. One close observer describes what ensued: "Hal, not quite understanding...the problems or the history, went charging up to see [Democratic Congressional leaders] Byrd and O'Neill...and started talking about how the chairman had this hot idea...to create this policy council and lay out the 'Democratic alternative.' Well, it took him about one week, and the Democratic leadership was up in flames. They were saying what the hell is this new guy Manatt doing? Doesn't he know that Democratic policy is made by House Democrats and Senate Democrats." It thus fell on Eugene Eidenberg, brought in as the DNC's executive director in the spring of 1981, to untangle the situation and put the policy council on a new footing. Eidenberg and Manatt settled on an approach similar to that chosen by Strauss in 1973: appoint a policy council consisting *only* of elected officials.[86]

It should be noted that the council organized by Strauss, referred to here, was quite different from the one set up by Butler. Although Butler's attempt was spurned by the Congressional leadership, there were other Congressional activists who saw to it that a "genuine *party* agenda"[87] was developed in 1960. However, with the nomination of John Kennedy, the Democratic Advisory Committee was absorbed into the Kennedy campaign. The type of advisory council envisioned and implemented by Butler is unique to and a necessary component of an out-of-power party. Price suggests that the failure of the Democrats "to work through their policy approaches while they were out of power" contributed to the difficulties of the Carter presidency.[88] In other words, it is important than an out-party make policy while their presidential sun does not shine. However, without direction and leadership dedicated to party instead of personal fortunes, no such policy will be articulated or forthcoming.

One of the recommendations made by the Committee on Political Parties of the American Political Science Association in its development of the Responsible Two-Party System model was for the formation of just such a party council of "perhaps 50 members, composed of repre-

sentatives from such units as the national committee, the congressional
parties, the state committees, and the party's governors."[89] William
Keefe further describes the ideal party council in this way:

> Meeting regularly and often, the policy council would examine
> problems of party management, prepare a preliminary draft of the
> party platform adopted for submission to the national convention,
> interpret the platform adopted by the convention, screen and rec-
> ommend candidates for congressional offices, consider possible
> presidential candidates, and advise such appropriate party organs
> as the national convention or national committee "with respect to
> conspicuous departures from general party decisions by state and
> local party organizations." ... The essence of the council's task
> would be to blend the interests of national, congressional, and state
> organizations in such a way as to foster the development of an
> authentic national party, one capable of fashioning and imple-
> menting coherent strategies and policies.[90]

This, the ideal, was never fully realized by the Democrats. "Only the
Republicans have given policy development high priority as a national
committee function."[91] There had been a rather active and effective Democratic Policy Council in 1969–70, under the direction of Hubert Humphrey, the defeated party presidential candidate. There were several
other attempts at policy councils, but they rarely reached the point of
effectiveness of the Butler group. The Sanford Charter Commission had
"importuned the national party to take responsible positions on matters
of policy, ... a role it had attempted to fulfill through such agencies as
the Democratic Advisory Council (1956–60) and the more recent Democratic Policy Council (1970) but one which some congressional and other
party leaders felt it had no business playing."[92] The charter did not
"require," it merely pointed out the benefits of such a council and suggested that there be one. Like the national midterm conventions, the
policy councils would take on the shape designated by the current party
chairman. Strauss was very wary of the policy council, and in 1973 he
formed the Democratic Advisory Council of Elected Officials. This body
rarely met and was "less active and less influential than the policy councils that had preceded it. Strauss's fear of offending Congress and his
wariness of fractious policy debates led him to deemphasize the entire
effort, virtually shutting down the full council. ... "[93] Manatt had never
put himself forward as a policy maker, but he did give high priority to
the formation of the policy council. He knew it was important, but he
did not appear to know the history of such groups, nor did he reckon
with the magnitude of Congressional egos. His concept of the policy
council was a good idea allowed to go randomly astray.

By the time the first meeting of Manatt's attempt at a policy council was held in mid-October 1981, the name of the group had been changed to protect Congressional relations and certain proprietary attitudes— exactly of the sort met by Paul Butler some twenty-five years earlier. "Out of deference to the sensitivities of Senate Minority Leader Robert C. Byrd (D-W.Va.), the word 'policy' won't even appear in its title. It will be the Democratic Strategy Council," wrote columnist Dave Broder.[94] (At the time the House and Senate leadership snubbed the Policy Council in 1956, "Tip" O'Neill had only been in the House for two terms, and Robert Byrd had not even been elected to the Senate, so their reluctance to participate in the Manatt meeting was not based on personal prior experience.) Manatt had invited not twenty but one hundred participants to convene in Baltimore at the Hyatt Regency Hotel, situated on the shore of the newly rejuvenated Harbor Place, on Friday, October 16, 1981. The beginning of the conference was less than auspicious. As Broder observed, "when the Democratic National Strategy Council convened its first meeting on Friday night, no one was certain that it might not be the last."[95] Manatt was taking a "gamble," as Broder said, in assembling the participants who were federal, state, and local elected officials. The "gamble" lay in the possibility of opening up old ideological war wounds along with the nervous twitch that accompanies the "social issue" disease.

This meeting was called while the Hunt Commission was still at work, and although there was some news coming out of its deliberations about the inclusion in the delegate selection of a high percentage of state and local elected officials, nobody had seen the final draft of the rules, and the local politicians, just as the Congressional party members, were wary of what they might be asked to agree to. Manatt was careful to describe the meeting as "organizational in nature." He told reporters that it would be late in 1982 before the council would be ready to "adopt a set of policy alternatives."[96] (If the council ever *did* adopt such a set of principles, it did not report such to the National Party Conference in 1982. In fact, the council as such did not even have a place on the three-day program.) Rather than working on substantive policy issues in October 1981, the council would concentrate on 1982 campaign strategies. According to Paul Taylor's report, "Some party leaders, such as Speaker of the House Thomas P. (Tip) O'Neill Jr. (D-Mass.) and Senate Majority Leader Robert C. Byrd (D-W.Va.), have been cool to the idea of an official DNC policy council, and have been advocating this fall that, as the loyal opposition, the Democrats should simply stand back for now and give the president time to hang himself."[97] Such a strategy, from the do-nothing-and-maybe-it-will-go-away school of management, held incipient dangers, according to Walter Heller, former chairman of the Council of Economic Advisors under Carter. "Heller said the president's economic program is laden with contradictions, but warned the Democrats 'not to delude ourselves into thinking Reaganomics will self-destruct politically.' "[98]

The Senate Democrats had met two weeks prior to the convening of the Strategy Council at a three-day conference at Canaan Valley State Park in the mountains of West Virginia to discover, in Sen. Alan Cranston's words, "much more unity than we anticipated. The main consequence is we are committed to searching for issues where we can stand together."[99] Forty-one of the forty-six Democrats remaining in the Senate after 1980 met to listen to panel discussions given by leading experts and political scholars on energy, the economy, defense, foreign policy, and political demography. Senator Byrd, not yet used to his role as minority leader, stated, "We're meeting among ourselves and we've grown closer."[100] It might seem strange that the Democratic senators had not been "meeting among themselves" as a matter of course in their daily work in the Senate, but Byrd's style of leadership as majority leader had not been one that relied on "participatory management." If the senators worked together, as they certainly did, it was rarely with Byrd as a participant. Perhaps this meeting among themselves seemed not only novel but also sufficient to the Congressional members of the party. However, their exclusive attitude and proprietary claim on policy must have been a frustration to Manatt, who was trying to rebuild a party which had virtually succumbed while holding steadfastly to those very attitudes.

Senator Byrd was particularly obstinate, fearful that the Strategy Council would usurp or preempt Congressional policy-making prerogatives. To assuage him, the word *policy* was dropped from the council's title. Furthermore, the question of whether the council would ever issue policy statements in the Party's name was left hazy.[101] Manatt was sensitive to the feelings of the Congressional Democrats, and indeed, they *had* called for more notice and assistance from the National Committee office during the time they were smarting most from defeat and humiliation. O'Neill had even stated that the House Democratic Caucus should review the candidates for Manatt's job. The apparent snub and recalcitrance on the part of the Congressional branch of the party regarding the Strategy Council must have placed a strain on Manatt's patience. Although he had been clumsy in his initial approach to the Congressional members, he had replaced the ineffective Kwalwasser and had made concessions in shaping the council after the Strauss model. Apparently Manatt was able to control whatever exasperation he might have felt; he went on with the council meeting, seeking to mend fences by inviting both Byrd and O'Neill to speak at the opening session. They did, and launched the council meeting in what David Broder termed a "tidal wave of rhetoric."[102]

None of them hung around long, which did not disappoint the organizers. While they wanted the legitimacy the big names could confer, they did not want the council to become an arena for 1984 presidential politics, and they did not want to focus national attention on the younger-generation Democrats who represent the party's long-term future.[103]

Although Manatt had announced that the council was to serve a policy-making function, he had been forced to change the focus from substantive to organizational, after "prolonged negotiations with nervous congressional leaders about its make-up and powers."[104] In the final session of the two-day council meeting, the press was barred, but a report out of the meeting stated that there was general agreement on two major points: "the Democrats need clear national themes to prevail in the 1982 election and the strategy council itself needs more closed sessions if it is to come up with the themes."[105] Here we see an attempt, probably well conceived, to see that if the "knives were not going to be kept under the table," as they probably would not, at least it would not be done in public. Not only would a public fracas and bloodletting be embarrassing, but there also were other aspects to be considered. David Truman has observed that "decisions of such an advisory committee [which are] not made in public" are probably not much different from those made under scrutiny, but at least the pressure is removed that comes from being "placed in a position, whether justifiably or not, of asking or commanding without success."[106] Manatt announced that task forces were to be appointed to focus on the national economy, federal-state-local relations, foreign policy, and defense. These task forces were to report at the midterm conference to be held in June. There would at that time be discussion and possible formal ratification of the new policies to come from the conference delegates.

These recommendations were not forthcoming at the midterm conference, at least not in the form predicted by Manatt. There was no formal report from any of these task forces and there was no vote on any ratification of a set of prescribed policies. If any set of policies was submitted for consideration at the midterm conference, they may have been incorporated into the workshop sessions, but nothing was identifiable as having come from the task forces formed at the Strategy Council meeting in Baltimore.

At the end of the council, when participants were once more making statements for publication, Rep. Michael Barnes of Maryland said, "There are clearly strong disagreements among us on many issues, but there is a feeling we can—and must—get our act together."[107] Rep. Charles Rangel of New York summarized the deliberation at the council meeting:

Our common thread today is that we're losers. In the past, we've
never had to get along; we've been able to get by just tolerating
each other. Now we've reached the point we have to find out what
we do agree on. And we have to find out how to handle the issues
where we don't agree.[108]

Senator Byrd had said that "we're meeting among ourselves and we've
grown closer"; Rangel said "we have to get along." Apparently in the
Democrats' search for themselves, they were beginning to find each
other, but they were strangers when they met.

Organizing the Midterm Conference

During the first two years of Manatt's administration of the Party, the
search for a mission and a message seemed always to elude him and
the National Committee. The high hopes held for the development of
policy at the National Strategy [nee Policy] Council were dashed on the
rocks of Congressional egos.

Manatt hoped that the midterm miniconvention would "serve to set
the themes for the fall 1982 campaign."[109] Historically, midterm conventions had been controversial since the first one, which was authorized by the 1972 National Party Convention.

The party's leaders appeared annoyed by this historic first and its
conservatives, having failed to prevent it from being held at all,
did manage, in a series of hotly contested votes, to force its res-
cheduling from midsummer of 1974 to a month *after* the November
congressional elections so as not to embarrass the party's candidates and to confine its deliberation to *only* the provisions of the
[Sanford Commission] charter itself. Unexpectedly, the course of
political events, and especially the administration's inability to deal
forcefully with the deepening recession and inflationary price spi-
ral, had these same conservatives and party regulars loudly at-
tacking the restrictions as the convention drew near, a move that
eventually succeeded in opening the convocation to at least the
discussion of relevant contemporary issues.[110]

The Sanford Commission report recommended that the midterm conferences be made mandatory rather than optional and set the time,
composition, and format for the agenda of each. This recommendation
met with a great deal of controversy and opposition. "Unquestionably,
[Robert] Strauss distrusted the whole idea of a midterm convention. He
would have liked to abolish or ignore it." Ultimately, the charter, as
adopted, *"allowed* (the optional alternative) for midterm party confer-

ences to be held, with the time, place, agenda, and final decision of their
being convened left in the hands of the National Committee."[111]

When the question of a midterm convention arose early in the spring
of 1981, there was some hesitancy on the part of the regulars, who feared
that more bloodletting and self-flagellation might ensue, thus further
weakening the wounded party. James Sundquist was one who thought
that there was a danger in a midterm convention being held at *any* time.
"I think we are better off without one, the off-year races are very local."[112]
However, there were those with a more sanguine view of the midterm
meetings, who think that especially in the case of a party in power, such
devices as midterm conventions are a means for making the "president
more responsible to his colleagues in Congress and to the members of
his party."[113] Longley believes that the fears surrounding such conferences are largely unfounded. He sees that the "midterm conventions
have expanded the orbit of national party operations and provided an
additional setting for activity by party supporters."[114] Perhaps it was
just such expansion of "party activity" that prompted Sundquist and
others to recommend against holding the 1982 convention. They may
have been remembering not only the controversy surrounding the first
miniconvention in 1974 but also that of the more recent, second midterm
convention held in Memphis in 1978, which Jimmy Carter described as
"one of the most painful experiences of his life."[115] It was this 1978
gathering which "became a showcase for Sen. Edward M. Kennedy's
first full-scale attack on the domestic policies of the Carter administration."[116] It was also at this Memphis convention that the United Auto
Workers, under the leadership of Douglas Fraser (co-chair of the Hunt
Commission), in collaboration with other liberal groups, attempted to
defy the Carter policies and to push through a critical liberal resolution.
It was only the dogged work of Vice-President Mondale, trading on
personal power, which saved the Carter forces from public confrontation
and denunciation. "Nobody wanted to go through another gathering
like that, especially the Democratic members of Congress who are looking ahead to the fall campaign. Many urged Manatt to cancel the mini-
convention."[117] Manatt could hardly do that, since the Democratic National Committee voted in May 1981 to honor a resolution which, having
slipped by the Carter tactical forces, had been passed by the 1980 New
York Convention mandating just such a convention.[118]

In accepting the responsibility to mount a midterm convention in 1982,
the Democratic National Committee decided to make substantial changes
in the format and intent of the meeting. Meeting in Denver in June of
1981, the National Committee voted to change the date to one in late
spring or midsummer, *before* the midterm elections, and to reduce the
number of delegates by about half of the number who had attended
previous such gatherings. The delegates would include all members of

the National Committee and an equal number chosen by state central committees. There were to be some one hundred at-large delegates to even out representation of women and minorities, in case those groups were not adequately represented in the original selections.[119] Although the Hunt Commission had not even been announced when these rules were set, the DNC appeared to see the wisdom in involving a wide constituency, but at the same time, it wished to maintain some control over just who might attend. "Conferees were not selected by grass-roots Party participants, as they have in the past. Nervous members of Congress were assured that they would not be embarrassed by the demands of single-interest groups."[120] In deciding that the state party committees should choose 369 of the convention delegates, the National Committee wanted to give a degree of control to those "people who ought to set the party's mid-term election course." Manatt told a news conference that the Democrats are "not in any way turning their backs on the participatory process," but Broder reported that the "action was seen by many others as a landmark in the changing attitudes and procedures of the Democratic Party." He quoted South Carolina Committeeman Donald Fowler as saying that the "1978 conference was an assembly of the rabble," but Billie Carr of Texas, a reformer and leader of the "rabble," warned against the change in the selection process and the reduction in numbers; "You will have people demonstrating outside because they can't get in."[121]

The conference would be not only smaller, with its 973 conferees as compared with the 1,633 who met in Memphis, but also less expensive.[122] Economy in producing the conference was no inconsequential consideration for a party that had just paid off its 1968 debt, left from the campaigns of Humphrey and Robert Kennedy, and that had assumed $600,000 of the $1.25 million owed by the Carter-Mondale campaign at the end of the 1980 election.[123] Another significant change in the 1982 meeting was its change of name. Just as Manatt, for tactful and tactical reasons, had changed the name of the *Policy* Council to *Strategy* Council, he changed the name of the midterm *convention* to midterm *conference*. This change of name was supposedly to allay the fears of Congressional candidates that the meeting represented an *official* body of the party— just in case, after all the planners' carefully laid plans to keep things under control, the rabble got unruly and passed resolutions or binding actions with which the vulnerable House and Senate campaigners would have to travel for the next four months. Thomas E. Cronin has commented on the attitude toward midterm gatherings by members of Congress, who often approach them "with a lukewarm to opposed stance":

There are two reasons for this. First, it can complicate congressional elections (especially if the conventions are held before early November), by raising issues that a legislator would rather not run on or have to take a side on. Second, the platform or policy clarification role to some extent competes with, and even threatens, the responsibilities of the congressional party caucuses.[124]

Probably the most remarkable aspect of the Philadelphia conference, held appropriately in the city of both Independence and Brotherly Love on June 25–27, 1982, was that nothing much happened. There were a lot of speeches, innumerable parties, some crowded and emotional discussion groups, and most spectacularly, a "beauty contest" of the 1984 presidential hopefuls. Manatt was masterful in keeping the lid on the conference. He presided at the sessions with wit and poise. Drew comments that the conference was made up of carefully selected people and that "there was some heavy guidance from the top, but a Party that has absorbed as much diversity as the Democrats is by nature on the brink of—and sometimes in—chaos. The Democrats had been drowning in democracy."[125] A journal account of my own observations of the conference appears in the following chapter. It is offered to give a sense of the flavor and tempo of the conference and not as a critical assessment of the activities, which did, at times, border on chaos. Drew has summarized the accomplishments of the Philadelphia parley this way:

> What was most important about the conference in Philadelphia was that a number of big interests and several people with large egos and much at stake and a lot of people with little history of subordinating their particular goals to a common one managed to get together and consent to work for a larger purpose. In their so doing, the Party began to regain its morale and its bearings.[126]

It was to be the Democrats' finest hour of the two years after the debacle of November 1980. Although this era of good feelings did not last very long, at least they had momentarily found themselves.

Summary

Manatt's style of becoming the vocally partisan "organization" man and his affirmation of Jim Hunt, a state governor, to head the Commission on Presidential Nomination showed him as recognizing the weakness of the lack of participation by professional party leaders. The recommendation by the Hunt Commission for the return of Congressional Party members and State Party leaders to active participation in the national nominating conventions was a step toward "professionalization" of the Party, which could lead to a more cohesive and stable organization.

One of Manatt's strongest characteristics was his willingness to innovate. His setting up of the technology for a direct mail fund-raising mechanism was a major step toward solvency for the Democrats. Although the Democratic Party was still far behind the Republican Party in total amount of funds raised, Manatt did show a 45 percent increase in the treasury over the previous year of 1980. The addition of over 100,000 names to the donor lists was also a significant improvement. The innovative aspect of Manatt's leadership was also evidenced in his willingness to negotiate and to change course on the purposes of the National Policy Council when he met with resistance from members of Congress. Of course, it may be well argued here that the idea of the "policy" council was poorly implemented and that the result was clumsy ignorance in action. However, there had been precedent for such councils, and certainly the calls for "new ideas" and shared party goals were not to go unheeded by the new chairman. The search for a mission was to be ever elusive for Manatt and the National Party during the first two years after the 1980 defeat. In assessing the lack of productive behavior surrounding the National [Policy] Strategy Council, one can also discredit the Congressional leadership, who put personal political interest above the interest of the Party. This attitude on the part of the Congressional Democrats was not unique, being similar to one experienced by National Chairman Paul Butler in the late 1950s. However, just because it had happened before did not make it appropriate or less destructive.

Manatt's revival of the National Training Acadamies may have contributed to the gain of twenty-six Democratic House seats in the 98th Congress. We have no direct evidence to substantiate this, but since the average gain for an out-of-power party in an off-year election is ten seats, we could surmise that the extended services offered to state and local candidates by the National Party was helpful. The most important benefit will probably lie in the long-term payoff of such educational programs, that is, if they are continued and reinforced.

Besides the policy council debacle, the least effective of Manatt's endeavors was his attempt to persuade the states to abide by the rules of the Hunt Commission in holding primaries within the "window" period. Although some political scholars have criticized the restriction of the primary season, stating that it will lead to a "national" primary, there are others, such as Ranney, who see this as beneficial. In any event, the Democrats had laudable motives in wanting to shorten the season, but the state party leaders were not able to control their proprietary impulses. Once again we see evidence of the inability, or at least the unwillingness, of state party leaders to accept the "nationalization" of the Party. Manatt did as well as could be expected in attempting to get state and local party members involved, but there are historical as well as organizational barriers to this ... perhaps when the National Party is

able to send money instead of directives, the states will be more amenable to cooperation.

Probably the main accomplishment of Manatt's first two years was
the staging of an uneventful midterm conference. He was willing to give
in to Congressional Party members in changing the intent and impact
of the gathering by changing the name from *convention* to *conference*. The
organization of the conference, with almost half of its delegates being
chosen by state Democratic committees, and a careful managing of the
agenda helped to produce a sense of commonality among the participants. Manatt handled "prima donna" behavior on the part of presidential hopefuls at the conference with tact and skill, giving in when
he had to in the interest of harmony.

As for looking at the system of the National Party segment of the
Democratic Party, we can see that the main accomplishments lay in
further reforms to involve more party regulars, retiring a long-standing
campaign debt, establishing the framework for direct mail fund-raising
and increasing the list of known donors, beginning an educational program for party workers and candidates, and, at long last, holding a
national meeting which was not torn with divisiveness and strife.
Charles Manatt's skills and talents were all instrumental in the success
of these ventures.

On the negative or random side, the search for a mission or a unifying
policy was highly frenetic and nonproductive. Every time the Democrats
came together to find out what they stood for, they seemed to be sur-
prised at finding each other. Instead of facing up to the tough task of
determining their reason for being, they retreated to plotting strategy
in order to win elections—but they never seemed to be able to tackle
the big question of *why* anyone should want to elect them.

Notes

1. Cotter and Hennessy, 105.

2. *New York Times*, 22 March 1981, 21.

3. For a detailed account of these events see Jack W. Germond and Jules
Witcover, *Blue Smoke and Mirrors: How Reagan Won and Why Carter Lost the Election
of 1980* (New York: Viking Press, 1981), 191–208; Elizabeth Drew, *Portrait of an
Election: The 1980 Presidential Campaign* (New York: Simon and Schuster, 1981),
221–60.

4. Polsby, *Consequences*; Crotty; Byron E. Shafer, *The Quiet Revolution: Reform
Politics in the Democratic Party, 1968–1972* (New York: Russell Sage Foundation,
1984); James W. Ceaser, *Reforming the Reforms: A Critical Analysis of the Presidential
Selection Process* (Cambridge, Mass.: Ballinger Publishing Co., 1982).

5. Polsby, *Consequences*, 73. For a provocative essay on the types of party
reform, see also Nelson W. Polsby and Aaron Wildavsky, *Presidential Elections:*

Strategies of American Electoral Politics, 6th ed. (New York: Charles Scribner's Sons, 1984), 208–66.

6. *Report of the Commission on Presidential Nomination*, by James B. Hunt, Jr., Chairman (Washington, D.C.: Democratic National Committee, 1982), 1.

7. Douglas Fraser here should not be confused with *Donald* Fraser, who was a member of the House of Representatives from Minnesota at the time he served on the McGovern-Fraser Commission.

8. *Washington Post*, 3 July 1981, 10.

9. George F. Will, "Pushing and Pulling the Party Together," *Washington Post*, 5 March 1981, A19.

10. Polsby, *Consequences*, 180.

11. Haynes Johnson, "Party is Trying to Chart Political Realities of '80s," *Washington Post*, 18 May 1981, A19.

12. *Report of the Commission*, 4, 506.

13. Ibid., [i].

14. Ibid., 2.

15. Ibid., 3.

16. Ibid., 6–7.

17. Polsby, *Consequences*, 5.

18. Ibid., 54–55.

19. *Report of the Commission*, 7, 27, 17.

20. *Delegate Selection Rules for the 1984 Democratic National Convention*, Adopted by the Democratic National Committee, March 26, 1982 (Washington, D.C.: Democratic National Committee, n.d.), 8, 12.

21. *Report of the Commission*, 12–13.

22. Ibid., 28.

23. Ibid., 56.

24. Ceaser, 46.

25. *Report of the Commission*, 3.

26. Drew, *Portrait of an Election*, 225.

27. *Report of the Commission*, 6.

28. Ibid., 9–10.

29. Ceaser, 55–70; Crotty, 193–237; Polsby, *Consequences*, 55–75; Rubin, 90–106; Austin Ranney, *The Federalization of Presidential Primaries* (Washington, D.C.: American Enterprise Institute for Public Policy Research, 1978).

30. *Report of the Commission*, 10.

31. Ibid., 19.

32. Ibid., 19–20.

33. Ruth Marcus, "Stubborn: DNC and Vermont May Prefer, But New Hampshire Insists," *Washington Post*, 24 January 1983, A4.

34. *Report of the Commission*, 56.

35. Marcus.

36. Ibid.

37. David Broder, "Democrats' New Calendar, Rules May Produce Early Winner," *Washington Post*, 22 August 1983, A2.

38. Mark Shields, "Democrats, Seize the Rules," *Washington Post*, 21 August 1981, A29.

39. *Report of the Commission*, 14.

40. Ibid.

41. Mark Shields, "The Democrats' Boutique Politics," *Washington Post*, 11 February 1983, A23.

42. *Report of the Commission*, 14.

43. Ibid.

44. Austin Ranney, "Political Parties: Reform and Decline," in Anthony King, ed., *The New American Political System* (Washington, D.C.: American Enterprise Institute for Public Policy Research, 1978), 238–39.

45. Dom Bonafede, "For the Democratic Party, It's a Time for Rebuilding and Seeking New Ideas," *National Journal*, 21 February 1981, 317.

46. *Report of the Commission*, 12, 22.

47. Robert G. Torricelli and Tom Donilon, "Reforming the Democrats' Reforms," *Washington Post*, 24 August 1981, A17; David G. Broder, "Democrats and Unintended Consequences," *Washington Post*, 17 January 1982, A6; Gillis Long, "Shaping Up the Democrats," *Washington Post*, 5 February 1982, A27.

48. Elizabeth Drew, "A Political Journal," *New Yorker*, 28 March 1983, 66.

49. David S. Broder, "Democrats, Gearing Up for '82, Launch National Training Academies," *Washington Post*, 28 September 1981, A9.

50. Bibby and Huckshorn, 227.

51. John F. Bibby, "Party Renewal in the National Republican Party," in Gerald M. Pomper, ed., *Party Renewal in America: Theory and Practice* (New York: Praeger, 1981), 110.

52. Charles H. Longley, "National Party Renewal," in Pomper, ed., *Party Renewal*, 85.

53. Drew, "Political Journal," 225.

54. Austin Ranney, "The Evolution of the Democratic Party's National Organization: Characteristics, Causes, and Consequences" (Paper delivered at joint meeting of Commission on Party Structure and Delegate Selection and Commission on Rules, Washington, D.C., 19 November 1971), 5.

55. Louise Sweeny, "Democrats' Boss Has No Time for 'Goofiness,' " *Christian Science Monitor*, 8 September 1983, B8–B11.

56. Gerald M. Pomper, "The Contribution of Political Parties to American Democracy," *Party Renewal*, 9–10.

57. Democratic National Committee, *Official Proceedings of the 1982 Democratic National Party Conference* (Washington, D.C.: Democratic National Committee, 1982), 211.

58. *Insider's Report*, Democratic National Committee newsletter, 2 (Jan./Feb. 1982): [2].

59. Broder, 29 September 1981, A9.

60. Flyer, Democratic National Training Academy, 1625 Massachusetts Ave., N.W., Washington, D.C., 20036 [June 1982].

61. *Insider's Report* (Jan./Feb. 1982): [2].

62. Ann F. Lewis to party members, Washington, D.C., 25 June 1982. Personal files of Caroline Arden, Arlington, Va.

63. Longley, 84.

64. Polsby and Wildavsky, 53.

65. Clymer, 1 March 1981, sec. 4, p. 2.

66. *Campaign Funds—A Widening Gap*, Special Report, No. 98–1 (Washington,

D.C.: Democratic Study Group, U.S. House of Representatives, 5 January 1983),
1, 9.
    67. Ibid., 1.
    68. Ibid., 2.
    69. Polsby and Wildavsky, 149.
    70. Martin Schram, "Why Can't Democrats Be More Like Republicans?
They're Trying," *Washington Post*, 23 March 1982, A2.
    71. Elizabeth Drew, "A Reporter at Large: Politics and Money—I," *New
Yorker*, 6 December 1982, 101.
    72. *Campaign Funds*, 2.
    73. John C. Culver, letter, Democratic Study Group, Washington, D.C., 18
November 1981. Personal files of Caroline Arden, Arlington, Va.
    74. *Insider's Report*, 1 (Washington, D.C.: Democratic National Committee,
n.d.).
    75. Schram.
    76. "Political Notes," *Washington Post*, 11 October 1981, A5.
    77. "Social Security Appeals by Democrats Assailed," *New York Times*, 19
December 1981, 28.
    78. Ibid.
    79. Schram.
    80. Ibid.
    81. *Campaign Funds*, 3.
    82. "Democrats Day," *Washington Post*, 3 October 1981, C6.
    83. David B. Truman, *The Congressional Party: A Case Study* (New York: John
Wiley & Sons, 1959), 301.
    84. Ibid., 301–2.
    85. Price, *Bringing Back the Parties*, 273.
    86. Ibid.
    87. Ibid., 268.
    88. Ibid., 271.
    89. William J. Keefe, *Parties, Politics, and Public Policy in America*, 2d ed.
(Hinsdale, Ill.:Dryden Press, 1976), 159.
    90. Ibid.
    91. Price, 270.
    92. Crotty, 253.
    93. Price, 271.
    94. David S. Broder, "Democrats' Policy Session a Big Gamble," *Washington
Post*, 19 October 1981, A4.
    95. Ibid.
    96. Paul Taylor, "Democratic Alternative Not Ready," *Washington Post*, 16
October 1981, A7.
    97. Ibid.
    98. David S. Broder, "Top Democrats Struggle to Find Fuel for a Political
Comeback," *Washington Post*, 18 October 1981, A3.
    99. "Democratic Senators Meet on Mountain, Find Unity But Not Strategy,"
Washington Post, 5 October 1981, A2.
    100. Ibid.
    101. Broder, 19 October 1981.

102. David S. Broder, "Democrats Launch a New Policy-Making Council," *Washington Post*, 17 October 1981, A7.

103. Broder, 19 October 1981.

104. Broder, 17 October 1981.

105. Broder, 19 October 1981.

106. Truman, *Congressional Party*, 302.

107. Broder, 19 October 1981.

108. Ibid.

109. David S. Broder, "Democrats Agree on '82 Philadelphia Parley," *Washington Post*, 18 September 1981, A6.

110. Crotty, 248–49.

111. Ibid., 251, 253.

112. James L. Sundquist, Remarks before the Woman's National Democratic Club, 27 March 1981, Washington, D.C.

113. Pomper, "The Contribution of Political Parties," 16.

114. Longley, 82.

115. Elizabeth Drew, "Reporter at Large: The Democratic Party," *New Yorker*, 19 July 1982, 77.

116. David S. Broder, "Democrats Aiming for Maximum Control over Mini-Convention," *Washington Post*, 6 June 1981, A3.

117. Ibid.

118. "Democrats Seek Changes in Conference Set for 1982," *Washington Post*, 5 May 1981, A7.

119. Ibid.

120. Drew, 19 July 1982, 78.

121. David S. Broder, "Democrats, In Turnabout, Shrink Size of '82 Mid-Term Convention," *Washington Post*, 6 June 1981, A3.

122. Elizabeth Drew gives the count of conferees at 897, but a count of those listed in the *Official Proceedings* amounts to 973 "Conference Participants and Replacements."

123. "Democrats Pay Off '68 Debt But GOP Has Money Edge," *Washington Post*, 4 June 1982, A2.

124. Thomas E. Cronin, "The Presidency and the Parties," in Pomper, ed., *Party Renewal*, 189.

125. Drew, 19 July 1982, 94.

126. Ibid.

4

The Search for
Community

"Neat but not gaudy" may have been the goal of the conference planners, but by the time the 973 conferees, 1000 members of the press,
members of Congress, presidential hopefuls, professional staffs, ven-
dors of tacos, buttons, and bromides, as well as just plain old-fashioned
political toadies and tosspots had gathered in the steam bath which is
Philadelphia in late June, there were over 6000 people in and around
the Civic Center. Credentials were hard to come by, and they were
checked carefully by a zealous security falange outside the hall. Potential
candidates were everywhere. There was no doubt that, even without
the ninety-plus degree weather, there was going to be a hot time in the
old town *every* night.

Texas Committeewoman Billie Carr's prediction that there would be
people demonstrating outside the hall was correct; on the other hand,
they were not there trying to get in as participants but rather to catch
the attention of the television porto-packs and the credentialed individuals who were allowed on the same side of the street as the Civic Center.
Those who assembled on the very sunny side of the street, across from
the hall, did so for the most part extremely peaceably. There were women
wearing the symbolic green-and-white of the ERA campaign. With only
three days to Endsday for the passage of the Equal Rights Amendment,
its proponents wanted the conferees to know: "The vote you cast may
be your last! Remember ERA!" There were black activists who appeared
to be a purely local group marching to the same drummer whenever
and wherever there was attention to be had. They were particularly
unhappy with Averill Harriman and some association with "German
Fascist Butcher-Barons." It was never quite clear what their cause was,

but the security forces around the Civic Center put on their helmets and stood in parade-rest formation at the steps leading to the hall whenever this group took over from the women in green and white.

Inside the hall itself there was an enormous amount of activity and intensity. The city of Philadelphia may have figuratively rolled out the red carpet for the Democrats, but the Civic Center managers had taken the precaution to take up the Center's traditional red floor covering, and the feet of the faithful tramped through the dust and grime. Few appeared to care. On Friday afternoon, June 25, at 2:38 P.M., Manatt called to order the noisy throng which included thirty-three state governors and lieutenant governors and fifty-two members of Congress among its official participants and alternates. All Democratic state party executive directors, members of DNC committee commissions, and "members of Congress who [were] not otherwise selected as participants [were] entitled to floor access during the Conference."[1] Any and everybody who could gain floor access on Friday afternoon wanted to be there to see and be seen. It was almost impossible to be heard, and Manatt was forced constantly to "shush" the participants present. Saturday was to be the beginning of the speeches by declared presidential candidates. Position on the program had been determined by lot, and Alan Cranston had drawn the first slot.

There had been a bit of a ruckus just prior to the conference when Ted Kennedy refused to appear on the same day as the other candidates, but this was worked out by allowing him to give the closing address to the conference on Sunday. It all had to do with the use of a Tele-PrompTer, which Kennedy said he needed and which the DNC said was too expensive, and besides that why did he need a TeleprompTer in order to speak from the heart to an auditorium of the faithful? There was closed-circuit television for those excluded from the floor on Saturday, that is, if one could find a monitor. The one in the press room was not working. Those fortunate enough to find a monitor probably saw and heard much more of Saturday's proceedings than those in the noisy hall.

Cranston's speech centered on the economy in its opening portion; the Cranston wit came through in his remark that "Ronald Reagan is depending on charisma alone, and he is giving charisma a bad name." Cranston, for obvious reasons, could not depend on charisma, and he soon launched into his major campaign theme calling for an immediate freeze on the production and deployment of nuclear arms.

Several speeches intervened after Cranston's, giving some of the party faithful, including former Party Chairman John White, a moment or two in the limelight. It is doubtful that anyone in the hall heard anything that was said until Manatt announced, "Fellow Democrats, I am proud to present, former Vice-President of the United States, Walter F. Mondale." Mondale spoke, and it was the first and last time that undivided attention was given to a speaker that afternoon. Even the paterfamilias "Tip" O'Neill had not commanded such attention. Mondale touched all the bases. He dwelt mostly on the economy, but he did not miss the questions of the ERA, the excesses of special-interest money in politics, and arms control. Although he said he favored a freeze on nuclear production, he supported a strong defense system. Right down the middle of the road, he drew on the words of the preamble to the Constitution and drew his loudest applause with the following:

> To establish justice; not just order, but justice. To provide for the common defense *and* the general welfare. It doesn't say to provide for the common defense *or* the general welfare; It says both.[2]

The hall went wild. It was difficult for Manatt to regain the attention of the participants, but eventually they settled somewhat so that Sen. Ernest Hollings could begin his address. In his thick Charleston accent, the senator admitted that he knew that "in the minds of many, the presidency has been ruined for a Southerner, but Richard Nixon didn't ruin California for Ronald Reagan. Besides, Jimmy Carter is looking better every day."[3] Hollings drew little applause in the course of his speech, but he made no effort to play to the gallery. He took a hard line on stepping up defense, and gave lip service to the nuclear freeze. His was by far the most scholarly of the speeches, and he invoked Madison from the *Federalist Papers*, along with other intellectuals such as Archibald MacLeish and Adlai Stevenson. His was not the most popular speech, but it was by far the most substantive in content and in giving the assembled an idea of where the candidate stood. The afternoon had been billed as a "beauty contest" of candidates, the speeches being the talent portion. Hollings's speech was as though a hopeful Miss America had just executed a brilliant Beethoven concerto between a tap dancer and a baton twirler. The performance was splendid and sincere but not a crowd pleaser. The afternoon droned on. Sen. Gary Hart spoke with passion and intensity, seeming to add to the heat of the stifling hall. Participants squirmed and swabbed brows. Hart invoked the names of Franklin and Eleanor Roosevelt, Martin Luther King, and John and Robert Kennedy, all dead and all in the political public domain. He admonished the Party to return to the liberal principles of yesterday. There was little in Hart's speech that gave evidence of having been written in 1982 rather than 1932, save the reference to banishing the "nuclear demon back in to its cave and seal[ing] it up forever."[4] Hart, the dragon slayer, didn't say much, but the consensus outside the hall was that he looked very attractive while saying it. By the time Sen. John Glenn took the platform, it was well after 6:00 P.M., far into the cocktail hour, and the participants were getting very restless. There were countless parties and receptions to attend, and Glenn had a hard time capturing and holding attention. He is by no means a dynamic speaker, and his speech was laden and leaden with turgid prose. He had one masterful statement which drew loud applause from the frustrated feminists:

> The President says appointing Sandra O'Connor to the Supreme Court proves his commitment to equal rights for women. But we Democrats say there is a huge difference between making one woman a Justice and bringing justice to American women.[5]

Glenn spent more time on the economy than he did on defense. His one nod to the prevailing issue of the nuclear freeze was to state: "We must seek a limiting verifiable freeze on nuclear weapons." He went on to demand an involvement of all nations in an effort for arms control.[6]

Reubin Askew, former governor of Florida who had also announced his candidacy, chose not to address the conference. He spent his time in one-on-one conversation with individuals and groups. He was everywhere, walking up to any group in which more than three were gathered. He played especially hard to any identifiable contingent of Young Democrats. Askew gave one the impression of a freshman at a fraternity mixer who is eager, but doesn't have an alumnus sponsoring him and doesn't know he needs one. He just went around smiling and shaking hands, sure that there would be at least six bids in his mail by morning.

Perhaps the most attention-getting event of the afternoon was when Manatt announced that Alexander Haig had just resigned as Secretary of State. At first the noisy crowd thought it was some kind of Manatt joke or contrivance just to get them to pay attention. However, when members of the press corps began to adjust their earphones, listen for a second, and then leave the hall, they knew it was true. This event almost upstaged the entire proceedings of the day. It certainly distracted media attention. If one could ascribe careful cunning rather than acute pique to Haig, one might think that he planned it that way.

The crowd, surfeited with rhetoric, left the Civic Center and set about the real business of such a gathering, which is in the renewing of old acquaintance, pressing the flesh, and being courted by candidates. The organizers may have changed the name to protect the Congressional squeamish, but the "participants" were acting like delegates. There were parties all over the city that night:

> Like warring kings who gave feasts for their courts, each candidate laid out the cheese and the chicken wings. One way to tell the seriousness of each presidential candidate was to size up his cocktail party. Most of the rooms in which the parties were held were

sweltering and all were packed; Democrats, in the magnanimous spirit of a party out of power, invited everybody.[7]

Saturday Workshops

Saturday, June 26, was a workday for the participants. Although there had been training and strategy sessions held prior to the plenary session on Friday, Saturday's agenda presented the meat of the conference. There were seven workshops dealing with party goals and principles to be held. These workshops were to "offer participants an opportunity to discuss public policy changes and to adopt a consensus statement that reflects the Party's broad statement of goals and principles. Statements [would] also outline the clear differences between Democrats and Republicans on the issues."[8]

Participants were given a chance to choose the workshops they wanted to attend prior to the conference. Choices had to be in to the DNC Conference Committee before April 30, 1982. They were asked to submit a draft statement to the Program Committee Task Force for any of the seven workshops. It was requested that the statements be concise and that they "reflect the Party's goals and principles."[9] The deadline for submitting these statements was April 16, 1982. The Program Task Force, chaired by Lynn Cutler, vice-chair of the DNC, sent draft workshop statements to all participants by June 4, with a deadline for amendments and alternative statements due by June 18, 1982, only one week prior to the Philadelphia meeting. Any amendments which the Task Force deemed worthy would be included in the draft workshop statements.[10] These amendments were not distributed to the participants until the close of the plenary session late on Friday afternoon. Further amendments could be added before 8:00 P.M. that evening if they were accompanied by signatures of 10 percent of the workshop participants.[11]

It is difficult to accept that the participants had time and inclination to give the workshop statements and amendments the study they demanded. However, after an afternoon of unending oratory and a night of revelry, the participants were back in the various meeting rooms of the Civic Center by 9:00 A.M. on Saturday. Admission to the workshop meeting rooms was not as strict as it had been to the main convention hall on the previous day during the candidate speeches, and participants and observers moved freely and frequently among the sessions. The two most heavily attended workshops were those on Foreign Policy, Defense and Arms Control, "America's Security in the 1980's" and Promoting Economic Growth and Opportunity, the attendance pattern echoing the candidates' emphasis of the day before. Senator Paul Tsongas chaired the session on foreign policy, and Senator Bill Bradley presided over the deliberations on economic growth. Each workshop followed a

similar pattern, with statements from the panelists and then floor discussion and questions from the duly credentialed and assigned participants.

The session entitled Investing in Our People, chaired by Rep. Paul
Simon, drew many of the reform activists to its deliberations, and the
discussion that came from the floor was often emotional and heated.
An equal amount of passion, but of a more aggressive nature, emerged
in the workshop on Citizens Rights and Personal Safety. This session,
chaired by Eleanor Holmes Norton, covered such diverse issues as
women in policy-making positions, respect for regional languages and
cultures, justice for all, organized crime, and "a voice of freedom stifled."
From a brief attendance at the meeting, it was difficult to determine that
any voice was stifled. This workshop must have been planned to accommodate all the issues and groups who stand alone and don't fit anywhere
except in the all-embracing arms of the Democratic Party.

The workshop on Agriculture, Rural America, Food and Nutrition,
though covering a variety of issues, was at least more focused than those
that tried to be all things to all forgotten people. Roxanne Conlin chaired
this meeting, which appeared to have attendees who were vitally involved in the topics rather than just there for the show. In the discussions
emerging from the workshop on Promoting Energy Security and Pro-
tecting Our Environment, it became evident that Reagan's plan for abolishing the Carter-created Department of Energy would be a major
campaign issue in 1984 if the workshop participants had their way. They
saw "the challenge of energy" as "a rallying point for national renewal,
building the foundation of a more secure, productive America."[12] The
group also got in some good anti-Reagan licks concerning the administration of EPA, and appropriating Reagan's Press Secretary Jim Brady's
remark about Reagan's lack of understanding of photosynthesis, there
was even a section in the workshop proposals on "Killer Trees—the
Republican Assault on Clean Air." By far the most lively of all the reports
out of the workshops, the Energy-Environment statement, bore the sure
mark of the wit of one of its panelists, Rep. "Moe" Udall.

Rep. Allen Ertel of Pennsylvania chaired the workshop on Making
Government Work Better. It was in this session that the Democratic faith
in government as an "instrument of our common good" was reaffirmed.
The proposals coming from the session consistently returned to the same
thesis:

> The Democratic Party views government as an extension of the
> people, created by them and good or bad in its effect as they make
> it so. It is an expression of the people's will and common purpose
> and, properly guided and managed, a tool for defense of the public

interest, a catalyst for economic development in private markets, and a guarantor of equal rights and opportunities.[13]

The old and cherished Democratic progressive ideals were stated anew in the proposals coming from the workshop participants. There was enough campaign rhetoric supplied there for any and all future candidates, whoever they might be.

Conversations With Conference Delegates

As the Saturday session went on, not all participants in the conference found their way into one of the crowded hearing rooms. Many found this to be time for renewing contacts, calling special interest rump sessions, and in general just milling about. The "beauty contest" participants toured each session, waded into groups larger than four, and smiled and shook hands with everybody in sight. The candidates were easily identifiable. All, except Reubin Askew, wore the vivid orange face make-up which would make them presentable for the television camera, in case one happened to turn its red eye in their direction. Ted Kennedy brought his own crew. His entourage could create a crowd and compress it just by moving through the hall with camera dollies and klieg lights. Manatt was ubiquitous and obviously enjoying himself. He could be seen escorting Mondale through the lobby crowd at one minute and five minutes later he had Fritz Hollings in tow. Manatt gave the impression of a man who had everything completely under control and was happy with the results of his labors.

Manatt was not the only one who was pleased with the way things were going. David C. McClung, committeeman from Hawaii, who had been a party officer since long before Manatt cut his political teeth with the Young Democrats, said that he saw the conference as an event that was bringing about a consensus, something that had been lacking since 1968. He saw the 1972 and 1976 Democratic conventions as "fiascos." McClung thought that as a result of winning the White House in 1976, along with good majorities in the House and Senate, the Democrats "got fat and sassy" and did not work hard enough in the 1980 election. He felt that there were some valuable lessons learned in defeat, especially the realization that "hey, maybe I'd better talk a little better to my fellow Democrat."[14] McClung thought that the Hunt Commission's recommendation to make delegates of all members of the National Committee a good one; he also approved of allowing financial assistance for young people to attend the convention. He felt that the Party had too long neglected the recruitment and training of new members. He summed up this point of view in a colorful metaphor: "The only reason the toilet flushes and the water runs is because there was water in the tank in the first place."[15] McClung did not think that there is much value in courting organized labor, "they rarely bring out the vote, anyway." His fellow participant, Sam Dawson of Texas, disagreed. Dawson, who is political director for the National Steelworkers in Washington, thought that although labor had been driven away from the Party, some may return, and it will be to the benefit of both the Party and to the individual union member. He saw the unions as the "people's lobby," adding that "out of all the constituency groups and organizations, we're the only ones who have the bucks to do it."[16]

Sherry McGowan, committeewoman from Kansas, was pleased with her participation in the workshop dealing with personal safety. She felt that the issue paper and the resolutions coming from that session gave that portion of the platform recommendations a sharper "cutting edge." She was concerned that members of Congress in her workshop had admonished that the Party had to move further to the right. She felt that if there is a movement it should come from the center out to the left. She said that some had wanted to muzzle the left-wing members of the Party, but she thought that would have a detrimental effect, in that our "ideas come from the left." However, McGowan recognized that members of Congress and members of the DNC have a primary obligation to represent the people back home. She thinks that local "issue conferences" such as those held in Kansas are a good way to encourage grass-roots participation and are an excellent means for getting ideas generated and disbursed. "We must train Democrats to *think* and write papers," she added. Her assessment of the period following the Reagan victory and the Democrats' loss of the Senate was that it represented a "grief cycle" for the Democrats. She said the Party went through all the classic manifestations of grief, including denial, self-loathing, and guilt. She saw the time of the midterm conference as that of the "acceptance and positive reconstruction" phase of the cycle. McGowan said, "We are still talking about the same things, people's needs haven't changed, but I think we are changing in the way we are talking to each other. Some of us are even starting to listen."[17]

McGowan's fellow Kansan, Richard A. Pinaire, who serves on the DNC's Platform Accountability Committee, agreed with her that elected officials need to represent the interests of their constituents. However, reconciling the desires of one's constituents with inconsistent tenets in the Party's platform has caused certain members of the committee great difficulty. The Platform Accountability Committee has been charged with the responsibility of studying various ways to make elected Democrats more accountable to positions on issues as set out in the Party platform. Pinaire believes that it is inappropriate to require that each elected official support each and every tenet contained in previous Party platforms because to do so would stifle the development of new ideas for the Party. Pinaire added that the Party must change and evolve but that such change should occur at a measured pace. "In recent years, platform committees have been unduly influenced by various special interests and pressure groups," Pinaire observed. He went on to add that many of the proposals presented by special interests had merit but many did not have broad appeal to the electorate. Accordingly, he could not find fault with a member of Congress who adopted a position favored by a majority of his constituents as opposed to an inconsistent position that may be adopted by the Party in its platform. He feels that the most virulent political disease at the moment is political apathy. He said that this stems from the fact that the people see government at all levels as unresponsive. Pinaire said it was this problem that led him to become involved in studying platform accountability, but he had little hope that the Platform Accountability Commission would solve that problem. He was not as enthusiastic about the present condition of the party as his colleague McGowan, but he felt, along with Sam Dawson, that getting organized labor back into the Party was a very positive step towards rebuilding the Party. "Organized labor can bring financial support to the Party and their involvement can demonstrate the importance of belonging to parties to people on the street, based upon results that are achieved by reason of their involvement."[18]

If Sam Dawson saw his labor constituency as "the people's lobby," Jessie Rattley, committeewoman from Virginia, and her fellow Virginian, Henry Marsh, at that time mayor of Richmond, saw their Black Caucus as the "conscience of the Democratic Party." Rattley said that although she is very active in the Black Caucus, she feels that she represents "*all* the people of Newport News, across the board." She said Reagan's agriculture policies had been especially harmful to her district and that the small shipbuilding companies were suffering, the Republican's tending to award contracts to the larger, more affluent companies. Rattley said she was most impressed by Mondale's speech of the day before, especially the "part about providing for the common defense *and* the general welfare—both of those are very important in my district."[19] Her colleague Marsh was not as sanguine or as all-encompassing in his affection for the Democratic Party. Mayor Marsh felt that many of the issues which were being debated in the workshops were really issues of race, but "they aren't saying that." Marsh felt that the Party was selling the black cause short while taking their "95 percent voting strength for granted." Marsh warned that the Party had best change that attitude and "realize that politics is the art of the possible and it's possible for blacks to mount their own platform and slate. If somebody doesn't *really* listen to black voices soon, this country is going to go down the tube."[20] (Three days after the interview in Philadelphia, Marsh was under siege in Richmond. A group of white business leaders supporting a newly elected black city council member, Roy West, wielded enough influence to topple Marsh from his post and elect West as mayor. During his administration, Marsh had altered the mayor's job from a largely ceremonial office to one of power and change. It was West's vote that was the deciding one in Marsh's ouster. Perhaps Marsh had taught his political lesson too well—black Mayor Roy West certainly had shown it was possible to learn the art of politics, and that art probably lay in coalition building.)[21]

Ted Kennedy Addresses the Conference

Sunday, June 27, dawned hot, bright, and bleary-eyed for the Democrats in Philadelphia, but their increasing enthusiasm and mutual affection could not be dimmed by mere hangovers. They had another day to revel in the excitement of political superstars, and the hard work of passing amendments and adopting the issue papers was behind them. There was to be no debate from the floor on the policy papers. They were to be presented to the participants by the chair of each workshop and accepted without discussion or a vote. The haggling, debating, amending, voting, and adopting had all taken place the day before in the workshop sessions. The main convention hall was filled by a half-hour into the proceedings on Sunday morning. The Kennedy speech was scheduled for about noon, and everybody wanted to be there, whether to exult, take notes, plot an opposing strategy, or just to bask in the television limelight. Senate Minority Leader Robert Byrd, House Majority Leader Jim Wright, and former Party Chairman Robert Strauss preceded Kennedy on the program. They were given scant attention by the participants. Everybody was waiting for the main event. Even Jim Wright, known for his stirring oratory on the floor of the House, had difficulty gaining and keeping attention.

Finally, Manatt asked that "everyone in the aisles now either hunker down or else just go in an area where other people can see ... we've got some good news, and that is the space shuttle is up, and it's doing fine, and the crew is well. So that's the good news."[22] He did not finish the statement with the expected, "and now for the bad news," but the implication was there whether it was intended or not. Manatt, the polished professional, did not miss a beat; he proceeded to introduce Senator Kennedy.

After the beginning pandemonium died down, Kennedy launched into a well-written speech, which, although it lacked the luster of the one he had given at the 1980 Democratic convention, drew applause some fifty-two times during its course. His best delivery and most effective statement came when he addressed the question of the Party's search for new ideas:

We do not seek new ideas solely for the sake of their novelty. For us the test of an idea is not whether it is new or old, but whether it is right or wrong. And for those old ideas which are right, we must continue a never-ending fight.[23]

If he did nothing else, Kennedy reminded the Democrats of their moral duty in a way in which the Black Caucus, with its stridency, had failed to do.

The only actual votes taken on the floor of the conference were those supporting resolutions of gratitude to the city of Philadelphia and for adjournment, which the Democrats did at 4:14 P.M. on Sunday, June 27, 1982. Everybody went home tired but very happy with the conference and, for the most part, with each other.

Notes

1. *Rules for the 1982 National Party Conference*, adopted by the DNC Executive Committee, 14 January 1982.

2. Democratic National Committee, *Official Proceedings of the 1982 Democratic National Party Conference*, (Washington, D.C.: Democratic National Committee, n.d.), 78.

3. Ibid., 79.

4. Ibid., 83.

5. Ibid., 85.

6. Ibid., 86.

7. Elisabeth Bumiller, "The Happy Days: Politics Aside, The Democrats Had Fun in Philly," *Washington Post*, 28 June 1982, C3.

8. *Rules for the 1982 National Party Conference*.

9. Ibid.

10. Ibid.

11. Democratic National Committee, 87.

12. Ibid., 177.

13. Ibid., 163.

14. David C. McClung, interview held during meeting of Democratic National Party Conference, Philadelphia, Pennsylvania, 26 June 1982.

15. Ibid.

16. Sam Dawson, interview held during meeting of the Democratic National Party Conference, Philadelphia, Pennsylvania, 26 June 1982.

17. Sherry A. McGowan, interview held during meeting of the Democratic National Party Conference, Philadelphia, Pennsylvania, 26 June 1982.

18. Richard A. Pinaire, interview held during meeting of the Democratic National Party Conference, Philadelphia, Pennsylvania, 26 June 1982.

19. Jessie M. Rattley, interview held during meeting of the Democratic National Party Conference, Philadelphia, Pennsylvania, 26 June 1982.

20. Henry Marsh, interview held during meeting of the Democratic National Party Conference, Philadelphia, Pennsylvania, 26 June 1982.

21. *Washington Post*, 30 June 1982, A1–7, and 2 July 1982, A1.

22. Democratic National Committee, 200.

23. Ibid., 203.

5

The Congressional Search for a Common Identity

The essential irony of political parties in the American legislative system is this: while party identification is perhaps the most important determinant of voting behavior in elections as well as legislative voting, the sort of unified, efficient party organization which would seem to be a necessary part of such a system is lacking both at the electoral and the legislative level.[1]

This chapter examines how the Congressional Democrats went about their search for a common identity, an ideological message that would include the myths, symbols, and beliefs of the Party and a voice to carry that message to those who voted for them as well as to those who did not. Since these elements of the centripetal momentum could come only from some sort of leader or group of leaders, close attention is given to the Party's elected leadership as well as to that leadership which emerged, called forth by other imperatives. James McGregor Burns observed that when the presidency is not held by the majority party in the Congress, "the elected congressional leaders usually move closer to the seniority leadership of the congressional party."[2] Burns, writing some ten years prior to the dramatic Congressional reforms of the 1974–75 period which changed the seniority and standing committee system, noted that "the difficulty for the elected leaders, in contrast to the other sets of leaders, is that they lack firm institutional bases of their own. . . . If the majority leader and his whips lack a President to back them up, they are generally, and over the long run, drawn into the vortex of the senior leaders."[3] Where Burns had once seen a vortex, the 1981 Congressional leadership saw only a void. An examination is made of how existing groups became revitalized and how new ones evolved as the Democrats in the House sought to fill that void. The Senate presented a peculiar and particular problem. For the first time since the 83rd Congress of 1953–54, the Republicans controlled the Senate. It was in the less structured setting of the Senate that it was possible to observe how coalitions evolved and how individuals attempted to assume a leadership role in this body, which has been called by Norman Ornstein and others the "presidential incubator."[4]

In observing the Democrats' search for identity and ideology, it was important to examine publications and policy statements that were made by the leadership, the various groups, and/or individuals in the Party of both houses about what that ideology might be. A search was made for evidence of a strategy on the part of the Congressional Party for regaining and increasing power by winning elections in 1982. The findings from this research are presented in this chapter.

Individualism in a Majority Party

There are two pre-existing conditions that exacerbated the distress of the walking wounded of the Democratic Party in the Congress after the 1980 election. One was the intense individualism of all members of Congress which had developed in the years after the Congressional reforms of the 1970s. The other was the fact that the Democrats had for a very long period of time been a stable, majority party. They did not know how to lose, and when they did, they were each very much alone. The members of the U.S. Congress are what Thomas Mann terms "political entrepreneurs."

> While legislative styles differ—members are more or less active, ideologically motivated, solicitous of constituency interests, and inclined to defer to colleagues—they are all likely to view themselves first and foremost as individuals, not as members of a party or as a part of a president's team.[5]

David Mayhew states this same point even more bluntly: "The important point here is that a congressman can—indeed must—build a power base that is substantially independent of party."[6] Of course, in November 1980, for those who did lose and for those in the Senate who did win or were still there but now in a *minority* party, individual responsibility for defeat was very difficult to accept. John Kingdon has explained this attitude as the "congratulation-rationalization effect," where winners will congratulate themselves upon winning, but blame their defeats on factors beyond their control.[7] Although Speaker Thomas P. O'Neill had long held that "all politics is local," he admitted that in

1980 "there were coattails."[8] The coattails the Speaker referred to here were not those of Ronald Reagan, which may have carried some Republicans *in*, but the coattails of Jimmy Carter, which O'Neill was convinced carried many Democrats *out*.[9]

The rather long-term stability which the Democrats had enjoyed in the Congress would prove to be a burden for them as they tried to recover and regroup in the 97th Congress. As Mann points out:

> Large, relatively stable majorities tend to become divided and self-centered; they come to take for granted the rewards of majority status and lose sight of the party's collective performance.[10]

Somehow, the Democrats would have to learn how to come together as a minority party in the Senate and as a weakened majority in the House. Charles Clapp has observed that "a minority, to have any effect, must stand together."[11] My research gave me reason to believe that the Congressional Democrats in 1981 were in doubt as to where they stood as a party on ideology. This was no new phenomenon. Stewart had also observed in the mid–1970s:

> The Democrats are unlikely to remain satisfied with a long-term lease on Capitol hill if they keep receiving no-vacancy notices at the White House. Yet the transformation of a congressional majority into a presidential victory can be difficult, especially if familiar ideological guideposts can no longer be relied upon as clues to political success.[12]

The lack of ideological guideposts made the way of the Congressional *minority* even more treacherous.

Whereas Kingdon's opinion that "loss of the White House results in lack of an administration legislative program and consequent inactivity by that party's leadership"[13] may be true over an extended period of time—during which a long-term minority party has learned the art of opposition, which, by its very nature, is reactive rather than active—we would not expect to find lethargy in a party that has just recently become a minority. Indeed, my paticular thesis, which offers that parties under stress will become particularly *active*, was substantiated by the behavior of the Congressional Democrats immediately following their losses in the 1980 election. Drew observed, "There is a great deal of ferment within the Democratic Party. . . . After the 1980 elections, the Democrats went into an emotional collapse . . . [and] many Democrats simply lost their bearings."[14] Clinton Rossiter, in commenting on the behavior of out-of-power parties, wrote, "It often seems that American politicians are happier out of power than in it."[15] Rossiter, too, may have been commenting

on parties that experienced the stability of the minority for a long period
of time. What they may have been "enjoying" was not being out of
power, but merely being stable. The Democrats were definitely *not*
happy about being out of power in either the White House or the Senate.
Meg Greenfield, editorial page editor of the *Washington Post*, commented
on the Democrats' reaction to being a "minority" party:

> The Democrats were thrashing around . . . trying to rearrange
> themselves . . . what we were witnessing was the early struggle,
> confused and uncertain, of a political opposition to create itself.
> What was interesting about it was the tension between those pre-
> pared merely to pursue ancient and reflexive grievances against
> the Republican right and those more wary, who believe the terrain
> is new and therefore more treacherous for those planning an as-
> sault. Not that these different sentiments are found only in different
> groups of critics. More typically they are found at war within the
> same individual.[16]

Interrelationship of Ideology and Leadership

Critical to the creation or *re*-creation of the Congressional Democratic
Party were the interrelated centripetal elements of ideology and leadership. The desire for leadership is inherent in any political party. A
leader or leaders is what Maurice Duverger terms one of the "practical
necessities" in the organization of power. Duverger contends that the
dominant belief of a group will be the determining factor in attributing
legitimacy to the leader. He sees this "belief" criterion as relative, according to the type of political party, but holds that "parties must in
consequence take the greatest care to provide themselves with leadership
that is democratic in appearance."[17] Duverger goes on to point out that
"practical efficiency" drives the parties in the opposite direction:

> Democratic principles demand that leadership at all levels be elec-
> tive, that it be frequently renewed, collective in character, weak in
> authority. Organized in this fashion, a party is not well armed for
> the struggles of politics.[18]

As clumsy and inefficient as the reformed Congress may be in determining and sustaining leadership, this democratic inefficiency is a fact
of political life, and one that the Democrats found particularly troublesome in the early days of their new status as an out-of-power party.

However, as with many other aspects of democratic government, the
inefficiency in Congressional workings is not without its greater benefits,
a point found throughout Madisonian political thought and philosophy.

Take note in Duverger's commentary that the leaders are chosen by virtue of their espoused beliefs. This implies the concept of the free marketplace of ideas—what Jefferson saw as truth's "natural weapons, free argument and debate."[19] According to this reasoning, the leaders are chosen *because* of their beliefs, with the beliefs most commonly held by the group winning out, thus bringing their leaders with them. The belief comes first, and the individuals who have the most appealing or acceptable beliefs are the ones who emerge as leaders. The very young Woodrow Wilson gave us something similar to this in his essay on cabinet government:

> . . . *debate* is the essential function of a popular representative body. In the severe, distinct, and sharp enunciation of underlying principles, the unsparing examination and telling criticism of opposite positions, the careful, painstaking unravelling of all the issues involved, which are incident to the free discussion of questions of public policy we see the best, the only effective, means of educating public opinion. . . . Crises give birth and a new growth to statesmanship because they are peculiarly periods of action, in which talents find the widest and freest scope. . . . None but the ablest can become leaders and masters in this keen tournament in which arguments are the weapons, and the people the judges. . . . Eight words contain the sum of the present degradation of our political parties: *No leaders, no principles; no principles, no parties.*[20]

So we see that ideas, principles, and the ideology that emerges from them are inextricably bound to the emergence, selection, and endurance of leaders. In 1981, the Democrats found themselves to be particularly bereft of "ideas." Although they may have found it to be a dubious luxury, as an out-of-power party, they now had the time to cast about for new approaches to old problems and to redefine the principles and subsequent policies that would most appeal to the constituency they wished to represent, serve, maintain, and increase.

The Desire for a Spokesman

For the party newly out of power, lacking the president to set goals and establish priorities for the regime, the desire for a single leader may be pressing. However, it is not necesarily desirable to move too quickly, lest the winnowing effect on conflicting ideas be lost. Yet, many consider that one of the most essential personages for an out-of-power party is a party leader or spokesperson, often referred to as the "titular" leader. Cotter and Hennessy opine that "the position of titular leader is largely mythological . . . only when a defeated presidential candidate can keep

his visibility, a party nucleus, and public support does the theory of
titular leader fit the brutal facts of political life."[21]

The "brutal fact" for the Democrats in the days following their defeat
was that by no one's measure could Jimmy Carter fill the role of leader,
titular or otherwise. He would not maintain any sort of visibility, a fact
that must have been of at least *some* comfort to those Democrats still in
the Congress. Still, the persistent question remained: who would lead
and who would speak? Drew saw this desire for a spokesman also as a
"myth":

> A fair amount of mythology—and obliviousness of history—sur-
> rounds the Democrats' dilemma. One myth is that the congres-
> sional opposition party can, or should, coalesce around a single
> spokesman.[22]

It has been well established that myths are a central part of American
politics,[23] and no less so in the case of an out-party spokesman. Cotter
and Hennessy have observed that "the party out of power is peculiarly
at the prey of public demand that it have a spokesman."[24] Myth is an
integral part of ideology. It is almost impossible to determine the origin
of a myth—uncertainty of beginnings is one of the criteria for separating
myth from fact. It is possible that the desire for a spokesman stems from
the Constitutional imperative for an executive, and although presidential
selection is one of the functions of party in the American political system,
it is only *one* of the functions, and by no means the most important,
although modern-day emphasis on the presidency may have given that
impression. For the purposes of this study, it is idle to speculate on the
origins of the myth of the titular leader. The importance of a myth lies
in its prevalence and pervasiveness. Dan Nimmo and James Combs state:
"A myth may be true, false, or both. The key characteristic of myth,
however, is that it is a dramatic representation of past, present, or future
events that people *believe*."[25] So, whether the need for a spokesman was
a myth or not, the Democratic members of Congress perceived that the
need was real, and that was enough to send them in search of a speaker,
even if it was not THE Speaker.

In commenting on the role of the national party chairman as a possible
spokesman for the Party, Bibby and Huckshorn observe that by doing
so the chairman "could probably strengthen the position of certain elements within his party, but he would have little power to induce intraparty agreement with his policy statements. And, *if furthering party unity
is a prime objective*, [emphasis added] policy statements by a national
chairman can hinder its achievement."[26] For these and other considerations, Manatt wisely took himself out of the running as party spokesman. Not only was Manatt's personality and experience not geared to

such a role, but also the message came loud and clear from the members of Congress that if any one would speak, it would be one of them. What emerged was a wide-screen version of a daily drama to be seen and heard in the halls of Congress where "each members wants to exercise power—to make the key policy decisions."[27]

The Many Faces of Congressional Rhetoric

Certainly not all of the rhetoric coming from the Democratic members of Congress in the early months of 1981 could be considered potential ideology. Much of it was self-serving grandstanding. Some of it was an attempt to rally the fallen and to raise morale. Some was clearly aimed at furthering the political ambitions of individual members as they auditioned for a spot at the top of the Democratic ticket in 1984. However, there were occasions, especially during the midterm party conference, when members of Congress could combine all these motivations and elements. This posturing and pronouncing is a part of the process not only for determining what ideas and principles will "sell," but also for determining which of the leaders emerging from the "presidential incubator" will "sell" to the wider audience of the American electorate.

Sen. Edward Kennedy, a more or less perennial presidential hopeful, began his bid for the role of party leader early in December 1980, when he said with dramatic hyperbole that the November election had cost the Democrats "half a political generation." He went on in a rallying cry for unity: "I think we Democrats need all the help we can get—governors, congressmen, state party officials, a new national committee chairman."[28] It is not clear if Kennedy was really speaking more often and more loudly than others in the early days after the defeat or if he was just more likely to be covered by and quoted by the press.

Kennedy was not alone in seeking a wider audience than just his Congressional colleagues. Senator Byrd, deposed majority leader of the Senate, made sure he too was covered by the press. He continued the weekly Saturday morning press conferences which he had established as his conduit for the party line when the Democrats had controlled the Senate. At the first of these press conferences to be held after the November 4 losses, reporter Kathy Sawyer observed Byrd as seeming "generally chipper and philosophical about the Democratic fall from power." Sawyer went on to describe the senator's words and demeanor:

> His fire engine red sports shirt was a bright contrast to the gloomy pall that has spread among his colleagues on the Hill. He urged the party to broaden its ideological approach and to "give attention to reorganizing, to fund raising in ways that will have an impact on congressional races".... He vowed that Senate Democrats

would be supportive of the Republican leadership, though there would be some "constructive disagreement." He noted with apparent relish that "Mr. Reagan is going to have to explain his broken campaign promises if he can't make things work. . . . I will be the first to compliment him if he can do them . . . Let's just see."[29]

Apparently Byrd was going to take the tack of giving the Republicans enough rope for a self-hanging. This was not exactly the strategy espoused by some other, more activist senators. Joseph Kraft saw the possibility of the Senate becoming the "bully pulpit of modern American politics." Kraft described what he termed "the outline of a new Democratic opposition":

Three wings—one on the left headed by Edward Kennedy, one in the middle headed by Henry Jackson, and one on the right headed by Ernest Hollings—are discernible. Jockeying for position among these groups will probably dominate Democratic politics for the foreseeable future.

Several conditions assert the preeminance of the Senate as the headquarters of the Democratic opposition. . . . Congress is the one place where Democrats can offer systematic and coherent alternatives to the foreign and domestic policies the Republicans will lay before the country. . . . The Senate, by contrast [to the House] offers a natural forum for a free-for-all. Discipline ranges from minimal to non-existent.

The present Majority Leader, Robert Byrd of West Virginia, is a nuts-and-bolts man, long on rules and procedures as distinct from the enunciation of broad political positions. He did not work hard either for the national ticket or for other senators during the recent campaign. If he is designated as Majority Leader, (which is by no means certain) it will be mainly because his dullness makes it easy for so many to outshine him.[30]

Kraft was to be correct in some of his observations, but not that the Senate or its leaders would emerge as the voice of the Party. His assessment of Byrd's style was quite correct, and perhaps also his conjecture that Byrd would be chosen as minority leader because he was not apt to upstage any of his colleagues who might be vying for the spotlight.

Internecine Struggle for Leadership in the Senate

As early as March 1981, Helen Dewar of the *Washington Post* saw the Democrats "frustrated at almost every turn as they try to adjust to the unfamiliar role of the loyal opposition, Senate Democrats are groping for new strategies, new ideas, a new image—everything, it seems, except new leaders." In recounting Byrd's election to the post of minority leader, Dewar pointed to "rumblings of dissatisfaction" with Byrd's leadership both from the right as well as the left. There was some talk of replacing him in 1983:

> "If," as one of them put it, "we can ever get our own act together enough to decide where and how we want to be led." . . . Byrd lacks the dynamism and public presence that a party on the rebound needs to articulate its policy alternatives. Byrd was further characterized by a colleague who said "He's been real nervous in the saddle . . . sort of insecure. . . . He's always having meetings."[31]

Late in January 1981 reports came out that confirmed the discontent in the Senate with Byrd's abilities and policy positions. A group of ten moderate-to-conservative senators "chaffing under the party's identification with liberal causes have begun caucusing quietly in an attempt to expand their influence . . . and nudge the Senate Democratic leadership to the right," reported the *Washington Post*.[32] Apparently what had stirred the senators to coalesce against Byrd was Byrd's lame-duck effort as majority leader, just after the November elections, to win passage for a fair housing bill championed by Sen. Edward Kennedy. Although Sen. David Boren of Oklahoma was quoted as declaring that the senators' actions were not to be interpreted as a "challenge to the leadership," one of his colleagues stated: "We hope Byrd gets the message and recognizes that the party is not just Kennedy and Co. . . . Byrd operates on the squeaky wheel principle . . . and we are going to squeak."[33] This group of senators had some difficulty in deciding how much open opposition it would offer the established leadership. Neither could they decide whether to convene as a formal caucus or to just keep their Wednesday meetings in Senator Boren's office on an informal basis, so as not to give the appearance of a revolt against the leadership. There was more talk in the spring of that same year about this informal group. By this time Senator Hollings had emerged as the leader of the caucus, and it was surmised that there was a strong possibility he would lead the movement to challenge Byrd's leadership and possibly depose him as minority leader in 1983. Reportedly this coalition believed "that the party needs more aggressive leadership . . . and [that] they could win support from some liberals who are unhappy with Byrd."[34]

Apparently even the splinter coalitions in the Senate had difficulty in deciding who should be in charge. This internal vacillation to be found in the insurgents probably contributed to Byrd's remaining as minority leader not only in the 97th but also in the 98th Congress. Although all this internecine struggling did nothing to enhance the minority image of the Party, it was a necessary experience, as the Democrats were learning to be an opposition party. In the long run it could have a beneficial effect. The positive manifestations of the "bully pulpit" are not to be felt or discerned overnight. The reconstruction of a defeated party and the reformation of ideology demand patience and persistence. Revolution is spontaneous and dramatic; reformation is slow and boring to those who experience it. Reformation holds drama only for the historian. As Stephen Bailey observed of the Republicans when they were the humiliated minority party in the mid-sixties:

> Their present painful disorientation and their ideological cacophony is a necessary prelude, if they stay in the political business at all, to a new sense of mission and party purpose. When this sense develops, a new and tighter leadership and a new integration of disparate party organization will emerge in both houses. . . .[35]

Considering the Democrats' recent volatility in institutional reform at the cost of ideological reform, it is not surprising that there were few indications that any such sense of mission and purpose was developing among the Senate Democrats in the first two years of their minority.

Rumbling and Fumbling Around the House

The situation in the Democratic-held House was somewhat different, but certainly no better than that found in the confused Senate. In the search for a leader or a spokesman, the Democrats in the Congress and in the electorate would naturally look to the Speaker of the House. The person holding this position not only holds the power of party leadership but also is the third-ranking individual in succession to assume the power of presidential leadership.

Although he saw himself as the "leader of the opposition," Democratic Speaker of the House Thomas P. O'Neill, Jr., had great difficulty in asserting himself in the early days of the 97th Congress.[36] As Mark Shields observed in August 1981, "For six months now, the criticism of the man has been as inconsistent as it has been insistent. Take your pick: he is either a hopeless liberal, out of touch with the times, or he is too quick to cave in to, or cooperate with the conservative opposition."[37] In looking back over the first nineteen months of the Reagan administration and O'Neill's leadership in the House, columnist Margot Hornblower recalled the "Repeal O'Neill" buttons which appeared early in 1981 as "the Speakers' flock was downcast, grumbling that at 68, 'Tip' was too old, tired, out of touch. Some called for his resignation." Horn-

blower also cites the activity of O'Neill's colleague Les Aspin of Wisconsin when he wrote to constituents:

> Tip O'Neill is a good friend of mine . . . a loveable old bear. . . . But
> now, I regret to say, Tip is reeling on the ropes. Tip grew up in
> the Depression. His politics have always been straight out of the
> New Deal. In 1981, the New Deal doesn't carry a lot of water. Tip
> doesn't understand the explosions that have been going off since
> November. He's in a fog.[38]

O'Neill well may have appeared to be in a "fog" to many of his
colleagues who expected something else of him. Aage Clausen suggests
that there is ambiguity to be found in the concept of party leadership
in the "image of the party leader as a consensus manipulator . . . a party
leader may find it useful to spend at least as much time looking back at
his troops to assess their policy field positions as he does in marching
forward on a new policy front."[39]

In looking back at his fogbound troops in the early spring of 1981,
O'Neill decided to let his men fight the battle the way they saw it in
their own immediate trench. He states: "As Speaker, I could have refused to play ball with the Reagan administration. . . . But in my view,
this wasn't a politically wise thing to do. Despite my strong opposition
to the president's program, I decided to give it a chance to be voted on
by the nation's elected representatives."[40] When the first budget came
out of Chairman Jim Jones's House Budget Committee, reflecting the
Democrats' response to the Reagan budget proposals, O'Neill says that
his colleagues "were eager to compromise with the admnistration."[41]
O'Neill had made some compromises of his own, which were to have
dire consequences for the Party and for the budget process for years to
come. He had allowed Jim Wright to convince him that Phil Gramm of
Texas should be appointed to the Budget Committee. This appointment,
and Gramm's defection from loyalty to the Party, would cause the Democratic leadership much anguish and embarrassment. O'Neill admits
that he was not prepared for what happened.[42]

To many, O'Neill did not give the appearance of looking after the
Democratic Party's best interests. Columnist David Osborne of the po-
pulist, progressive journal *Working Papers for a New Society* commented
on the House leadership:

> House Speaker Tip O'Neill is accurately described by Republicans
> as their best weapon in Congress. As one Democratic insider put
> it, "Tip governs by gut and instinct more than intellect, and his
> gut and his instinct were formed in a past era. . . . He doesn't have
> much toleration for new ideas in any form. . . . He likes junketing,

he likes the limelight, but he doesn't like the work that goes with
it."[43]

O'Neill did appear to be weak and very ineffectual in mounting any
sort of coherent strategy to combat the Reagan influence in the House.
O'Neill had made a bad political decision in placing Texas freshman
Gramm on the Budget Committee. Gramm rewarded his benefactor
Wright and O'Neill by joining Republicans on the committe in chal-
lenging the chairman of the Budget Committee, Jim Jones. Gramm carried the message of the Reagan administration wholeheartedly into the
committee deliberations. When Gramm's attempts to pass a substitute
to the Jones budget failed, he joined with Republican Delbert Latta of
Ohio to offer a substitute budget plan which backed the Reagan blueprint
to the full House. The Speaker, the majority leader, and Jim Jones, chair
of the Budget Committee, together could not prevent the Democrats
from caving in on May 7, 1981, when "sixty-three Democrats joined all
of the House Republicans to overwhelmingly endorse the Reagan budget
plan, sponsored by Latta and Gramm. The vote was 253–176."[44] O'Neill
admits that the "damage done by Gramm-Latta was enormous."[45]

There was more humiliation to come in the budget reconciliation process, set for May 15. Gramm and Latta teamed up once more to propose
Gramm-Latta II. This proposal would use the reconciliation process not
only to bring further cuts desired by the Reagan administration but also
to set a limit on program authorizations that would affect the authorizing
committee's power permanently. The Democratic leadership had
wanted to vote separately on the programs in the reconciliation bill, but
the Republicans were determined to put it on a fast-track up-or-down
vote. The Republicans stuck solidly together and were joined this time
by twenty-nine Democrats to pass the reconciliation bill *in toto*. After
the vote, Speaker O'Neill despondently said, "I've never seen anything
like this in my life, to be perfectly truthful.[46] In his memoirs, O'Neill
sees this time in 1981 as "absolutely the lowest point in my career."[47]
Richard Cohen, commenting on the activity surrounding the budget
process of 1981, wrote: "A well-coordinated attack that relied more on
artful presidential persuasion and Democratic disarray than a detailed
discussion of the issues has given President Reagan a momentous victory
on the budget."[48]

Jim Wright had tried to head off the disloyal miscreant Gramm by
going on his own directly to President Reagan with a proposal of compromise on the budget. By his own admission, Wright was "operating
on his own, without consultation either with Speaker O'Neill or Ways
and Means Chairman Rostenkowski."[49] This episode, occurring early in
the first Reagan administration, offers a dramatic and telling example
of just how ineffectual and fragmented the House leadership and dis-

cipline was at that time. By any measure, it was not among one of the Democrats' greatest maneuvers as an opposition party, and O'Neill got much of the blame. He said later that he had planned it that way all along:

> We were fighting an opposition that was supremely confident that they were doing the right thing and so proud of their victories that they couldn't conceive that what they were doing was wrong and that disaster was ahead of them . . . we had a plan every inch of the way, and the plan was to win the final ball game.[50]

If O'Neill really had a plan "every inch of the way," some of that best-laid plan went decidedly agley—the Gramm appointment serves as a dramatic illustration of this fact.

Horatio at the Bridge

For all of his blowhard bumptiousness, O'Neill became the most consistent, albeit ineffectual, voice of the party. He said this about his image as spokesman:

> I looked at myself as kind of Horatio at the bridge. Somebody had to stand out there and stay with the basic creed of the Democratic party, the concern for the needy and the handicapped and the golden ager. Somebody had to speak out and stop being an apologist as many in our party were.[51]

There was certainly nothing novel or exciting in this Democratic ideology pronounced by the Speaker. The symbols evoked were hardly those which would attract new followers or would rally any except the most faithful of the moribound party.

However, as early as August of 1981 Joseph Kraft thought he saw a "fine flowering of a great political culture [finding] embodiment in the Democratic leadership of the House of Representatives." Kraft listed O'Neill as being "especially well-placed to bind the generations together," and Majority Leader Jim Wright as "well equipped to make common cause with other Democrats in battling high interest rates and monopoly concentration." Kraft went on to point out that O'Neill's style had wisely been to avoid confrontation with the very popular president. But Kraft was critical of the younger members of the Democratic majority who "had no patience with that approach. . . . They goaded the Speaker into defining policies in a way that set up direct challenges on budget cuts and taxes. . . . So they fought and lost everything."[52] We see here an example of a phenomenon observed by Clapp:

A strong sense of partisanship may, in fact, make it difficult for a congressman, especially a junior one, to adjust to the tendencies for accommodation and moderation which epitomize the activities of a legislative body. It may intensity his criticism of the party leadership. He may react sharply and angrily to the defeat or serious modification of proposals in which he is concerned, especially if he believes the leadership is not sufficiently aggressive in pursuing victory.[53]

O'Neill may have thought that he emerged as the spokesman for the Democrats, but in truth there was no one voice which could be heard as bringing "the message." O'Neill's oblique and ofttimes mixed messages were just not being received by the members of his party in the House. The members had been independent too long, and O'Neill could not find a way to catch their attention, much less control or discipline them.

Shifting Coalitions

Coalitions, formed along both regional and ideological lines, waxed and waned in the House. The "Boll Weevils" who jumped ranks and voted for Reagan's economic program were welcomed back into the fold by the leadership.[54] The younger "Atari Democrats" advocated a shift away from the traditional Democratic position of providing resources and support for heavy industry by encouraging assistance to the high-technology and service industries of the "Information Age."[55] Like so many disturbed ants, the Democrats were haphazardly scurrying about on the Hill, following no leader and going nowhere.[56] Mayhew has observed that:

It should be obvious that if they wanted to, American congressmen could immediately and permanently array themselves in disciplined legions for the purpose of programmatic combat. They do not. Every now and then a member does emit a Wilsonian call for program and cohesion, but these exhortations fail to arouse much member interest. The fact is that the enactment of party programs is electorally not very important to members (although some may find it important to take positions on programs).[57]

In 1981 the Democrats gave us case evidence of Mayhew's conclusion. To the Party's detriment, it was fragmented and fractious "business as usual" on the Democratic side of the House.

Lack of Discipline in a Majority Party

A lack of discipline within a party and a lack of power on the part of the leadership is another by-product of a party which has enjoyed a long period as a stable majority. Edmund Beard and Stephen Horn found in their 1975 study of attitudes in the House that "the Democratic leadership in the House doesn't exist . . . the Democratic leadership wouldn't know how to apply pressure."[58] Clapp notes that the Congressional leadership must rely on persuasion and personal appeal rather than on pressure, sanctions, or discipline; therefore, members feel little constraint to take orders from the Party. Members will also tend to serve the Party in direct proportion to how well the Party has served them. Clapp quotes one member as saying, "If we depended on the party organization to get elected, none of us would be here. Because the organization is not too helpful, it doesn't have much influence with us."[59]

The lack of financial suppport, as well as the tendency for members to view their success at having been elected as a personal achievement, contribute to the tendency toward individualism mentioned earlier in this chapter. The strong pull toward individualism and toward responding to constituency rather than party has been noted by a number of commentators, although, as Vogler points out, "congressmen indicate a desire to support their party even when other pressures, such as constituency opinion or ideology, lead them often to oppose their party in floor votes."[60] The party, as such, can at best serve only as a "cue giver." Kingdon found that members "like to 'go along' with the leadership when they can,"[61] but there are many reasons why they will ignore the clear call of the Party's leader to vote along certain party lines. Keefe observes:

> Party loyalty . . . is more than a veneer. By and large, members prefer to stay "regular," to go along with party colleagues. But they will not queue up in support of their leaders if the conditions appear "wrong," if apparently there is more to be lost than gained by following the leadership.[62]

Clausen describes the situation this way:

> The difficulties confronting an attempt to pinpoint the effect of party on the decision-making process of the individual in Congress are a bit more challenging than I would prefer. There is, first of all, no easily interpretable and definitive set of documents that state the party program; nor is there any statement of a party ideology, nor even a set of discrete party policy views, for either

the short or the long term. Attempts along these lines occur every four years at the national conventions, and on occasion party leadership groups outside of Congress may suggest a program. In neither case do senators and representatives line up for instructions.[63]

The Search for Policy and Principles

The lack of a party statement of principles, of goals or a clearly articulated policy, was something that caused much concern among the Democrats in and out of the Congress even as early as December 1980. There was a good bit of talk about the Party being bereft of "ideas." Price has observed that "the congressional parties, like the national committees, are likely to take a more active role in policy development when they are not in the majority and/or do not have a president in power."[64] Although Julius Turner and his successor Edward Schneier, Jr., stated that "American parties are notoriously non-programmatic," and although Clausen despairs that "few politicians, indeed few persons of any description, possess either the talent to develop, or the desire to abide by a clearly formed ideology," the Democrats went full speed ahead in all directions in search of a policy.[65] Dom Bonafede characterized this period in the Democrats' rebuilding process thus: "The almost frenetic activity can be viewed as both a sign of vigor and a reflection of the divisions within the party. This ambivalence extends to the approach the party should take in its rebuilding program."[66]

Democrats in Retreat and Reflection

Although many were called, it was the Congress that declared itself chosen to define the Party's ideology. It is likely that this declaration stemmed more from custom than from conviction. Manatt's attempt to reinstitute the Democratic Policy Council was documented in an earlier chapter. His efforts failed when he had resistance from the Congressional Party members. The Congressional resistance was so intense that Manatt was forced to rename the group the Democratic Strategy Council. The Democratic Senate members went up to the mountain just a short time before Manatt's first session of the Strategy Council, but the eager House members had gone into retreat less than two months after the 1980 November defeat. About one hundred House members and their spouses gathered for a three-day seminar at a downtown Washington hotel to listen to papers and discussions on "The Future of America," "The State of the Economy," "Foreign Policy," "Energy Issues in the 1980's," and "Democrats: An Endangered Species." Majority Leader Jim Wright was quoted as saying that he expected the session to be a "roving, general discussion of all facets of the political scene." The meetings were closed to the press, but a list of the participants included "a constellation of academic and Democratic stars" such as Duke University professor James David Barber, economists Barry Bosworth and Walter Heller, political consultant Michael Barone, Harvard University foreign policy professor Ernest May, Joseph Pechman of the Brookings Institution, and Marian Edelman of the Children's Defense Fund.[67]

For the Record: "The 1981 Democratic Party"

A few days later, on February 6, Michael Barnes, a popular young member of the House from Maryland, took the floor of the House to address his colleagues on the state of the Democratic Party. Barnes said omnisciently:

> It should be reported that the Democratic Party is not in a quiescent state; all over this country Democratic leaders and activists are meeting to discuss the future of the Democratic Party ... there is a serious reevaluation underway of all the themes, ideas and policy positions which have traditionally guided the Democratic Party.[68]

Barnes then inserted into the *Record* the text of a paper written by party activists Stephen Schlossberg and Ted Van Dyk entitled "The 1981 Democratic Party." This paper dealt with recommendations for the presidential nomination process, the need for money and technical assistance, selection of a national party chairman, and policy development. In the area of policy development, the authors clearly stated:

> One should not expect the Democratic Committee to produce sharply-honed policy proposals. . . . The DNC should provide the framework for dialogue and rethinking through a reconstituted Democratic Policy Council. . . . [The Policy Council,] however, should not aspire to issuance of finished Democratic Policy Proposals. No, new thinking and initiatives will come from individual Senators and Congressmen, from state officeholders, from writers and academics, and from independent centers of policy development. . . . The DNC should provide a forum for thinking and communication. . . . But it should bear in mind that others in the party have primary responsibility for policy development.[69]

This statement did not say exactly who *was* in charge here, but did say it *was not* the DNC. An arrangement such as Van Dyk and Schlossberg recommended could lead only to more fragmentation and ambiguity. It did. As Clausen has observed, "the 'out' party may send off public relations signals promising alternate policy programs, but somehow the subsequent signals always seem to weaken and fade away, like a well-tutored old general."[70]

Tapping Internal Resources: Democratic Caucus and DSG

Although Clausen does not believe that many politicians possess the talent to develop an ideology, the Democrats in the Congress, especially in the House of Representatives, are not without resources to draw upon in shaping a party philosophy and policy. The Democratic Caucus, with its appointive powers and its strong alliance with the leadership, could provide the framework and the staff assistance necessary to do the job.[71] The Democratic Study Group, a service and coordinating organization for Democratic members of the House, "has become the primary source of legislative research for the Democratic Members and staff."[72] In 1969, the Democratic Study Group "launched a concerted effort to revive the long-dormant Democratic Caucus as the basic arbiter of Democratic policy and power in the House . . . the effort transformed the House of Representatives and sparked a similar, but not largely successful, movement in the U.S. Senate."[73] There is a Democratic Steering and Policy Committee within the DSG, but its principal function is to make recommendations to the Caucus regarding members' committee assignments. "The committee also has authority to make recommendations regarding party policy . . . for House or Caucus action."[74] This Steering and Policy Committee is made up of the Speaker, majority leader, caucus chairman, the whip, twelve regional representatives, and eight members appointed by the Speaker. There can be no doubt that the leadership has a channel through which they can direct policy recommendations to the full Caucus. Yet, Price concludes, even with this "concerted attention . . . to the roles and resources of party leadership, . . . the party's limitations as an integrative force remain at least as impressive as its successes in counterbalancing the centrifugal forces of member individualism and subcommittee government."[75] Charles Jones has described one of the sources of the difficulties faced by the Democrats in shaping cohesive policy as what he terms "front end power" acceding to the leaders. This power gives the leaders the privilege of making committee assignments and referring legislation, but it does not provide the power for "organizational policy integration."[76]

Committee on Party Effectiveness

It was out of the Democratic Caucus that the most effective instrument for shaping a "new" policy was drawn. Acting swiftly on a recommendation from the group of House members who went into retreat in

Washington in January 1981, Caucus Chairman Gillis Long appointed a special Committee on Party Effectiveness.[77]

The Committee on Party Effectiveness was made up of "more than 30 Members who represent[ed] every philosophy and region within [the] Caucus." The group met weekly for over twenty months to produce their final set of documents which would, as Long wrote, "renew our commitment to the fundamental principles of the Democratic Party—to equal opportunity, to economic growth and full employment, and to a strong national defense." Of seven issue papers presented, the one dealing with economic policy was probably the most innovative. This paper, written by Long, Timothy Wirth, and Richard Gephardt, represented many of the attitudes and values of the "Atari Democrats." It recommended increased investment to "retool our basic industries and to expand growing industries in the high technology and information sectors."[78]

The other issues tackled were Housing, Small Business, Women's Economic Issues, the Environment, Crime, and National Security. The National Security paper recommended strategic arms control negotiations "consistent with maintenance or overall parity with the Soviet Union,"[79] and although it criticized President Reagan for failure to curb nuclear proliferation, it did not recommend a nuclear freeze.

The coverage of issues was fairly representative of the traditional concerns of the highly "inclusive" Democratic Party. For the most part, the papers were both diagnostic and prescriptive, although the solutions offered represented a rather safe, middle-of-the-road, centrist approach. Margot Hornblower of the *Washington Post* reviewed the report and found that there was "little in the generally worded reports to stir controversy in this election season."[80] Controversy was one commodity the Democrats could do without in September 1982, only weeks away from the midterm elections. Regarding the rather bland, "centrist" cast of the caucus committee report, it is interesting to note that in 1966 the young Republicans of the Ripon Society stated emphatically: "The GOP cannot regenerate and rebuild itself without making an unapologetic commitment to the center of American politics. . . . Meanwhile the Republican party waits to see it if can work the miracle of organization without ideology."[81]

Generalities notwithstanding, it is to the credit of the Caucus committee that it was able to produce a document which said *something*, if not *everything* . . . in truth, it was probably much better that it did not try to say everything. Ideology, by its very nature, is composed of generalities and ambiguities. It must appeal to the masses on many levels, meaning only what people think it means.

Whatever its shortcomings, *Rebuilding the Road to Opportunity* was by far the most coherent set of principles that the Democrats produced, although Price states that at first "Speaker O'Neill and his staff were somewhat 'nervous' about the caucus committee." Price quotes Alvin From who served as the executive director of the committee as saying that "much of it [the Report] is still at the level of rhetoric." Price goes on to note that after the 1982 election, the caucus directed the standing committees "to report within three months on their disposition with respect to proposals in the caucus report that fell under their jurisdiction."[82] The Long committee may have been rebuilding more than "the road to opportunity" for the citizens of the country . . . they had the potential for rebuilding the road to opportunity for the Democrats, if the ideas in the report ever moved beyond the "level of rhetoric." An interesting and perhaps revealing future study regarding how well the Democrats used and promulgated their developing policies would be found in comparing the points in *Rebuilding the Road to Opportunity* and the final reports of the National Party Conference task forces with the 1984 Democratic platform and the campaign statements of the 1984 presidential nominee.

Tsongas, Simon, and Hart as Authors of Policy

During the early months and years of the Democrats' attempts to rebuild, there were three particularly conspicuous entrepreneurial examples of policy development. Sen. Paul Tsongas of Massachusetts had his own road show with his collection of essays entitled *The Road From Here: Liberalism and Realities in the 1980s*, published in 1981. Another entry was Rep. Paul Simon's *The Once and Future Democrats: Strategies for Change*, which came out in 1982. Sen. Gary Hart of Colorado published his entry, *A New Democracy: A Democratic Vision for the 1980s and Beyond*, in the spring of 1983. These published works by members of Congress were an attempt to present particular and personal points of view to the wider audience in the electorate. Published by established commercial presses, the works allowed the authors to state their cause and at the same time to possibly stake their claim to a leadership position, unencumbered by party line.

Of the three, Tsongas's work is by far the most thoughtful. Stating that he hoped "to define a direction for the future," with a core of "realism," Tsongas wrote from the perspective that liberalism "was living off its legacy." He stated that he viewed the Democratic Party as offering a "base of compassion essential for the functioning of any democratic society." But he saw compassion not as an end in itself but as a "softening" agent for free market forces. Tsongas declared that his objective was "realism—some of it Republican in its origins—combined with the value system of the Democratic liberal tradition."[83] He seemed to be describing Adam Smith with a heart transplant. The work is somewhat tedious to read, sprinkled throughout with baseball analogies and allusions. Its general tone is rather gloomy, which may be stylistically intended to express the essence of no-nonsense "realism." Robert Kaus, senior editor of *The American Lawyer*, commented on Tsongas's style: "Those who attempt to actually read this book will discover that the benefit of an unfiltered glimpse into Tsongas' mind is not without its aesthetic penalties . . . [some] passages read like Tsongas found them in a bad fortune cookie."[84]

As Professor Norman Ornstein commented in his review of Tsongas's work: "If there *is* a future for the Democratic Party and for liberalism, it will first have to resurrect a more positive vision of America's future than we find in *The Road from Here*."[85] Although the bulk of Tsongas's recommendations dealt with domestic economic policy, his chapters on foreign policy and international trade were the most provocative and well reasoned. This work, too, tends to move toward the center, away from extreme Northeastern liberalism. At least Tsongas added some concerns to the usual ritual liberal litany. Tsongas introduced some novelty here, but he lacked an essential vitality. The messasge was different, but it was not particularly cohesive either in exposition or delivery.

Paul Simon's work was more direct and upbeat in its message. He began by saying, "This book is a call to the Democratic party to correct our deficiencies, but not to sell our soul." Simon sent very much the same message as Tsongas by calling for "compassion tempered by common sense."[86] Where Tsongas urged "realism," Simon urged "common sense." Simon stated the case for the Democrats rather succinctly:

> What the Democratic party needs—what the nation needs—is not an avalanche of additional information. We generally have adequate data to make decisions. The question is one of attitude. The oldest political party in the land must neither automatically embrace or automatically reject the decisions of the past. But the Democrats dare not reject the tradition of concern.[87]

Much of Simon's work is anecdotal, which contributes to its readability but not necessarily to its credibility. However, Simon does have some very specific recommendations which could be translated into legislative policy. He urges "greater compassion, improved productivity and enrichment of the quality of life in every direction."[88] Simon's is a humanistic approach to bringing all the "tribes" of the Party together under one national banner. He has hopes for the Party and calls for the Party to bring a spirit of optimism to the general electorate:

> Government, among other functions, must give people hope. A solid Democratic program that stresses productivity, economic jus-

tice, and the improvement of quality in the nation is one to which all Americans can look with hope. The Republican program substitutes nostalgia for hope, a dream of a yesterday that never really was, for a vision of what this nation and this world might become.[89]

Simon came forward as a cheerleader and urged the Democrats to use their adversity to a sweet national purpose.

Although Gary Hart's book was published after the period of time of this study, a review of it is included here in order to present further evidence of the search among the members of Congress for a direction for the Party and a place in the leadership which might determine that direction. Hart offered his own list of what the Democratic Party should stand for: "equal rights and opportunities, real progress in the standard of living and the quality of life . . . justice . . . and a promise of hope for our young people, our unemployed, our poor, our disadvantaged, our elderly." Hart did not miss a beat in reciting the litany. His vision for the future included "universal education," a simplified tax system, "industrial modernization," open trade, rebuilding of the "infrastructure," a "health plan" which would guarantee "full health and nutrition programs for every American child," policies to clean up air and water, development of United States energy resources, military reform, and "comprehensive nuclear arms control."[90]

Hart's most well-reasoned and reasonable proposals come in his essay "Restoring Industrial Vitality," but even here he mixes many uncontrollable variables to present a scenario for the future. There is more futuristic rhetoric than reason in the bulk of Hart's plan. I characterize it as the "Tinkerbell Approach" to policy development: It *might* work if all the children would just *believe* hard enough and clap their hands.

So, with Hart's contribution, the essential qualities for a successful politician and a successful party could be found in the triumvirate: Tsongas the Realist, Simon the Optimist, and Hart the Opportunist.

The Ever-Elusive "New Ideas"

For all of the efforts, both individual and cooperative, there were just not very much many "new ideas" coming out of the Congress in 1981–82. The evidence suggests that what the Democrats were *really* looking for were new approaches and novel solutions to old and enduring problems. Therein may lie a clue to the Democrats' difficulties . . . it is nearly impossible to know if one has found something if one does not know *what* one is looking for.

Martin Kaplan, a guest scholar at the Brookings Institution, commented on the Democrats' quest for novelty:

The notion that the Democrats have to come up with "new ideas" is the shrewdest Republican ploy since the nomination of Ronald Reagan. . . . There's no question that the Democrats took a drubbing in 1980. But it wasn't the Republicans' new ideas which beat them, and it won't be Democrats newer ideas which will return them to power in 1984. . . . If the Democrats choose to be judged on whether they've come up with new ideas, they should at least realize that they have allowed the Republicans to set the terms of the contest . . . sharp politicians know they should never fight on turf they haven't chosen themselves. . . . In private, when they're not issuing statesmanlike appeals for new ideas, Democrats admit this is what it all comes down to. Walking past the White House after a National Press club luncheon where three economists had laid out some ideas under Center for Democratic Policy auspices, one well known Democrat connected with the Center acknowledged that he'd just heard nothing new. Nor did that bother him. . . . "There was nothing new in the ideas that brought Reagan to power, either," he explained. "The point of all this isn't to come up with new ideas. The point is to have the best blue smoke and mirrors."[91]

Michael Barone was more encouraged by what he saw and heard in the Democrats' search for a possible new approach if not for new ideas. He saw the change in nomenclature from "public works" to "rebuilding the infrastructure" as the Democrats changing from a "politics of distribution to a politics of production, from a politics that focuses on distributing society's wealth to the unfortunate to a politics that focuses on producing more wealth."[92] The truth lay somewhere between these two extreme views. The fact that the Democrats were engaged in reevaluation of their policies and in a search for new approaches was healthy. What they lacked was a central forum for evaluating their policies, the will to set realistic priorities and a chorus in unison, with a conductor, to send the message forth. There was latent talent in the Party as evidenced by the willing and sometimes creative approaches sought by organized groups in the Congress and by individual members. Undisciplined though the Congress may have been, there was no lack of talent. However, there was a lack of direction.

Rejuvenating Congressional Campaign Funding

It was not just in policy development that the Democrats in the Congress sought creative new approaches to old problems. In 1980, Democratic candidates actually outspent Republicans by $3 million, although in total receipts the Republican Party committees had outraised the Democratic Party committees by $109 million, or $128 million for Republicans to the Democrats' $19 million.[93] How to reconcile such a discrepancy in expenditures over receipts? Simple, when we consider that we are talking about Democrats. Individual Congressional candidates had known for some time that they would have to fend for themselves in fundraising. This fact of life for Democratic candidates was partly due to the campaign reforms in 1971, ironically enacted by Democrats to combat the kinds of excesses of the Nixon campaigns, amended through 1979. The individual fund-raising imperative was further impelled by the emphasis of the Democratic National Committee on supporting presidential candidates rather than Senate and House hopefuls. It was another case of Democrats acting as individualistic entrepreneurs. Rob Gurwitt of the *Congressional Quarterly* summed up the Democrats' dilemma in this way:

> While the GOP was building a huge fund-raising base and developing the resources to support its candidates nationwide, House Democrats relied on the $1 million to $2 million they could raise in their time-honored fashion, and lagged far behind their opponents in making use of developing campaign technology. The 1980 elections, which cost them the presidency, the Senate and 33 House seats, demonstrated just how far behind they were.[94]

Part of the Democratic fallout in 1980 was the House seat of James C. Corman of California. Corman had served as chairman of the Democratic Congressional Campaign Committee from 1961 until his defeat in November 1980. Corman's job as chairman was taken over by Tony Coelho, also of California, who was just beginning his second term in the House. Gurwitt characterized the DCCC as "being reborn in Tony Coelho's image—aggressively optimistic, relentless in its fund raising and eager to make friends on all sides of the political spectrum."[95] Coelho saw that his task was to "institutionalize" the Campaign Committee. He stated that the primary concerns of the DCCC were "to save our majority, and to ensure our long-term viability." Coelho attributed the "close working relationship between the House Leadership and the DCCC" as enabling him to "accomplish the first goal and to make significant progress on the second."[96]

Coelho accomplished something that the House leadership had not been able to do in its efforts to bring Democrats together in a unified front to oppose the Reagan administration's economic program—he made an ally of Texan Kent Hance, who had cosponsored the Reagan tax cut bill in 1981. Hance "used his contacts in the oil industry to help Coelho's committee the following year. 'There should be participation in the Democratic Party by labor and business, and liberals and conservatives and everyone,' argues Hance."[97] Although Drew had observed that money seemed to be a divisive force for the Democrats, Coelho, the cheerleader, was bringing them together and showing a profit to boot.

Apparently Coelho was psychologically well suited and politically well placed to revitalize the DCCC. He did do that to a degree, although his actions were not without criticism by some hapless candidates in 1982. Coelho chose to build on strength and used the technique of "targeting," that is, giving "a larger percentage of the gifts . . . to more vulnerable incumbents and Democratic challengers identified by the committee as possible winners." Coelho explained, "Our primary goal is to save incumbents, but it's to *save* incumbents, not to funnel money to them. There's an important difference."[98]

Besides the change in distribution of funds, the DCCC established "several aggressive political programs," such as filmed responses to the president's State of the Union addresses, opposition research on Republican candidates, establishment of an automated system for implementing direct mail fund-raising and for collating Republican campaign statements and voting records. Other innovative efforts were evidenced in the establishment of a media center to "develop an in-house media production facility that would be available to all Democratic candidates" and in the filing of "equal time lawsuits" in the hopes of getting better response timing from the television networks.[99]

The media center, funded by a $400,000 contribution from Pamela and Averell Harriman, was, in Coelho's words, "the DCCC's most exciting development." "For the first time ever," he enthused, "a national Democratic committee has a major asset—we actually own something now."[100]

There were other "exciting" developments in the DCCC during Coelho's first two years. He expanded the full-time staff from nine in 1980 to twenty-six in 1983, with over half of those individuals working at raising funds.[101] The DCCC did show a dramatic increase in fund-raising in 1982, as compared with 1980. They went from the $2.0 million collected in 1980 to a total of $6.3 million in 1982. However, this $4 million increase did not result in an appreciable increase in funds given *directly* to candidates. Candidates received $649,000 in 1980 and $779,000 in 1982. As a report from the Democratic Study Group, which supplied these figures, stated, "The discrepancy between the big increase in DCCC receipts (204%) and the relatively small increase in assistance to candidates (15%) is a reflection of the economics of direct mail fund raising. Direct mail can bring in huge amounts of money, but it is extremely costly and requires heavy reinvestment of returns in the early stages."[102] Coelho was making capital investments in the House Democrats' "long-term viability."

Senate Campaign Committee Improvements

The Senate Campaign Committee did not go to the lengths of "institutionalization" promoted by its counterpart in the House. However, in 1982 the Senate campaign forces showed "the biggest improvement on the Democratic side" by raising more than triple the amount it had in 1980 and by doubling its assistance to senatorial candidates. The Senate Campaign Committee raised $5.6 million in 1982, as compared to $1.6 million in 1980. It provided thirty Democratic Senate candidates with assistance totalling $2.4 million, "a 146% increase over the $971,000 provided in 1980."[103] This gain was still not enough to take back the control of the Senate in 1982, but the Democrats did manage to keep the Republicans at a relative stand-off. The Democrats did not gain any seats in the Senate, but the roll of the Senate of the 98th Congress shows that the Republicans gained one, bringing their total to fifty-four. Essentially this was not a real gain for the Republicans, because the seat they picked up was the one vacated by the retirement of Independent Harry Byrd of Virginia. Byrd had almost always voted with the Republicans in recent years, and when his seat was filled by Republican Paul S. Trible, Jr., there was no actual change in the balance of power. The real accomplishment of the Democratic Senate Campaign Committee might be measured by the fact that they stayed even with the Republicans, although the Republicans gave their senatorial candidates $9.3 million, "or nearly four times as much as the Democratic Committee gave its candidates."[104]

Innovative Funding from the DSG

The Democratic Study Group tried an innovative technique for support of Congressional candidates in 1982. It set up a "revolving fund" for candidates in close races, who were allowed to borrow directly from the fund. Those who won were responsible for paying back the loan in full. Losers' debts were forgiven. The DSG reported:

> Some 58 candidates received loans totalling $165,000. A total of $50,000 in loans to 18 losing candidates was subsequently converted to contributions. The remaining $115,000 in loans to 40 winning candidates is being repaid and will therefore be available to assist candidates in 1984.[105]

For all its novelty, this "revolving" fund was a rather pitiful attempt to bring off the electoral equivalent of the miracle of the loaves and the fishes. For those who received a loan from the DSG, each candidate got less than $3000. The federal campaign law permits a campaign committee to contribute up to $36,880 per district race. In 1980 the average Democratic candidate for the House spent $188,000.[106] However—as Ann Lewis of the Democratic National Committee had said, "We can't match the Republicans on their contributions, but we can give our people the tips they need to make the most of the resources they have"—the DSG did provide other types of assistance in the form of polls conducted for fifty-seven candidates. These polls would probably have cost about $500,000 apiece if done by commercial firms. "However, candidates were only required to pay actual costs which totaled less than $100,000 due to the use of trained volunteers to do the interviewing."[107] The DSG reckoned that it had saved the candidates nearly $400,000. The DSG also provided candidates with DSG reports on major issues and with information on their opponent's records. Some losing and narrowly winning candidates in 1982 said that the issue papers and research were nice, but money would have been nicer.[108]

Summary

The luxury of having been a party with long-term stability became a liability for the Democratic Party in the Congress as the members sought to regroup and find new direction during the first two years of the Reagan administration. This fact, combined with the attitude of extreme individualism on the part of party members in both the House and the Senate, worked to exacerbate the Democrats' distress in trying to find a common purpose and sense of unity. In their discomfiture, party members went in all directions to find solutions, failing, for the most part, to pause to identify the problems that might have led to their defeat and disarray. Some, especially the leadership of both the Senate and the House, advocated a "wait and see" approach, whereas others took the tack that the 1980 election was a clear call for them to fall in line with the stringent economic policies of the Reagan White House.

Congressional Party members were impatient with the fact that it takes time and much thrashing about in debate before new leaders with acceptable principles emerge. So eager were they for a leader that they were willing to follow the leader of the other party. There had been few incentives from the Democratic Party in the past to encourage the Congressional Democrats to find any unity in party loyalty to a particular legislative program. When the Democratic House leadership attempted to work out a compromise on the 1982 Reagan budget, they could not maintain voting discipline along party lines. Having never had to serve as a part of a minority "opposition" party, many members had no experience in working together to formulate or promote a cohesive policy.

It was in the search for a uniquely Democratic Party policy that there was the most activity both on the part of groups and individuals. The

Democrats saw themselves as bereft of "new ideas" and energetic leadership. This view, in itself, could become a self-fulfilling prophecy if held too long and voiced too loudly to the American electorate. The apparent passivity in articulating policy on the part of the Senate Minority Leader and the Speaker of the House led many to volunteer as a spokesman before they even had anything to say. They searched for a medium without having a message to transmit. Though this behavior could prove beneficial to the Party's rebuilding efforts over a longer period of time, it had no positive effect for the Party in 1981–83.

It was in the relatively stable organizational component of the Congressional Party that the House Democrats were able to find the mechanism for developing their most cohesive policy statement. The House Democratic Caucus was called upon to activate one of its rarely used functions of determining policy and a course of action. At the instigation of a group of younger members of the House Democrats, who had gone into retreat to thrash things out early in January 1981, the Democratic Caucus established an ad hoc Committee on Party Effectiveness. It was this committee, chaired by Caucus Chairman Gillis Long, which produced the policy paper *Rebuilding the Road to Opportunity*, advocating a fundamental change in emphasis for the Democrats from the policy of redistribution of the nation's wealth to that of creating more wealth through increased productivity. Centrist in cast, it was by far the most coherent statement of purpose produced by the Democrats in the first two years of their struggle to find a testament of party faith. Unfortunately, the "Road to Opportunity" did not lead them anywhere, because not every member wished to travel with the recommendations of this party document. Especially detrimental to their cause was the fact that the Speaker of the House, Thomas P. O'Neill, was among those not getting on the road. Although the Committee on Party Effectiveness had produced a policy which addressed some new approaches to solving economic problems, it did not have a mechanism for promulgating its proposals directly into the Democratic Party at large. The Senate and House leadership had spurned the overtures of the National Democratic Committee for the establishment of a broad-based Policy Council. Once more, the spirit of individualism and proprietary attitudes in the Congressional Party hampered the Party's progress toward rebuilding a united partisan front.

Besides the development of a relatively innovative economic policy, the House Democrats came forward with one other significant achievement. Once again, use of their established party organization within the House made it possible to produce results. The revitalization of the twenty-year-old House Congressional Campaign Committee under the direction of Tony Coelho allowed the Democratic House members to procure the machinery for a direct mail fund-raising program which would have long-term benefits. Coelho also obtained support from Pamela and Averill Harriman to set up a media center for the production of campaign promotional materials. Although many House incumbents would have preferred more direct financial aid, the investments Coelho made in technological equipment would provide more lasting benefits to more members over a longer period of time. Even the Democratic Study Group was willing to try innovative measures in setting up its revolving-loan fund for Democratic candidates.

There was, indeed, a great deal of activity in the Congressional Party in 1981–82. Much of it was highly random and nonproductive. However, the very fact that the Democrats were engaged in reevaluation of their policies and in the search for new approaches and leaders was beneficial, providing momentum to the centripetal forces which were yet to coalesce around a center. Their cause would have been better served if they had been able to keep their squabbles and internecine struggles for power a little less public. They did produce a reasonable approach to an economic policy. However, they lacked a central forum for evaluating their collective and individual policy alternatives, and they lacked the concerted will to set priorities. Their greatest shortcoming was in their inability to determine who was, or who should be, in charge. There was no lack of individual talent, but there was a lack of direction.

Notes

1. David J. Vogler, *The Politics of Congress* (Boston: Allyn and Bacon, 1974), 83.

2. James MacGregor Burns, *Deadlock of Democracy: Four-Party Politics in America* (Englewood Cliffs, N.J.: Prentice-Hall, 1967), 255.

3. Ibid.

4. Norman J. Ornstein, Robert L. Peabody, and David W. Rohde, "The Changing Senate: From the 1950s to the 1970s," in Lawrence C. Dodd and Bruce I. Oppenheimer, eds., *Congress Reconsidered* (New York: Praeger Publishers, 1977), 17.

5. Thomas E. Mann, "Elections and Change in Congress," in Thomas E. Mann and Norman J. Ornstein, eds., *The New Congress* (Washington, D.C.: American Enterprise Institute for Public Policy Research, 1981), 53.

6. David R. Mayhew, *Congress: The Electoral Connection* (New Haven: Yale University Press, 1974), 38.

7. John W. Kingdon, *Congressmen's Voting Decisions* (New York: Harper & Row, Publishers, 1973), 166.

8. Neil MacNeil, "The Struggle for the House of Representatives," in Ellis Sandoz and Cecil V. Crabb, Jr., eds., *A Tide of Discontent: The 1980 Elections and Their Meaning* (Washington, D.C.: Congressional Quarterly Press, 1981), 79.

9. Everett Carll Ladd, "The Brittle Mandate: Electoral Dealignment and the 1980 Presidential Election," *Political Science Quarterly* 96 (Spring 1981): 1–25; MacNeil, 79–80; Germond and Witcover, 314–19.

10. Mann, 36.

11. Charles L. Clapp, *The Congressman: His Work As He Sees It* (Garden City, N.Y.: Doubleday & Co., Anchor Books, 1963), 365.

12. Stewart, 105.

13. Kingdon, 108.

14. Drew, "Reporter at Large: The Democrats," 130.

15. Clinton Rossiter, *Parties and Politics in America* (Ithaca, N.Y.: Cornell University Press, 1960), 47.

16. Meg Greenfield, "A Stirring Among the Democrats," *Washington Post*, 5 March 1981, A9.

17. Maurice Duverger, *Political Parties: Their Organization and Activity in the Modern State*, trans. Barbara and Robert North (New York: John Wiley & Sons, Science Editions, 1966), 133, 134.

18. Ibid., 134.

19. Thomas Jefferson, "Statute of Virginia for Religious Freedom," in Edward Dumbauld, ed., *Political Writings of Thomas Jefferson: Representative Selections* (Indianapolis: Bobbs-Merrill Co., American Heritage Series, 1955), 35.

20. Woodrow Wilson, "Cabinet Government in the United States," in Albert Fried, ed., *A Day of Dedication: The Essential Writings and Speeches of Woodrow Wilson* (New York: Macmillan Co., 1965), 75–78.

21. Cotter and Hennessy, 104–5.

22. Drew, "Reporter at Large: The Democrats," 130.

23. Dan Nimmo and James E. Combs, *Subliminal Politics: Myths and Mythmakers in America* (Englewood Cliffs, N.J.: Prentice-Hall, 1980).

24. Cotter and Hennessy, 104.

25. Nimmo and Combs, xii.

26. Bibby and Huckshorn, 216–17.

27. Lawrence C. Dodd, "Congress and the Quest for Power," in Dodd and Oppenheimer, eds., *Congress Reconsidered*, 272.

28. B. Drummond Ayers, Jr., "Kennedy Says Democrats Face Difficult Comeback," *New York Times*, 17 December 1980, 28.

29. Kathy Sawyer, "Byrd Faults Party Panel in Handling of Election," *Washington Post*, 16 November 1980, A5.

30. Joseph Kraft, "The Struggle Inside . . . ," *Washington Post*, 16 November 1980, L7.

31. Helen Dewar, "Democrats Sticking With Byrd While they Seek New Strategies," *Washington Post*, 14 March 1981, A6.

32. Helen Dewar and Richard L. Lyons, "10 Senators Team Up to Nudge Democrats to Right," *Washington Post*, 31 January 1981, A4.

33. Ibid.

34. *National Journal*, 18 April 1981, 365.

35. Stephen K. Bailey, *The New Congress* (New York: St. Martin's Press, 1966), p. 51.

36. Thomas P. O'Neill, with William Novak, *Man of the House: The Life and Political Memoirs of Speaker Tip O'Neill* (New York: Random House, 1987), 340.

37. Mark Shields, "Don't Underestimate Tip O'Neill," *Washington Post*, 7 August 1981, A15.

38. Margot Hornblower, " 'Horatio At the Bridge': O'Neill Fought Back, Feels Like a Winner," *Washington Post*, 10 October 1982, A12.

39. Aage Clausen, *How Congressmen Decide: A Policy Focus* (New York: St. Martin's Press, 1973), 123.

40. O'Neill, 344.

41. Ibid.

42. Price, 67; *Congressional Quarterly Almanac*, 97th Cong., 1st Sess., 1981, vol. 37 (Washington, D.C.: Congressional Quarterly, 1981), 248; O'Neill, 345; David Broder, "Those Wayward Democrats," *Washington Post*, 12 July 1981, C7.

43. David Osborne, "Can This Party Be Saved?" *Working Papers for a New Society* 9 (July-August 1982): 38.

44. *Congressional Quarterly Almanac*, v. 7, 1981, 252.

45. O'Neill, 345.

46. *Congressional Quarterly Almanac*, v. 7, 1981, 263.

47. O'Neill, p. 346.

48. Richard E. Cohen, "The 'Fun and Games' Are Over—Now Congress Has to Enact the Cuts," *National Journal*, 16 May 1981, 888.

49. David S. Broder, "Diary of a Mad Majority Leader," *Washington Post*, 13 December 1981, C5.

50. Hornblower, A12.

51. Ibid., A13.

52. Joseph Kraft, "Democrats, After Defeat," *Washington Post*, 4 August 1981, A15.

53. Clapp, 24.

54. David S. Broder, "Hill Democrats Grant Amnesty to Boll Weevils," *Washington Post*, 17 September 1981, A1.

55. Thomas B. Edsall, " 'Atari Democrats' Join Party Conflicts Revived by Gains," *Washington Post*, 7 November 1982, K1.

56. Michael Barone, "The Battle for the Democratic Party," *Washington Post*, 30 November 1982, A23.

57. Mayhew, 90–99.

58. Edmund Beard and Stephen Horn, *Congressional Ethics: The View From the House* (Washington, D.C.: Brookings Institution, 1975), 75.

59. Clapp, 397, 352.

60. Vogler, 91.

61. Kingdon, 116.

62. Keefe, 137.

63. Clausen, 121.

64. Price, 279.

65. Julius Turner, *Party and Constituency: Pressures on Congress*, rev. and ed. Edward V. Schneier, Jr. (Baltimore: Johns Hopkins University Press, 1970), 236; Clausen, 101.

66. Bonafede, 319.

67. "Democrats In House Gather for Party Unity Discussions," *Washington Post*, 31 January 1981, A3.

68. U.S. Congress, House of Representatives, Representative Barnes, speaking on the state of the Democratic Party, *Congressional Record*, 97th Cong., 1st Sess., 6 February 1981, E417.

69. Ibid., E418–19.

70. Clausen, 121.

71. Price, 65.

72. Democratic Study Group, "Organization and Operations" (Washington, D.C.: Democratic Study Group, n.d.).

73. Ibid.

74. Democratic Study Group, "Special Report: Democratic Campaign Committee and Democratic Steering and Policy Committee," no. 97–63 (Washington, D.C.: Democratic Study Group, 1982), 5.

75. Price, 66–67.

76. Charles O. Jones, "House Leadership in an Age of Reform," in Frank H. Mackaman, ed., *Understanding Congressional Leadership* (Washington, D.C.: Congressional Quarterly Press, 1981), 126.

77. Ibid., 280.

78. Committee on Party Effectiveness, Democratic Caucus, U.S. House of Representatives, "Preface," *Rebuilding the Road to Opportunity* (Washington, D.C.: Democratic Caucus, 1982), 1, 12.

79. Ibid., 119.

80. Margot Hornblower, "House Democrats Tackle the Issues—Generally," *Washington Post*, 23 September 1982, A13.

81. Ripon Society, *From Disaster to Distinction: A Republican Rebirth* (New York: Pocket Books, 1966), 94.

82. Price, 280, 281.

83. Paul E. Tsongas, *The Road from Here: Liberalism and Realities in the 1980s* (New York: Random House, Vintage Books, 1981), xiii, 32, 46, 47.

84. Robert M. Kaus, "Reaganism With a Human Face," *New Republic*, 25 November 1981, 29.

85. Norman J. Ornstein, "Paul Tsongas: A Liberal for All Seasons," *Washington Post Book World*, 13 September 1981, 6.

86. Paul Simon, *The Once and Future Democrats: Strategies for Change* (New York: Continuum Publishing Co., 1982), ix, vii.

87. Ibid., vii.

88. Ibid., 163.

89. Ibid., 169.

90. Gary Hart, *A New Democracy* (New York: William Morrow & Co., Quill Edition, 1983), 7, 14–15.

91. Martin Kaplan, "Elections Aren't Won by 'New Ideas,' " *Washington Post*, 29 November 1981, C3.

92. Michael Barone, "The Battle for the Democratic Party," *Washington Post*, 30 November 1982, A23.

93. James R. Dickenson, "$900 Million to Elect a Government?" *Washington Post*, 1 August 1982, B4; Democratic Study Group, *Campaign Funds—A Widening Gap*, no. 98-1 (Washington, D.C.: Democratic Study Group, 1983), 1.

94. Rob Gurwitt, "Democratic Campaign Panel: New Strategy and New Friends," *Congressional Quarterly*, 2 July 1983, 1346.

95. Ibid.

96. Tony Coelho to members of the Campaign Committee, Washington, D.C., 20 June 1983. Personal files of Caroline Arden, Arlington, Va.

97. Gurwitt, 1346–47.

98. Ibid.

99. Coelho letter, 20 June 1983.

100. Ibid.

101. Ibid.

102. Democratic Study Group, "Special Report," no. 98–1 (Washington, D.C.: Democratic Study Group, 1983), 1.

103. Ibid., 2.

104. Ibid.

105. "DSG Campaign Fund 1982 Election Report," DSG Campaign Fund, Washington, D.C., 5 January 1983.

106. Dickenson, 1 August 1982, B4.

107. Ibid.

108. Gurwitt, 1348.

6

Citizen Programs and the Search for Policy Alternatives

But who can say what the goals and purposes of the parties are? Their quadrennial platforms provide only hazy hints. And neither party possesses the intellectual and political discipline to convert this generalized rhetoric into realistic and distinctive policy alternatives.[1]

The "Extra-Legal" Party

The extra-legal party presents us with a conundrum. Whereas the groups that make up the extra-legal party have the capacity for continuity and autonomy of organization and membership to a far greater extent than either the national or Congressional parties, the extra-legal party can exist only in relationship to the other two, less stable, parties. It is a strange and sometimes uneasy relationship. The groups in the extra-legal party that I chose for my study were selected on the basis of commonality of the word *Democrat* in the name, a stated shared interest with the Democratic Party, and the date of the group's founding, which had to be within the immediate years preceding or surrounding the Party's decline.

I had anticipated that I would find these six groups in the extra-legal party to be operating more or less as auxiliary units, filling some of the unmet needs or inoperative functions of the other segments of the Party. Although some of the groups advertised themselves as serving in that capacity, it was not entirely the case. There is mutual interdependence, but the extra-legal party frequently gets far more than it promises to give. The best analogy I can find for describing the extra-legal party groups is that they are very similar to the crustacea of the subclass *cirripedia*. (The Latin means "feather foot.") This subclass includes the barnacles, which in their maturity have no locomotion of their own and must attach to a host in order to move about in search of food. These organisms are not true parasites, in that they attract food from the seawater around them and not from their transporting host. In its larval stage, the cirriped is free-swimming but must eventually attach itself in order to mature and survive. The most attractive hosts are whales, wooden ships, and floating timbers. A few barnacles will do a host no harm, but accrued over a number of years, the host finds its locomotion impeded, and the chance for survival for both the barnacles and the travelling host is diminished. The "feather-footed" friends of the Democratic Party which I examine in this chapter were attached to the Party for eight years or less. Fortunately for the Party, some never got a firm foothold, and one found an even more attractive host.

The selected groups in the extra-legal party were formed immediately prior to or during the 1976–80 Democratic administration or immediately after the 1980 defeat. Four were formed in 1981, one in 1972, and one in 1975. Four dealt with policy formation only, one with policy combined with fund-raising, one with fund-raising only. Of the four formed for the sole purpose of defining and promulgating policy compatible with Democratic Party ideology, only two were active or productive.

Difficulties in Studying Policy Groups

The task of assessing the efficacy of the policy-making organizations was not an easy one. As Raymond Wolfinger observes: "Policy formation is the heart of government and also the most difficult aspect for political scientists to study in any but an anecdotal fashion."[2] In order to add something of substance to the discussion of the formations and activities of these extra-legal policy groups, I combed the literature of policy sciences, problems of public policy research in the social sciences, and the relationship of ad hoc policy groups and established research organizations to political parties. There was precious little to be found. However, I did find some interesting perspectives in terms of elite theory views and the interrelationship of members of the formal parties and the extra-legal party.

I had surmised that one of the reasons subgroups or extra-legal party groups come into being is because the more formal party organizations are not functioning fully or effectively. Cotter, Gibson, Bibby, and Huckshorn say this is not necessarily so:

Political action committees have joined candidate campaign committees and private management and advisory firms to make available to prospective nominees and candidates resources that the parties are thought to have once monopolized. The easy response

to these developments is to take the general complexity and tur-
bulence of the changing political environment as evidence of the
atrophy of parties and the decomposition of American parties. But
the organizational complexity of American life is an old story, going
back to Alexis de Tocqueville's observation of the "immense as-
semblage of associations" in the new nation ... and it is not clear
that the party organizations will, or that researchers should, be
unduly intimidated by recent changes in the listings on the score-
card of electoral politics.[3]

I am not intimidated, but I respectfully take issue with Messrs. Cotter,
Gibson, Bibby, and Huckshorn. I agree that the emergence of groups
surrounding and latching on to a party does not mean that the party
functions are atrophying. If the party were not going somewhere, or at
least providing enough bulk to hang on to, the group would not attach
itself. However, I still hold that it is significant that the majority of the
groups which surrounded the Democratic Party following its defeat had
to do with ideology or policy formation. There obviously was a need to
be filled and there obviously was something to be gained by those who
would come forward and attempt to fill that need.

"Professionals" and "Elite-Amateurs" Described

I agree with Dye and Zeigler that "American parties do not present
clear ideological alternatives to the American voter" and that it is the
elites who actually shape ideology and policy, and who do so in their
own self-interest.[4] I also observed that the members of the groups in
the extra-legal party were what James Q. Wilson would identify as "amateurs." It was probably the elite-amateur status of the membership,
combined with the need by the Party for policy and purpose, which led
to the extra-legal party's preoccupation with ideological policy development. Wilson describes his "amateur" politician in this way:

> An amateur is one who finds politics *intrinsically* interesting because
> it expresses a conception of the public interest. The amateur pol-
> itician sees the political world more in terms of ideas and principles
> than in terms of persons. Politics is the determination of public
> policy, and public policy ought to be set deliberately rather than
> as the accidental by-product of a struggle for personal party ad-
> vantage.... The amateur takes the outcomes of politics—the de-
> termination of policies and the choice of officials—seriously, in the
> sense that he feels a direct concern for what he thinks are the ends
> these policies serve and the qualities these officials possess.... The

ultimate source of the amateur spirit is found in the expectations of the followers, not in the motives of the leaders.[5]

Wilson goes on to compare the amateur with the "professional" politician who sees politics as consisting of "concrete questions and specific persons who must be dealt with in a manner that will 'keep everybody happy' and thus minimize the possibility of defeat at the next election."[6] The most vivid examples of the amateur and the professional I have encountered thus far in this discourse are found in the amateur Ripon Society, referred to in chapter 5, which was formed as a "research and policy organization of young members of the business, professional and academic communities, [seeking] to rally the energies and talents of thinking young people to the cause of constructive Republicanism," and the unidentified "professional" who remarked to Martin Kaplan that what was said at the inaugural presentation of the Center for Democratic Policy was of little consequence since elections are not won by "new ideas," but according to who has the "best blue smoke and mirrors."[7] There will be many more examples of the elite "amateur" and a few of the "professional" as I present my observations on the six groups of the extra-legal party.

Examination of the Citizen Groups

In this chapter each of the six groups will be examined by describing its formation, stated purpose and goals, and how well it accomplished those goals in the two years following the 1980 election. An assessment of what each was able to offer the Party and what the group got out of it will also be presented. An attempt is made to ascertain what motives the groups may have had in offering their services to the Party and how successful they were in influencing the formal Party both in the national organization and the Congress. A large part of this discourse will deal with the three most active groups, the Center for [Democratic] National Policy, the Democrats for the 80's, and the Fund for a Democratic Majority. The reason for this is that these groups did the most; therefore there is more to say about them. However, there is significance to be found in what the other groups did *not* do, and an attempt will be made to account for that too.

The Center for [Democratic] National Policy

Late in February 1981, two days before Charles Manatt was elected as chairman of the National Democratic Party, a short notice appeared in the Washington Post "Executive Notes" column which stated that "a blue ribbon group of Democrats yesterday announced formation of an organization to think up new ideas for the party." The announcement stated, in the words of former North Carolina Gov. Terry Sanford, that the purpose of the Center would be "to look beyond the New Deal and Great Society toward the needs for the future."[8] The actual conception if not the birth of the Center had taken place in November 1980, scarcely a week after Reagan had been elected to the White House along with the Republican majority in the Senate. A small group of disillusioned and disenchanted Democrats gathered informally for lunch in Washington to find mutual comfort in companionship and to find consolation in talking not about what went wrong, but what to do about it. Among those present was Rep. Michael Barnes of Maryland, who proposed a revival of the old National Democratic Forum, which had existed in 1973–77 when the Party was out of power in the White House and, according to Barnes, had "provided intellectual stimulus and a means of serious issue discussion within the Democratic Party."[9] The National Democratic Forum had been established

> to reappraise basic premises that have dominated Democratic Party thinking since the New Deal. The group sponsored a well publicized national issues conference in Louisville, Kentucky in 1975. But since it was designed to focus Democratic thinking while the party was out of power, the forum was suspended when Carter was inaugurated.[10]

On December 9, 1980, Barnes served as convener of a procedural meeting, held in Washington, of former participants in the activities of the Forum. According to Maureen Steinbruner, who was present, there were some twenty-five to thirty people in attendance, who engaged in a free-flowing discussion.[11] Lester Hyman, former president of the National Democratic Forum, served as recording secretary for this meeting and wrote the minutes. Two directions were considered: that the Forum could work directly with the Democratic National Committee in developing strategies and policies *or* the Forum could resume the function it had held in the 1970s by holding public hearings and identifying issues. It was determined at this meeting that issue papers should be developed by certain individuals to be brought before another meeting of the Forum. There were no specific invitations issued for the subsequent meeting, but by word of mouth a number of people heard about it, and there was a sizeable turnout for the late January meeting when the issue papers were presented. One of these papers, "The 1981 Democratic Party," by Stephen I. Schlossberg and Ted Van Dyk, was the paper, cited previously in chapter 5, that was inserted in the *Congressional Record* by Michael Barnes on February 6, 1981. It may be recalled that these authors did not recommend any strong ties with the National Democratic

Party and emphatically stated that the National Committee should stay out of the policy business: "One should not expect the Democratic National Committee however, to produce sharply-honed new policy proposals. The moment it strays too far from fund-raising and technical assistance it becomes, by definition, a player in a potential factional struggle."[12]

This is an interesting statement, coming from Van Dyk who obviously had a vested interest in seeing that whatever shape the revitalized Forum took, it should be independent of the DNC. Although he did not mention the Center for Democratic Policy by name in his issue paper, he stated that the National Committee "should not aspire to issuance of finished Democratic Party policy proposals. No, new thinking and initiatives will come from individual Senators and Congressmen, from state officer-holders, [sic] from writers and academics, and from *independent centers of policy development* [emphasis added]." Another interesting aspect of Van Dyk's statement is the underlying assumption that a developer of policy is by "definition a player in a potential factional struggle." One could understand an "ideological" struggle in connection with policy, but it seems that "factional" would be more closely aligned with candidate selection and the winning of elections. Perhaps Van Dyk was speaking here from the perspective of the "professional" and not just the interested "amateur" that he appeared to be.

During the early months of 1981 the group continued to meet under Michael Barnes's leadership. They continued to work on the concept of the policy group, and by early February they were already thinking of it as something quite different from the old National Democratic Forum. Adam Yarmolinsky chaired a committee to produce the "Statement of Purpose—Center for Democratic Policy," which was revealed at a February 21 luncheon meeting and press conference. Van Dyk, who along with Barnes had served as a catalyst throughout the conception and planning process, led the meeting. Officers, staff, and initial members of the Board of Directors and the National Advisory Committee were named at this time. As Bill Peterson said in his comment in the *Washington Post*, "The group is a virtual who's who of the Democratic Party."[13]

Van Dyk was named president of the Center, Lanny Davis, secretary, Gregory B. Craig, treasurer, and David Ifshin, legal counsel. Other officers were added shortly thereafter: Keith Haller, former administrative assistant to Michael Barnes, as executive vice-president; Albert Eisele as communications director; Maureen Steinbruner, deputy director for research; Mary-Margaret Overbey, deputy director for finance; and Joan Ashton, office manager. Of these, only seven full-time positions received any salary. Those were filled by Van Dyk, Haller, Eisele, Steinbruner, Overbey, Ashton, and an administrative assistant.

The attention-gathering names associated with the Center were, most notably, Terry Sanford, chairman of the board, and vice-chairs Maxine Waters, Cyrus Vance, Sol C. Chaikin, and Cleta Deatherage. Waters, the only member of the Democratic National Committee in the group, was also assistant speaker of the California State Assembly; Vance was former secretary of state under Carter; Chaikin was president of the International Ladies Garment Union Workers, and Deatherage was chair of the House Appropriations Committee of the Oklahoma State Legislature. There was a mixture of both amateurs and professionals in this group, but there is no doubt that all were elites. They represented a prime example of the "governing elite" associated with private policy organizations described by Thomas Dye:

> The governing elite is "structured"—that it [sic], it is relatively stable over time. Issues and elections may come and go, but a fairly stable group of individuals continues over time to exercise a disproportionate influence over public policy. . . . Elected officials—the "proximate policy makers" whose actions give official sanction to policy decisions—knowingly or unknowingly respond primarily to the values of the elite.[14]

Further evidence of the presence of the Democrats' "ruling elite" can be found by perusing the list of 296 National Advisory Committee members. This roster includes such familiar names as Hodding Carter III, Warren Christopher, W. Michael Blumenthal, Stuart Eizenstat, Shirley Hufstedler, and Edmund Muskie of the Carter administration. Party perennials such as Adlai E. Stevenson III, Willard Wirtz, Newton Minnow, Nicholas Katzenbach, and Walter Heller were also on the committee. There was also a forty-member Board of Directors, which, according to Terry Sanford, represented a "broad range of outlooks, opinions and leadership experience that will help the Center achieve its goal of stimulating new ideas and fresh thinking about the central issues facing our country in the 1980's.[15]

By design, no incumbent senators, representatives, or potential presidential candidates were asked to serve on the board in order, according to Sanford, "to underscore the fact that the group will undertake no lobbying, have no direct political involvement and make no political contributions or endorsements."[16] There was one exception to this rule. Michael Barnes was a member of the National Advisory Committee. His presence was justified by Van Dyk because of Barnes's work in 1973 in the founding of the Democratic Forum and its successor, the Center for Democratic Policy.

There was probably a great deal more at work here than "political purity." The nonlobbying, nondirect involvement with a sitting legislator was crucial to the Center's maintaining its highly valued tax status

covered by 501 (c) (3) of the Internal Revenue Code. This status is re-
served for nonprofit, educational organizations which may receive donations that are tax deductible by the donors. The National Democratic
Forum enjoyed such a status, and when it was resurrected as the Center
for Democratic Policy, the tax status still pertained. All publications of
the Center carried the statement that the nature of the Center was that
of

> an educational, non-profit, tax-exempt public policy research or-
> ganization dedicated to developing alternative policy proposals and
> approaches to governance. The Center is independent of any po-
> litical structure or faction. It will express no single institutional
> viewpoint nor will it promote or lobby any program. Instead, it
> will reach out to sources of new ideas—and new variations of old
> ideas—and attempt to stimulate debate and dialogue among lead-
> ers at all levels of government, in labor and business, in the aca-
> demic world, in the media and in the voluntary sector, and to
> introduce those ideas into the public-policy process.[17]

In its initial announcement flyer entitled "Center for Democratic Policy: Asking Questions and Seeking Answers Regarding the Central Issues of the 1980's," the Center is described as being "independent of
any formal political structures," yet it characterizes its officers and advisory board as individuals who "believe *their political party* [emphasis
added], while remaining true to its dedication to human need, must
rethink its premises, programs and approaches to governance."[18]

One of the most articulate and popular members of the National Advisory Committee was Cathleen Douglas, widow of the late Supreme
Court Justice William O. Douglas. She went on the stump to raise funds
for the Center on April 13, 1981, before the members and guests of the
Woman's National Democratic Club in Washington, D.C. Douglas
shared the platform with Claudia Barnes, wife of Michael Barnes, and
Keith Haller, both representing the fledgling Center. Douglas presented
a reasoned argument for the support of the Center that day, stressing
the traditional values of the Democratic Party, "freedom and equality
and justice for all." She saw the Center as a means for finding new
solutions to old problems, some of the problems having been exacerbated by "well-meaning but inept attempts at solutions." Douglas cited
the emerging class of permanent poor and the national view of Democrats not responsive to individual initiative and productivity. She also
pointed out that Democrats were perceived to be "soft on crime."[19]

In answer to questions from the floor, Douglas and Haller pointed
out that the Center would elicit ideas from the masses by "reaching
out." Haller stated that one of the principal concepts of the Center was

"to create a decentralized structure." When asked if the Center would help to shape the 1984 party platform, Haller replied there would be no direct relationship. When asked how the Center would get the studies into the public domain, Haller responded, "We will work very hard."[20] These rather vague responses offer reason to believe that the Center for Democratic Policy structure, even in its initial stages, viewed itself as the model of an "elite" policy organization, as described by Dye:

> Policy questions are not decided by "the people" acting through elections, or through political parties, or through the operation of the interest groups. Rather the "elitist" model acknowledges only very indirect popular influence over the policy-making behavior of elites. Elite theory suggests that the structure of society itself is designed in such a way as to suppress the emergence of issues which might result in policies adverse to the interest of the governing elite. We have come to label this process "non-decision making."[21]

The Dye model presupposes the financial solvency and even wealth of the elites in the group, both individually and in the aggregate; however, the Center for Democratic Policy was far from solvent at the time Douglas and Haller were out soliciting funds in April 1981.

Although the Center announced in its initial publicity that it had pledges for at least half of its 1981 operating budget of $500,000, by mid-August of that year the money was coming very slowly. There had been some sizeable single contributions, such as one for $10,000 from the Harrimans, but there was still much to be done if the Center was to proceed with its grand scheme.

Funding would continue to be a critical problem for the Center throughout its early years. Staff had to purchase their own bookcases if they were to have them at all. Telephones were answered by volunteers. Typing services were provided by volunteers. Proofreading and major mailings were done by volunteers. There was little supervision or training done for volunteers, and the atmosphere at the Center's offices frequently resembled that of the campaign "boiler room" where the energy expended is far greater than the actual work produced.

When asked to characterize the motivations of the volunteers who worked at the Center, Steinbruner said that those who stayed did so out of an ideological commitment. Those who came hoping to be hired or looking for the social aspects of political activity did not last long. The Center used a fair number of student interns from American University and George Washington University who stayed a semester and got course work credit as well as experience.[22]

The salaried staff, especially Van Dyk and Steinbruner, appeared to work from an ideological impetus, with the prospect of a long-term association with the Center and its objectives. When asked how he perceived the Center's work and his place in it, Van Dyk replied that this was no six-month campaign effort to find ways to defeat or discredit Ronald Reagan.

> We hope to have some impact, but we have spent too long running against Hoover and for FDR. Our purpose is to develop new purposes for the party and the country. We have to get rid of the screamers left and right. We will not be trendy. We are not a movement or a cause, but a brain bank. We hope to be in business 20 years. I hope to be the head of a large research organization 20 years down the road from now.[23]

When asked why he thought he was chosen as the man to do the job, he said, "Because I know pretty much everybody left to right. They know my policy and they know I'm honest." Van Dyk describes himself as a "generalist and not arcane enough to be distrusted."[24]

Van Dyk was serving as the vice-president of the Weyerhaeuser Company in Seattle when he was first tapped for his position at the Center. Prior to that he had been a member of Hubert Humphrey's staff, an assistant administrator for the Agency for International Development, and a vice-president of Columbia University.

Maureen Steinbruner saw the Center as a realization of ideas and ideals which she had personally held since her student days in the 1960s and 1970s at the University of California, Berkeley, and at Harvard's Graduate School of Government. She said she had had a long association with policy organizations and that she had long felt that there was a void in this country for a liberal policy organization which would seek ideas from the broad range of liberal thinking. She stated:

> I am doing this because I think it is the right thing to do. I see one of our most significant problems as a lack of centralized policy. We must develop as a free standing institution. We must serve in dealing with all kinds of people in sharing information. The Democrats believe that there is such a thing as the public interest. I agree, and there must be some capacity for maintaining that interest.[25]

Polsby commented on some of the difficulties experienced by public policy organizations that aspire to function as an idealistic "free standing institution":

> A great and continuing problem for public policy research institutes concerns the inevitable tension between the desire to provide an

environment for independent work that stands on its own merits and the desire to put forward an organizational product. . . . An ideological or thematic focus can sometimes be detected in the published products of institutes, or in the briefings they give to congressional staffs and the newspapers, and can be observed in the composition of their study groups, trustees and advisory committees. . . . Some public policy research institutes aspire to greater breadth, however, and chafe at being stereotyped ideologically. Their leaders worry that the work of their organizations will not be received in the spirit in which it is prepared and that their sources of support, both intellectual and financial, will narrow down.[26]

James Sundquist, senior fellow of the Brookings Institution, sees difficulty in the production of pure social science policy research, especially when the researcher and the "research brokers aspiring for acceptance may find themselves getting into a tell-them-what-they-want-to-hear mood."[27] James Q. Wilson points to somewhat the same difficulty in maintaining the objectivity of a policy institute, such as that envisioned by the founders of the Center for Democratic Policy: "Getting good social science research is different from consulting good social scientists. The latter, unless watched carefully, will offer guesses, personal opinions, and political ideology under the guise of 'expert advice.' "[28]

The Center for Democratic Policy suffered from the pressures observed by the aforementioned scholars. Though the upper-level staff members seemed to work from a clear inner vision of the goals of the Center, that vision was not always projected to the board or to the public at large. The September 30, 1981, board meeting may have been a crisis point for the survival and direction of the Center. This is only speculation, drawn by inference, not observation. The board meeting was not open to the public; however the agenda was available. Item 8 on the agenda was "Changing the Center's Name." There had been speculation, based on some reports coming out of California, that the word *Democratic* in the Center's name was a deterrent to finding funding support. Some of the internal critics of using the word *Democratic* in the name said that this might lessen the effectiveness of the organization as an independent policy group which could not only attract nonpartisan intellectuals but also influence policy on both sides of the aisle in the Congress. There was the fear of the taint of ideologies that had failed or were worn out and of elections that had been lost.

Van Dyk himself said there were some doubts about using the party identifier when the metamorphosis was taking place back in January 1981, when the National Democratic Forum was being reborn into the new Center. He said that even then it was argued that the word *Dem-*

ocratic should be avoided.[29] Despite all the misgivings, the board voted
on September 30, 1981, not to change the name. However, at the December 1981 meeting, the board "voted unanimously . . . to rename the
Center [as the Center for National Policy] because, despite its role as a
tax-exempt, non-profit, educational institution, the word 'Democratic'
in its original title created the misconception that it was an official arm
of the Democratic Party or one of many recently formed political action
committees."[30]

It is remarkable that the Center, plagued with lack of funding, staff,
and physical office facilities and with a confused identity, accomplished
anything in its first year and a half of existence. However, it was able
to produce and publish four economic reports, mount a public forum
on telecommunications, and hold a well-attended public luncheon at
the National Press Club to present the first of its publications and their
authors. The Center took a rather innovative approach to the development of its policy papers. Several authors were chosen for each topic,
selected "after consultation among [the] Study Group Chairs, staff and
Program Committee, and review by [the] Board. In each case, balance
and diversity are the central factors."[31]

The quality as well as the approach varied in these papers commis-
sioned and published by the Center. Maureen Steinbruner commented
that the overall quality was rather good, "especially considering what
we pay our authors . . . which is nothing."[32] The papers were published
in a series entitled "Alternatives for the 1980's." On the day before the
introduction to the public of the first papers, dealing with economic
issues, at the National Press Club on October 14, 1981, Van Dyk and
some of the Center staff arranged a meeting with Speaker of the House
O'Neill and others of the Democratic leadership to present the ideas it
had generated directly to the Democrats in the Congress.

The Center's first publications received scant coverage by the *Washington Post*, with only seven paragraphs dedicated to the "new ideas"
that were unveiled.[33] The account of the launching of the first policy
papers fared better in the *New York Times*. Adam Clymer's full-column
story was headlined "Democrats Propelling 3 Strategies on Economics
into Battle of Ideas." In his story, Clymer described the Center, compared it to the American Enterprise Institute, commented on the papers,
and brought the reaction to them from Charles Manatt. Clymer quoted
Manatt as saying that the release of the studies "should put to rest any
lingering thoughts that the Democrats are short on ideas and alternatives
to the programs and policies of the Reagan administration."[34]

By the end of 1982 the Center for National Policy had published a
total of five sets of issue papers. These dealt with studies in productivity,
foreign policy, military policy, and tax and fiscal policy. It was the paper
on productivity that appeared to be the most influential in what would

emerge from the policy proposals coming out of the Congress. This paper called for

> increased productivity, in its most meaningful form . . . [enabling] workers to come close to their potential economic contribution. . . . The United States, in the spirit of private enterprise, must identify needs it can fill and take steps necessary to meet them. These steps will likely combine the efficiency of private enterprise and the incentives that the federal government can provide. The program suggested above, "The U.S. Private Sector in the Solution of World Problems," is one way it could be done. The ultimate question is whether we have the vision and will to do it.[35]

At least the scholars who worked for the Democrats recognized that want of will is just as debilitating as want of power.

As is often the case with any other noble or idealistic cause, the seeds of the Center's own destruction lay within it. Institutionally, the Center was designed to be beholden to no one group, articulating no systematic ideology other than "the public interest," and it was founded in the traditional American myth "that the American people have the capacity to reshape their political and economic system to address the country's highest priority needs and responsibilities effectively and compassionately."[36] The Center proposed only to develop alternatives to these ends. It disclaimed any stand that one idea is better than another, provided no mechanism for the promotion, promulgation, or implementation of those alternatives, and had no institutional mechanism for the measure of its success. Perhaps the fact that it was still surviving, although barely financially solvent at the end of 1982, was the most telling measure of its success.

There was no clear-cut mechanism by which the Center could transmit or translate its policy into action. If persuasion was their only means, they appeared to lack both the skill and the necessary entrée with decision makers. Another problem inherent in the design of the Center's purpose was the lack of a means for becoming self-sustaining and flourishing. In its politically immaculate state it rendered itself sterile, unable either to engender its own support or to reward those who would attach themselves to it. Their plans for a publishing program were vague, designed not to be a commercial venture. Their publications must be of a quality to meet the Center's high purpose and must focus on the issues determined by the Yarmolinsky Program Committee. There is scant reason to believe that with such a narrow publications program the Center would be able to compete in an already glutted publishing market. They would only wind up talking to themselves, finding little advancement for their primary objective of broad participation at all levels.

In the first two years of the Center's existence, the staff and hangers-on seemed determined to limit their public forums to a scholarly elite and known political clique which came out primarily in order to see and be seen. There is an important lesson to be learned from the experience of the Center's former self. When the Democrats once more gained control of the White House and the Congress, the National Democratic Forum ceased to function. With all of its illustrious names, the Center for [Democratic] National Policy served primarily as a halfway house for Democrats waiting to see which way the political winds were blowing and waiting perhaps for a return to power. If that could be the Center's only accomplishment, it would still not be a total loss, although it would not have become the institution its founders envisioned. Polsby speaks of the importance of what he calls "permeability" in American government:

> The permeability of American government means in the first place that there is a continuous two-way flow of senior personnel, in and out of governmental service. Public policy research institutes provide centers of recruitment for those on their way in, and a plausible, even honorable situation for those on their way out. Permeability means also a continuous flow of information and influence. . . . The character of our government, increasingly dominated by temporary political executives rather than career bureaucrats, encourages this dependency upon outsiders for intelligence, analysis, and advice.[37]

Polsby's remarks summarize the essence of the Center for National Policy's usefulness, although this "permeability" factor was not articulated in the Center's founding statement of purpose. This interdependence is the hallmark of the relationship of the extra-legal party with the less stable, though more fixed national and congressional parties.

Democrats for the '80s

In any interpretation of the phrase, whether in the vernacular or the categorical, Pamela and Averill Harriman were a "class act." The Harrimans were the embodiment of Dye and Zeigler's governing elite, "those [who] move easily in and out of government posts from their positions in the corporate, financial, and education world . . . and who participate in decisions that allocate values for society."[38] The organization that the Harrimans put together in the Democrats for the '80s combined both the policy-making and the fund-raising functions to be found in the extra-legal party. Although the group was affectionately known as "PamPAC,"[39] it engaged in far more than just raising funds

to assist Congressional candidates and the Democratic National Com-
mittee. The group was formed in December 1980 "to strengthen the
Democratic Party in funding, ideas, and organization." Members of the
Board of Directors included Averill Harriman, Edmund Muskie, Robert
Strauss, Bill Clinton, and Stuart Eizenstat. The Congressional Liaison
Committee was composed of Senators Robert Byrd, Alan Cranston, and
Daniel Inouye, and Representatives Thomas P. O'Neill, Jim Wright, and
Thomas Foley.[40]

Pamela Harriman, a member of the British aristocracy and formerly
daughter-in-law to Winston Churchill, and her husband, former chairman of the board of Union Pacific Railroad, U.S. Ambassador-at-Large,
and governor of New York, known as "the most durable link between
the United States and the rest of the western world,"[41] appeared on
April 13, 1981, before the Woman's National Democratic Club. This was
the same day that Keith Haller and Cathleen Douglas appeared to explain
and raise funds for the Center for Democratic Policy. The Harrimans
were also there to announce the founding of their organization and to
solicit funds for its support.

In her opening statement, Mrs. Harriman said that her group "sought
to open up a lively, thoughtful new dialogue for the future." She la-
mented that the Democrats had failed to get their message out in 1980.
"We lost the battle of communication, not the battle of ideas." She vowed
that she and her followers would make it possible so that the Democrats
"never again have to say that what we had was a failure to communi-
cate." Mrs. Harriman suggested that the Democrats for the '80s would
also be the source of some clearly articulated ideas which could be used
to "build a Democratic agenda in touch with people and in tune with
the times."[42] In a flyer given out at the April 13 meeting, the Democrats
for the '80s declared that the organization would

> be helping to define a workable, positive and imaginative program
> for America's future. We believe that there are new ideas which
> can combine Democratic principles, practical programs, and pop-
> ular support. We will encourage them, publicize them, and help
> put them to work.[43]

There would also be organizational assistance in planning strategy and
running campaigns. This advisory help would be made available to all
Democratic candidates and campaign volunteers. The group would
"support carefully-selected Democratic House and Senate candidates
who can win in 1982."[44] Democrats for the '80s not only would back an
effort to put Republicans "on the defensive," but also would challenge
the "New Right." In her speech, Mrs. Harriman made it clear that her
group would supplement the Democratic National Committee and by

no means compete with it. According to a story in the *Washington Post*, her relationship with Charles Manatt was "mutually beneficial." "She introduced Manatt, a party outsider, to Washington's Democratic establishment, and he in turn attends her fundraisers and so lends her PAC credibility. 'I couldn't have begun to know a small *portion* of the people she knows,' Manatt says."[45]

By virtue of being a self-confessed political action committee, Democrats for the '80s could not claim the nonprofit tax status enjoyed by the Center for Democratic Policy. Even with the handicap of not being able to collect tax-deductible contributions, the Harriman group raised $700,000 and had over 7,000 active members by the end of their first year.[46] A large portion of the funds raised came from a gala birthday party celebrating Mr. Harriman's ninetieth birthday on November 11, 1981. Some fifteen hundred of the Harriman's "closest friends" attended the party. According to an account in the *Washington Post*, the party was a spectacular success as far as bringing together the various parts of the Democratic Party, both past and present:

> Members of five White House administrations, the Senate and the House and some of the nations governors were among the 1,500 who came to the Harrimans' birthday party, a fete that turned into a flexing demonstration of Democratic might . . . there was an astonishing collection of famous people. It seemed that every other face has been on a magazine cover or at least a newspaper front page.[47]

Besides this large sort of fund-raising party, Pamela Harriman entertained at her Georgetown home with more-intimate "working dinners . . . to bring together elected officials and supporters of the Democratic Party to discuss [the] Party's strategy on energy, the economy, taxes and foreign affairs."[48]

One of the more interesting efforts of the Harriman group involved its direct opposition of the "new right" and especially the powerful National Conservative Political Action Committee, known as NCPAC. NCPAC had launched a particularly forceful television campaign against the reelection of Democratic Sen. Paul Sarbanes of Maryland, spending some $300,000 in the attack. Democrats for the '80s got into the fray and spent $20,000 to air "paid spots of [their] own calling NCPAC on its smear tactics. . . . NCPAC left such a trail of bad publicity that Sarbanes' leading Republican opponent, Representative Marjorie Holt, withdrew from the race."[49]

Another attack on the "new right" came in the form of a fourteen-page pamphlet entitled "The New Right: A Threat to America's Future."[50] This little booklet described just who was included in the "new right" and listed five of the largest organized groups: National Conservative Political Action Committee, The Fund for a Conservative Majority, Committee for the Survival of a Free Congress, The Congressional Club, and the Moral Majority. A brief profile of each organization was given along with the names of the most influential leaders and participants in each. Interestingly, there was no mailing address or locus for any of the organizations given. This information would have made the pamphlet more useful to researchers, but perhaps the Harriman staff did not wish to give too much information to those who might find themselves in agreement with the stated goals of the organizations. There is a page and a half of quotations from New Right leaders, excerpted from various newspaper accounts, which might have been useful to those developing campaign speeches, but there are some that can serve merely to provide amusement and, perhaps, a bit of political insight, such as the one from Terry Dolan, Chairman of NCPAC: "The only difference between Republicans and Democrats on a Presidential level is the Democrats tell you they're going to screw you and the Republicans tell you they're not going to screw you—and do it anyhow."[51]

The considerable attention the Harriman organization gave to fighting the ultraconservative right-wing groups points up one of the leading propositions of Dye and Zeigler's elite theory:

> Elites give greater support to democratic values than masses. Elites are also more consistent than masses in applying general principles of democracy to specific individuals, groups, and events. Extremist and intolerant movements in modern society are more likely to be based in lower classes than in middle and upper classes. The poor may be more liberal on economic issues, but when liberalism is defined in noneconomic terms—as support for civil liberties, for example—then the upper classes are more liberal and the lower classes more conservative. . . . Mass movements exploit the alienation and hostility of lower classes by concentrating upon "scapegoats." The masses are less committed to democratic "rules of the game" than elites and more likely to go outside these rules to engage in violence. Mass activism tends be undemocratic, unstable, and frequently violent.[52]

In June 1982, just in time for the midterm conference in Philadelphia, Democrats for the '80s came out with one of their more substantial and lasting contributions to the Democratic cause. In the Introduction to the 373-page *Democratic Fact Book: Issues for 1982*, Pamela Harriman wrote:

> The Democratic Fact Book: Issues for 1982 . . . is more than a partisan guide to the disheartening record of Reagan Republican-

ism at home and abroad. The message it carries for the American
people is a challenge to base their choice this fall on the facts of
the recent past and on the chance to put our country back on a
sensible course . . . the authors have documented the facts of Reagan Republicanism in its first 16 months. They have also outlined
a range of policy alternatives—not as prescriptions for all Democrats but rather to represent the variety of options and ideas before
the Party this year.[53]

"The authors" referred to here are not listed by name, but according
to the acknowledgments they included "women and men who gave of
their time, experience and knowledge to write—without compensa-
tion—the various sections of this book." Also acknowledged was the
"encouragement and support provided by the Democratic National
Committee, the Senate and House Campaign Committees, the House
Democratic Study Group and the Senate Democratic Policy Committee."
The work was supervised by Peter Fenn, executive director of the Democrats for the '80s. John C. Obert was the editor, with the help of Alfred
Friendly, Jr., as consulting editor and Will Smith as researcher. Peter D.
Hart, director of Research Associates, Inc., wrote a long essay on "The
Mood of America and the 1982 Elections" to set the tone of the work.
Hart reported that the major issues at the midterm election time were
the economy, the direction of national defense, social security, and the
role of government. He based his conclusions on the results of a survey
done by his firm during the first year of the Reagan administration. Hart
thought that issues would "assume greater importance in 1982, [and
that] the personalities of the candidates will have diminished in impact."[54]
     Whether this separation of issues from candidates would really occur
might be questioned by those who would view the party only in terms
of its presidential selection function. However, this separation is characteristic of the amateurs of the extra-legal party, who are more concerned with principles and ideology than with specific candidates.
Indeed, the extra-legal party groups of an out-party have a peculiar and
precious opportunity to offer these policy alternatives. As Wilson points
out, "The ultimate source of the amateur spirit is found in the expectations of the followers, not in the motives of the leaders."[55] Certainly
such a separation was both an organizational and practical political goal
of the Democrats for the '80s.
     In presenting themes for the Democrats to use in their campaigns,
Hart owned up to a strategy which the Democrats had been practicing
without admitting to it since November 1980—he urged Democrats to
be more like Republicans:

In 1980, the Republicans won from the courthouse to the White House on the basic theme, "Vote Republican for a Change." Regardless of ideology, region, or office, most Republican candidates used this theme in combination with their own strategy and issues to fashion a winning campaign. If imitation is the highest form of flattery, then the Democratic Party should be prepared to flatter the Republicans in 1982. While each campaign and contest will have its own issues and game plan, the ultimate goal should be to link individual strategies to four major themes.[56]

The themes were determined by use of survey data gathered by the Democratic National Committee, Democratic Senatorial and Congressional Campaign Committees, and Hart's organization. They determined that the Democrats should base their individual campaigns around the following propositions: Democrats serve as a balance to the Reagan administration; Democrats fight for the average working person; Democrats better understand government's legitimate role; and the overall goal for Democrats is to ensure a safer world.[57] Here we see a group offering a catalog of ideas to candidates for the choosing. In other words, those who would be leaders but were short on principles could pick causes which they might champion from an agenda set forth by some of the more idealisitic elite. In the particular case of the Democrats for the '80s, the elite were acting as intermediaries between the greater mass of the Democratic Party and the potential leaders.

Although the *Democratic Fact Book* does not address the themes specifically, the intent is implicit in the collection of essays and data which appears under the headings "The State of the Economy," "The State of the People," "The State of the Society and the Environment," and "The State of the Nation's Security." There are numerous subsections under each of these headings which provide a statement of the problem, with well-documented statistics when called for, the Reagan Republican record on dealing with the problem, and a list of specific Democratic alternatives to the solution of the problem. The work does not cover *everything* that might come up in political debate, but it is by far the most comprehensive, practical approach to issues and policy development produced by any single unit or segment of the Democratic Party. It was published at a cost of $70,000. Copies were given free of charge to the delegates of the midterm conference and were sold to others for a price of $10 per copy.[58] It was not within the scope of this study to determine how this publication was used by potential candidates and campaigners. The significance here lies in the fact that such a comprehensive and cohesive document was prepared by the extra-legal party, rather than by the more stable, institutionalized segments of the Party.

In the first two and half years of its activity, Democrats for the '80s raised $1.6 million, which was distributed across the board to Democratic candidates and causes. In the 1982 midterm election, Democrats for the '80s contributed $359,883 to candidates—"more than Terry Dolan's National Conservative Political Action Committee, which raised almost $10 million but gave out $263,171."[59] In terms of real goods and services, as well as intrinsic contributions that cannot be bought outright with money, Pamela Harriman and her group gave more to the Democratic Party in the aggregate than any other part of the Party, either the "real" or "extra-legal" party. There appears to be no accounting of how many candidates and campaign managers used the *Democratic Fact Book* in the 1982 campaign, but if they did not, it was their loss. The work was well conceived and has lasting reference value in itself.

There is no doubt that Pamela Harriman needed the Democratic Party. The destitute Party was the recipient of the expression of her noblesse oblige. However, it is almost impossible to measure what else Mrs. Harriman might have got out of her seemingly tireless efforts on behalf of the Party. Elisabeth Bumiller speculated on this question:

> It's hard to understand what motivates her. Why does she work 10 hours days when she could be riding in the country and going to lunch? Is it because she wants a political appointment in the next Democratic administration—or is she really committed to the party? But one sense you get from her is that she's preparing for the day when her husband is gone. She wants to be a part of the future, and she's trying to create her own niche.[60]

One has the feeling that whatever it is that Pamela Harriman wants, she will probably get . . . that is, everything but a sweeping Democratic victory in 1984. She could not do that singlehandedly. Besides, as Dye and Zeigler have pointed out: "[The elite] views public policy changes as a response to elite redefinition of its own self-interest, rather than as a product of direct mass influence. Finally, elite theory views changes in public policy as incremental rather than revolutionary."[61] Pamela Harriman can afford to wait.

The Fund for a Democratic Majority

There is little ambiguity about the purpose and intent of the Fund for a Democratic Majority, founded by Sen. Edward Kennedy in 1981. In a six-page letter addressed to "Dear Friend," Senator Kennedy requested that the recipient join him as a "co-founder" of the political action committee whose purpose would be

> to help Democratic members of both the Senate and House with the research, technical support, polling information, and fundrais-

ing technology that our opponents have so skillfully developed and deployed—in short, to provide a counter-balance to the overwhelming technological and organizational lead of the New Right which cost us so dearly last year.[62]

There would be no issuing of papers or policy statements. However, one of the devices for raising funds was a book coauthored by Senator Kennedy and Sen. Mark Hatfield entitled *FREEZE! How You Can Help Prevent Nuclear War* which was to be sent "to thank you for your contribution of $25 or more." This work was to "present our reasons for believing that a Nuclear Freeze is the *only* alternative to a course of destruction for the world."[63]

Kennedy stated in his initial letter announcing the fund that although he knew that he would be the "number one target of the New Right in the next election," he was "committed to more than a personal victory" for himself in 1982. He declared that none of the funds from the political action committee he was founding would go to his campaign. "The Fund's resources will be directed to vital races outside my own Senate re-election campaign in Massachusetts."[64] Kennedy said nothing about any resources which might be channeled toward his campaign for the presidency. However, on the day after his announcement that he would not seek the presidency on December 1, 1982, Kennedy sent out a letter, dated only "Thursday," that said, "As you know, I have decided not to seek the Presidency of the United States in 1984. But in making that decision, I have also made a second decision: that in giving up the campaign for a candidacy, I shall not, shall never, give up the campaign for a cause." Kennedy went on to say that he would direct his energies "to helping elect progressive Democrats," but no definition or criteria was offered to identify just what would constitute a "progressive" persuasion.[65] He also stated that in the 1982 midterm campaign the Fund had given

> critical support to over 400 progressive candidates and party organizations, including 22 Senate races, 26 gubernatorial contests, and 122 House campaigns. By Election Day, we had raised more than $2.5 million. We had contacted more than 3 million voters, attracted over 50,000 contributors, and developed one of the most advanced political computer systems in the country. And the result? Over 70% of the progressive Democrats we supported won on November 2nd.[66]

There is no mention of precisely how these winners were distributed, but in any event there were some 280 Democrats out there who were winners and beholden to the Kennedy efforts.

Much of the help that Kennedy offered the 400 candidates was what he termed a sort of "in-kind service program that will place experienced campaign personnel with candidates in key marginal districts." Another project provided candidates with television- and radio-spot productions.[67]

Kennedy made personal appearances for over 60 candidates in twenty-one states.[68] The states Kennedy visited were, for the most part, in the Northeast and the industrial Midwest or "rust belt" states. New Mexico, Colorado, and California were the extent of the Western states. His only forays into the South were in Kentucky and one stop each in Florida and Virginia.

The *1982 Annual Report* stated that the Fund was ranked as the eighth-largest independent PAC in the nation.[69] According to a *New York Times* survey of the top ten political action committees, with data gathered between January 1981 and October 13, 1982, the Fund's assessment of its standing was too modest. Considering total funds raised, the *Times* ranked the Fund for a Democratic Majority as ninth among the top ten of all PACs and seventh among independent PACs. The *Times* showed the Fund as having raised $2,126,200 and spending $1,803,300, with $134,000 going directly to candidates for the House and the Senate. This contribution to federal candidates represented only 6.3 percent of the Fund's income.[70]

It appears that Kennedy was spreading his assistance wide but not deep. By mid-July of 1983 John W. Leslie, executive director of the Fund, wrote that "the Fund has become the largest Democratic political action committee in the nation, and one of the fastest-growing and broadest-based organizations dedicated to electing progressive Democrats at every electoral level."[71]

The Fund for a Democratic Majority gave a little bit to a lot of people, but the principal beneficiary was Edward Kennedy, in terms of largess dispensed throughout the Party and political exposure in the personal appearances he made on the part of candidates. Kennedy would have a lot of political chits to call in whenever he might be ready.

Democratic Policy Center

One of the most intriguing puzzles I attempted to solve in my research involved the Democratic Policy Center. The search for answers took me further afield than any other portion of my study, and I returned with more questions than answers at the end of the journey.

The search began in April 1982 when I read a brief notice in the *Washington Post* that stated that Stuart Eizenstat, who had headed Carter's domestic policy staff, had been one of the hosts and the principal speaker at a luncheon in Atlanta on April 7, 1982. The other host for the "fund-raising luncheon" was Griffin Bell, former attorney general under Carter. The purpose of the luncheon was to raise funds for a "new 'think tank,' the Democratic Policy Center."[72] At that time, I made several attempts to reach Mr. Eizenstat by telephone at his Washington law office, but was never successful. Sometime later, I decided to try to obtain information directly from Mr. Bell. I wrote to him on February 21, 1983, and asked for information on the Democratic Policy Center. Mr. Bell responded on March 24, 1983, and suggested that I "get in touch with Stuart Eizenstat at his Washington office, which you will find in the telephone directory, and he can put you in touch with someone in the Democratic party structure in Washington. Should you be in Atlanta this week or next, you may wish to call Charles Kirbo here at this law firm and perhaps he can help you."[73] Taking Mr. Bell's advice, I attempted once more to arrange an interview with Mr. Eizenstat but was unable to reach him either by letter or telephone.

It was not until August 1, 1983, that I was able to arrange an interview with Charles Kirbo at his law offices at King and Spalding in Atlanta. Mr. Kirbo was very gracious in receiving me. I asked for any information he might be able to give me on the Democratic Policy Center. He responded that he was not certain that it really did exist. At that point in our interview he had his secretary place a call to Mr. Eizenstat in Washington. Unfortunately, Mr. Eizenstat was in court that particular morning. I asked Mr. Kirbo if I might have confused the Democratic Policy Center with a political action committee that Jimmy Carter had announced he was spearheading back in December 1981.[74] Mr. Kirbo assured me that the Carter PAC was "entirely related to Carter, with contributions from close friends to help him get out of debt and finance his offices in Plains and Atlanta."[75] I then asked if the Center might be somehow connected with the announced Carter presidential library and policy center to be administered by Emory University in Atlanta. Mr. Kirbo knew a great deal about that center and proceeded to show me architectural drawings of the proposed library and the topographic survey map of the controversial proposed highway leading to the center. I returned once more to asking Mr. Kirbo if he had attended the April 1982 luncheon and what he remembered about the announcement of the new Democratic Policy Center. He replied, "Yes, I was there, and what they planned was a center which would get out quality documents. It sounded like a good idea but I did not want to be a founder. . . . I haven't heard any more about it."[76]

It occurred to me at that point in the interview that the fund-raising luncheon might have been for the Washington-based Center for Democratic Policy, but Mr. Kirbo said that he did not think that was the case. Upon my return from Atlanta I tried unsuccessfully to get further information from Mr. Eizenstat.

What ever became of the "new think tank" announced by Eizenstat and Bell in 1982? I do not know. However, the significance of this rather futile pursuit is that there was activity among the elites of the Georgia Democrats, although not all of it was productive nor did any of it appear to benefit the Party as a whole.

Coalition for a Democratic Majority

In his classic work *The Real Majority* Ben Wattenberg wrote:

> In the Democratic Party, ... under the banner of New Politics there is talk of forming a new coalition of the left, composed of the young, the black, the poor, the well educated, the socially alienated, minority groups and intellectuals—while relegating Middle America and especially white union labor to the ranks of "racists." This position manages to violate *all* the axioms described in this book. Accordingly, if the search of the right-leaning Republicans can lead only to psephological fools' gold, then the march of the left-leaning Democrats must certainly yield up a prize of some new, even baser political non-metal; perhaps we might call it jackass pyrite. There would seem to be a greater likelihood of the Democrats doing themselves in than the Republicans. ... It is the out-party that will normally tend toward a more extremist position. ... If the Democrats do not commit suicide by throwing themselves upon the knife-edge of the Social Issue, they can lead a long life struggling to capture the center. This nonsuicidal scenario can easily include a Democrat in the White House in the not-too-distant future.[77]

This, written in 1970, embodies the philosophy and the intent of the organization that Wattenberg founded in 1972 and named the Coalition for a Democratic Majority. Wattenberg saw the "real majority" as "unyoung, unblack, unpoor," middle class and middle of the road politically.[78]

With a group of moderate-to-conservative Democrats, who were drawn together philosophically and by hope of the possibility of Sen. Henry Jackson's becoming a candidate for the presidency, Wattenberg and James O'Hara became co-chairmen of the group. O'Hara had served as chairman of the Commission on Rules, which in 1972 presented its recommended reforms to the Democratic National Committee. These reforms updated and improved convention procedures, thereby "limiting the potentially arbitrary exercise of authority by national leaders, the convention chairman, and whoever might control the national party bureaucracy at a given time."[79] Political scientist Austin Ranney, who had been a consultant to the McGovern-Fraser Commission, which worked simultaneously with the O'Hara task force, was a member and a frequent spokesman for the Coalition for a Democratic Majority.[80]

Earlier I pointed out that the members of the extra-legal party groups were largely "amateurs" in Wilson's definition and as such were more likely to be ideological. The Coalition for a Democratic Majority, though operating on a stated centrist ideology, was largely composed of Wilson's "professionals"—that is, those more interested in winning elections. Wattenberg and Scammon state very clearly at the outset of *The Real Majority* that theirs is a "psephological" approach to politics, or the politics that deals with "the study of elections."[81] The adoption of a centrist policy was a matter of pragmatic necessity to the Coalition for a Democratic Majority in order for the Democrats to return to power in the White House. In their "Epilogue" to the 1970 edition of their work, written in 1971 after the 1970 election, Scammon and Wattenberg assessed "The Threat and the Cure" for the Democratic Party:

> There is a central question that runs through. . . . *It is possible that the label of elitism—and the political poison it connotes—will move from the Republicans to the Democratic left?* To many, the left of the Democratic Party seems to be associated with a new elitism of the upper middle class. . . . To many, the leftists (and potentially, the Democrats) appear in smug opposition to so much that so much of America holds dear: social order, social stability, patriotism, and a rising standard of living. . . . A political party in the United States operates effectively between the two 35-yard lines of the political football field, wholly aware that there is a major substantive difference between one 35-yard line and the other, aware too that heading starkly for the end zone leads to a political fumble. A political party must keep itself aware that compromise and coalition are the essential tools of political action.[82]

The founders of the Coalition for a Democratic Majority urged the necessity of a "capture of the center . . . the capture of the allegiance of the masses of the votors [sic], unyoung, unpoor, unblack—middle-aged, middle-class, middle-minded," in order to win the presidency.[83]

So, with this clearly articulated philosophy and strategy did the Coalition for a Democratic Majority come to the aid of the beleaguered party in 1980–82? It did not. Whether they had given up on what they deemed a lost cause or whether individual self-interest became the major motivation of the members of the group or whether the untimely death of Senator Jackson late in the summer of 1983 had something to do with it, I cannot say. It was probably a combination of all of these factors, but suffice it to say that the Coalition for a Democratic Majority was conspicuously missing from the Democratic Party's search for itself. I wrote to Maria H. Thomas, secretary-treasurer of the Coalition, in July 1983, requesting annual reports, publications, or issue papers that might have been published during the time designated for this study. I received the following response, included here in its entirety:

> In response to your request for copies of CDM publications between November, 1980 and November, 1982, CDM did not publish anything during that period. Since many of our positions on foreign policy issues were coopted by the Reagan campaign and some of our Board members joined the Administration, our organization spent those years reassessing its goals and purposes. We are only now becoming active again.[84]

It is beyond the scope of this study to determine who went to work in the Reagan administration or why, but I find such a transition from a Democratic "majority" to a Republican administration significant. There is also significance in the fact that Wattenberg, Scammon, and Ranney have all found regular employment at the somewhat conservative American Enterprise Institute, where, as Polsby points out, "Democrats predominate among resident political scientists."[85]

Democratic Agenda

The Democratic Agenda is not a single group but a group made up of groups, most of which are about as far from Wattenberg and Scammon's thirty-five-yard line as Michael Harrington, the Agenda's convener, is from Averill Harriman. Founded in 1975, this umbrella group tries "to unite the democratic left behind a program responsive to the current crisis of the American system."[86] The stated purpose of the Agenda is

> to unite varied groups that do not always agree and are even sometimes diverted from the basic battle against corporate domination of the society into fighting with one another. It has always looked for that common denominator of economic interest that brings us together: without full employment, there will be no gains for unions, for minorities, women, environmentalists, people concerned with the third world, disarmament, and so on.[87]

To the members of the Democratic Agenda, large corporations are the source of all evil. The activists of this organization have, according to their own account, been a nagging and sometimes disruptive influence on the organized Democratic Party:

In 1976 we struggled at the convention to make the Democratic
party conscious that the old remedies were no longer workable. In
1977 we marched to the Democratic National Committee (DNC)
headquarters in Washington, D.C., to proclaim that if Carter kept
on with his inept version of an obsolete politics he would be defeated in 1980. At the Memphis mid-term convention in 1978 we
organized an impressive floor fight against Carter's policies, and
we were an important part of the progressive coalition at the 1980
convention.[88]

The Democratic Agenda is the embodiment of the "masses," which are
contrasted with the "elites" by Dye and Zeigler: "The masses are less
committed to democratic 'rules of the game' than elites and more likely
to go outside these rules to engage in violence. Mass activism tends to
be undemocratic, unstable, and frequently violent."[89]

If the groups from the Democratic agenda were represented at the
1982 midterm conference, they were distributed throughout the workings of the conference as individuals—there was no evidence of disrup-
tion or organized activism. It would have been difficult to identify these
individuals, since the Democratic Agenda had not, at that time, published a list of its membership. The newsprint flyer cited previously does
list some individuals and their organizations as "Democratic Agenda
Initiators," but these are given with the caveat that "these organizations
[are] listed for identification only. List in formation."[90] Repeated efforts
to obtain the final list were unsuccessful. Included on the "identification
only list" were such familiar Democratic names as Douglas Fraser of the
United Auto Workers and co-chair of the Hunt Commission, Representatives Ronald Dellums and John Conyers, and Julian Bond, Georgia
State Senator.[91]

Although the Democratic Agenda activists offer a lengthy program of
action to the Democratic Party, it is obvious that in doing so they expect
to get a great deal for themselves, collectively. They state that their
primary goal is to achieve full employment, but they do not see this as
coming about through increased productivity, as did the House Committee on Party Effectiveness. Two of their remedies are a high-speed
train system and a "renewable source energy industry with technology
on a human scale which can be used by neighborhoods and individuals
in order to create jobs in the United States, putting our fellow citizens
to work in areas of high unemployment producing goods and services
which, like high speed trains and alternate energy, will also help eliminate causes of inflation."[92] The ambiguity in the speciousness of their
logic here is surpassed only by their fractured syntax. The main message
of the Democratic Agenda was that "the American economy can work
again, that the needs of the American people can be met, their hopes

fulfilled—but only when they win substantial control over the major economic institutions of this nation.''[93] According to Harrington, this can be achieved by making the trains run on time.

In a more lengthy and articulate statement of the policies advocated by the Democratic Agenda, Harrington offered "Proposals from the Democratic Left" in an article in *Dissent*. Citing a Joint Economic Committee Report released in November 1981, Harrington states that the JEC "details many things that are wrong with [the railroads] but one statistic might stand as a paradigm for all the other [economic] problems.''[94] What caught Harrington's eye and imagination was the fact that the average speed of passenger trains in the United States has declined from seventy miles per hour in the mid–1950s to a current average of forty miles per hour. From this fact Harrington developed his thesis that publicly owned high-speed rail systems dispersed throughout the country could lead to the reindustrialization and subsequent economic revitalization of the country. He stated further:

> I believe, as a socialist, that corporations should receive subsidies as part of a plan for rebuilding America. I put the issue paradoxically to stress the practical importance of a generalization made earlier: that corporate America is going to be around for the foreseeable future and certainly during the next stage of the welfare state. They key strategy here, I believe, is to make any subsidies to corporations dependent upon their conforming to a democratically determined economic plan.[95]

The essence of the Democratic Agenda's message is summed up by Harrington in the following:

> Liberalism, which is as far left as America has ever gone, will have to go a good deal beyond itself if it is even to preserve what it has won. Socialism is not on the immediate agenda. But proposals that move in a socialist direction by democratizing the decision-making powers now held by corporations are very relevant.[96]

Harrington took a dim view of the emerging ideology in the Congress on the part of the "neoliberals," especially Paul Tsongas and Gary Hart, who Harrington feared "have a very real political future.''[97] The fear Harrington expressed here stemmed from his perception that there was really not much ideological distance between these two Democratic senators and Ronald Reagan:

> But why, then, group these neoliberals next to Ronald Reagan? Because their central point, their controlling assumption, is con-

servative; their liberalism is genuine but irrelevant; Hart and Tsongas are convinced that America's basic problem stems from over-
consumption and underinvestment.[98]

I offer that Harrington's basic problem stems from overstatement and
oversimilification. Yet there is no doubt that he has some ideas worthy
of consideration and that he can turn a neat phrase, as evidenced by
this one: "Neoliberalism, then, surely is better than Reaganism in that
it is more compassionate and even sensitive to equity considerations
about the distribution of income. Politically it might be called Reaganism
with a (somewhat) human face."[99]

With "feather-footed" friends like the Democratic Agenda hanging
on, the Democrats don't need Republican enemies. Harrington's group
presented more non-negotiable challenges and threats to the fragile
Democratic Party in the early days after the 1980 defeat than constructive
advice for a reasonable and incremental way out of the Party's dilemma.
As Dye and Zeigler have pointed out, "incrementalism" is the manner
in which organizational and political recommendations are accommo-
dated and decisions made.[100] Although the Democratic Party was in a
shaken state in the early 1980s, it apparently did not feel so devastated
that it would try anything, even very radical economic policies, as a
possible remedy. It may have been under stress, but it was not snapping
at anything that moved. This reaction was to the Democratic Party's
credit. It showed more strength than weakness. Schattschneider has
described the situation this way:

> It has been said, for instance, that the American people are so
> badly divided that it is impossible to organize cohesive parties, i.e.,
> that the special interests have disrupted the parties. The experience
> of American politics with the pressure groups does not support
> this conclusion. It is true that there is a great diversity of interests
> in the American nation and that modern society is complex. But
> this is true of other societies. The raw material of politics, i.e., a
> great multiplicity of interests, is nothing new and does not prove
> that the community is divided by impassable barriers. It is the
> business of the parties to deal with situations of this sort, to discover
> accords among the interests. . . . It is the task of statesmen to evolve
> policy amid conflicts.[101]

Summary

The groups that make up the extra-legal party have the capacity for
continuity, autonomy of organizational structure, and discretion over
membership to a far greater degree than either the National Democratic

Committee or the Congressional Party. Yet, none of the groups in the extra-legal party could have the influence and impact they have if they were not in some way attached to the less stable but more fixed segments of the parties. The extra-legal party groups become as barnacles attached to a whale—dependent on the larger body not for sustenance but for transportation and a place to be. The relationship between the less stable but more fixed segments of the Party and the extra-legal party is strange and sometimes uneasy.

Six groups were selected for examination in this case study of extra-legal party activity. These groups were attached, at one time or another, to the Democratic Party during a period of approximately eight years surrounding the Democrats resounding defeat in 1980. All had the word *Democrat* or *Democratic* in their organizational name, and all shared some of the traditional goals and philosophies of the Democratic Party. It was found that the majority of the groups were made up of "amateurs"— who find politics intrinsically interesting and who view the political world in terms of ideas and principles—rather than being composed of "professionals"—who are primarily interested in the winning of elections. It had been surmised that the reason there were more organizations emerging primarily interested in influencing policy was because the Democrats had been perceived to be bereft of new approaches to old problems and in need of "new ideas." This was found to be partially true, but during the course of the study, it became evident that there may have been a more salient reason that these groups were interested in influencing policy. It was found that most of the groups were made up of what we might call "elites." Elites are durable and tend to actually shape policy over time. Though the elites will be more likely to see the wide view of the world and to present the more idealistic principles, they ultimately serve their own self-interest by the ideology and policy choices they seek to influence. The group that was least effective in influencing the policy of the Party was made up of the "masses" rather than elites. The masses, lacking the wider view of the public interest, presented demands rather than "principles." The masses lacked the political polish and pragmatic patience of the elites.

Two of the groups were involved in fund-raising for candidates, so in that respect they were professionals, interested in winning elections. Ted Kennedy's Fund for a Democratic Majority provided small contributions to Democratic candidates across the board, but the most gain was realized by Kennedy himself, in collecting political obligations from those he helped and in extending his own considerable visibility. His group offered no "new ideas"; they just sent money. However, one of the fund-raising or political action groups, the Democrats for the '80s, organized and led by Pamela Harriman, contributed a great deal to the Party as a whole. It provided ideas, programs, and funds. It was by far the most effective of the groups and contributed more to the Democratic Party than it could possibly have gotten out of it. One of the groups organized prior to the Democrats' fall from power was admittedly organized around a "psephological," or winning-of-elections, approach to the development of ideology and policy. This was the very moderate, centrist Coalition for a Democratic Majority, which had been in existence the longest of any of the groups in the study. So conservative were the tenets of this group that by the time the Democrats were trying to regroup in 1981, many of the members of the Coalition had gone to work in the Reagan administration and others had retreated to the sanctuary of a conservative public policy institute. Therefore, they had nothing new to offer to the wounded party—only residuals.

The most ambitious of the new groups to form was the Center for [Democratic] National Policy. Just as with the Party to which it attached itself, it too had a difficult time in its search for an identity. The Center for Democratic Policy found that it was expedient to its fund-raising cause to drop the word *Democratic* from its name. Its founders encompassed a wide range of Democrats, but the Center had a very difficult time attracting funding. There was a lack of organization and focus in the administration of the Center, and its contributions in the form of issue papers never found their way directly into the mainstream policy channels of the more stable segments of the Party. The main contribution to the Party made by the Center was one probably not intended at the time of its founding. It served as a "halfway" house for out-of-power Democrats, allowing them to meet and to stay somewhat visible while they awaited a return to power. The Center provided what Polsby calls "permeability" to the Democrats.

There was one group that never got organized at all. Although it reportedly held one fund-raising luncheon, the Democratic Policy Center in Atlanta, Georgia, could never be located. The Democratic Agenda, formed in 1975 of a variety of subgroups representing the left-wing of the Democratic Party, was not its usual disruptive self at the Party's midterm conference, but its convener, socialist Michael Harrington, lambasted the Party with rhetoric and an avalanche of recommendations for redistributing economic power and control from the nation's large corporations to the "people." The centerpiece of Harrington's economic plan was a publicly owned high-speed railway system which would revitalize the industrial "rust belt" areas of the country. The Democratic Agenda demanded, it did not negotiate; therefore, its effectiveness with the more fixed Democratic Party was negligible.

Perhaps the best summary of the contribution and significance of the extra-legal party is found in the observation that the weakened Democratic Party was still able to attract, and to a degree move and sustain, groups as widely diverse as one led by the chairman of the Board of

Union Pacific Railroad and led by a political science professor who wanted a federally supported high-speed rail system. It is significant that one group had dropped off because the Party was not taking it where it wanted to go. It is also significant that the most service was given to the Party by the group who had the lest to gain. This was Pamela Harriman and the Democrats for the '80s. She was able to do what no other individual or group had done: she got Democrats from all parts of the Party to talk to each other. This was a major step forward in assisting the Party in its search for itself.

In the discrete time period devoted to the case study, assessing the long-term significance of the Democrat's extra-legal party is not only irrelevant but impossible. However, the findings indicate that the extra-legal party serves not the total Party but its own individual group members. The extra-legal party has the capacity for expressing opinions and the potential for developing principles and policy alternatives which might be taken up and incorporated by the institutionalized segments of the Party. In order to effect a lasting influence on the Party ideology, the particular extra-legal party must endure over a period of time. Those groups that will endure must be able to find enough sustenance from the political waters travelled by the main Party. Lacking this sustenance, the extra-legal party will either starve or drift away. A group of the extra-legal party which can be completely self-supporting and achieve independent mobility will cease to be an attached political barnacle and will become a free-swimming and separate political entity. The Americans for Democratic Action would be an example of this phenomenon.

In the study it was found that whereas one group fell away, there was no evidence that any of the other groups were nearing self-sufficiency, although the Center for National Policy was attempting to achieve autonomy. Groups in the extra-legal parties, like presidents, come and go. It is the organized, institutionalized Party that endures, in varying degrees of health and stability.

NOTES

1. Robert Shogan, "The Gap: Why Presidents and Parties Fail," *Public Opinion* 5 (August/September 1982): 18.

2. Raymond E. Wolfinger, "Policy Formation and Interest Groups," *Readings in American Political Behavior*, 2d ed. (Englewood Cliffs, N.J.: Prentice-Hall, 1970), 227.

3. Cornelius P. Cotter, James L. Gibson, John F. Bibby, Robert J. Huckshorn, *Party Organizations in American Politics* (New York: Praeger, 1984), 8–9.

4. Dye and Zeigler, 330, 325.

5. James Q. Wilson, *The Amateur Democrat: Club Politics in Three Cities* (Chicago: University of Chicago Press, 1966), 3, 5.

6. Ibid., 4.

7. Ripon Society, 9; Kaplan 29 November 1981, C3.

8. Bill Peterson, " 'New Right' Disillusioned With Reagan Breaks Into the Open," *Washington Post*, 25 February 1981, A3.

9. U.S. Congress, House of Representatives. Representative Barnes, speaking on the state of the Democratic Party, *Congressional Record*, 97th Cong. 1st sess., 6 February 1981, E417.

10. Rhodes Cook, "Learning from GOP Success: Chorus of Democratic Voices Urges New Policies, Methods," *Congressional Quarterly*, 17 January 1981, 139.

11. Maureen Steinbruner, interview held at the offices of the Center for Democratic Policy, 1333 New Hampshire Avenue, N.W., Washington, D.C., 10 April 1981.

12. *Congressional Record*, 6 February 1981, E418.

13. Peterson, 25 February 1981.

14. Thomas R. Dye, "Oligarchic Tendencies in National Policy-Making: The Role of the Private Policy-Making Organizations," *Journal of Politics* 40 (May 1978): 310.

15. Center for National Policy, *1981 Annual Report* (Washington, D.C.: Center for National Policy, 1982), 6.

16. Senator Kennedy quoted Sanford in presentation of remarks on the Center for Democratic Policy, *Congressional Record*, U.S. Congress, Senate, 97th Cong. 1st sess., 27 February 1981, S1678.

17. *Alternatives for the 1980's*, no. 1 (Washington, D.C.: Center for Democratic Policy, 1981), 29.

18. Flyer, issued by the Center for Democratic Policy, [Spring 1981]. Personal files of Caroline Arden, Arlington, Va.

19. Cathleen Douglas and Keith Haller, comments before the Woman's National Democratic Club, Washington, D.C., 13 April 1981.

20. Ibid.

21. Dye, 310.

22. Maureen Steinbruner, interview held at the offices of the Center for Democratic Policy, 1333 New Hampshire Avenue, N.W., Washington, D.C., 4 December 1981.

23. Ted Van Dyk, interview held at the Center for Democratic Policy, 1333 New Hampshire Avenue, N.W., Washington, D.C., 5 May 1981.

24. Ibid.

25. Steinbruner, interview, 4 December 1981.

26. Nelson Polsby, "Tanks But No Tanks," *Public Opinion* 6 (April/May 1981): 58.

27. James L. Sundquist, "Research Brokerage: The Weak Link," in Laurence E. Lynn, Jr., ed., *Knowledge and Policy: The Uncertain Connection*, Study Project on Social Research and Development, vol. 5 (Washington, D.C.: National Academy of Sciences, 1978), 138.

28. James Q. Wilson, "Social Science and Public Policy: A Personal Note," in Lynn, ed., *Knowledge and Policy*, 91.

29. Van Dyk interview, 5 May 1981.

30. Terry Sanford, "Chairman's Letter," *1981 Annual Report* (Washington, D.C.: Center for National Policy, 1982), 3.

31. Ibid.

32. Steinbruner, interview, 4 December 1981.

33. Caroline Atkinson, "Three Economists Offer Democrats Alternatives to Reagan's Programs," *Washington Post*, 15 October 1981, D15.

34. Adam Clymer, "Democrats Propelling 3 Strategies on Economics into Battle of Ideas," *New York Times*, 15 October 1981, sec. 2, p. 15.

35. Lester C. Thurow, Arnold Packer, and Howard J. Samuels, "Strengthening the Economy: Studies in Productivity," *Alternatives for the 1980's*, no. 2 (Washington, D.C.: Center for Democratic Policy, 1981), 27.

36. "Proposal for Support of the Center for Democratic Policy" (Washington, D.C.: Center for Democratic Policy, 1981), 3.

37. Polsby, "Tanks but No Tanks," 16.

38. Dye and Zeigler, 96, 326.

39. Jack Erickson, "The Democrats: Rebuilding With Support Groups," *Campaign & Elections* (Spring 1982): 5.

40. Flyer, Democrats for the '80s [March 1981]. Personal files of Caroline Arden, Arlington, Va.

41. Elisabeth Bumiller and Lois Romano, "The Ages of Harriman," *Washington Post*, 13 November 1981, B3.

42. Pamela Churchill Harriman, comments before the Woman's National Democratic Club, Washington, D.C., 13 April 1981.

43. Flyer, Democrats for the '80s.

44. Ibid.

45. Elisabeth Bumiller, "Pamela Harriman: The Remarkable Life of the Democrats' Improbable Political Whirlwind," *Washington Post*, 12 June 1983, L3.

46. Report from the Chairman, *Democrats for the '80's News '82*, Washington, D.C. (March 1982), 1.

47. Bumiller and Romano, B3.

48. *Democrats for the '80's News '82*, 1.

49. Ibid.

50. "The New Right: A Threat to America's Future," Washington, D.C.: Democrats for the '80s, n.d.

51. Terry Dolan, *Washington Post*, 10 October 1980, cited in "The New Right: A Threat to America's Future."

52. Dye and Zeigler, 327.

53. Pamela Harriman, "Memorandum to the Candidates," *Democratic Fact Book: Issues for 1982* (Washington, D.C.: Democrats for the '80s, 1982), 1–2.

54. Ibid., 373, 3.

55. Wilson, 5.

56. *Democratic Fact Book*, 5.

57. Ibid., 6–7.

58. James R. Dickenson and David S. Broder, "Political Notes," *Washington Post*, 20 June 1982.

59. Bumiller, L3.

60. Ibid.

61. Dye and Zeigler, 325.

62. Sen. Edward M. Kennedy, letter for the Fund for a Democratic Majority,

posted at various times throughout 1981–82. Personal files of Caroline Arden, Arlington, Va.

63. Edward M. Kennedy and Mark O. Hatfield, *FREEZE! How You Can Help Prevent Nuclear War* (New York: Bantam Books, 1982); Enclosure "signed" by "Ted," in undated mailing from the Fund for a Democratic Majority.

64. Kennedy letter, the Fund for a Democratic Majority undated. Personal files of Caroline Arden, Arlington, Va.

65. Edward M. Kennedy, letter from the Fund for a Democratic Majority, Thursday [December 2, 1982]. Personal files of Caroline Arden, Arlington, Va.

66. Ibid.

67. "The Democractic Report (Washington, D.C.: Fund for a Democratic Majority, 1982), 1.

68. Fund for a Democratic Majority, *1982 Annual Report*, 3.

69. Ibid.

70. "Independent Groups Lag on Candidate Donations," *New York Times*, 3 November 1982, A22.

71. John W. Leslie to Caroline Arden, 22 July 1983. Personal files of Caroline Arden, Arlington, Va.

72. "Personalities," *Washington Post*, 9 April 1982, D3.

73. Griffin Bell to Caroline Arden, Atlanta, 24 March 1983. Personal files of Caroline Arden, Arlington, Va.

74. "Carter Sponsors Action Group for Democrats," *Washington Post*, 3 December 1981, A10.

75. Charles H. Kirbo, interview held at King and Spalding Law Offices, Atlanta, Georgia, 1 August 1983.

76. Ibid.

77. Richard M. Scammon and Ben J. Wattenberg, *The Real Majority* (New York: Coward, McCann, & Geohagan, 1970), 280–81.

78. Ibid., 45.

79. Crotty, 242.

80. Price, 184.

81. Scammon and Wattenberg, 16.

82. Ibid., 316, 318.

83. Ibid., 319.

84. Maria H. Thomas to Caroline Arden, Washington, D.C., 30 August 1983. Personal files of Caroline Arden, Arlington, Va.

85. Polsby, 59.

86. "The Democratic Agenda," newsprint flyer published by the Democratic Agenda, [July 1982].

87. Ibid.

88. Ibid.

89. Dye and Zeigler, 327.

90. "The Democratic Agenda."

91. Ibid.

92. Ibid.

93. Ibid.

94. Michael Harrington, "A Path for America: Proposals from the Democratic Left," *Dissent* (Fall 1982): 417.

95. Ibid., 418.
96. Ibid., 407.
97. Ibid., 413.
98. Ibid.
99. Ibid., 414.
100. Dye and Zeigler, 333.
101. Schattschneider, 197.

7

Conclusion

"Cela est bien dit," repondit Candide, "mais il faut cultiver notre jardin."[1]

The Democratic Party has been called "the party of unintended consequences" by more than one of its followers and observers.[2] Certainly the Party had not intended to lose power and control to such an extent that it not only lost the White House and Senate in the 1980 election but also lost the capacity to regroup and recover in the two years after the defeat. Having indulged in reforms intended to open up the Party to wider participation, by 1980 the Democratic Party had ceased to be the Party of the masses and had become a mass party. Also by November 1980 it had literally lost its head. There was no locus of power, no "brain," no centralized switching system that could sort out the information and stimuli received by the various individuals and segments of the Party. The result was a highly random search by all who were affected.

Searching for Organization and Leadership

The logical place for centralized leadership and control was in the Democratic National Committee, and particularly in the national chairman. The various organizational reforms adopted by the Party, particularly the Democratic Charter, served to "nationalize" the Party, moving control and the potential for continuity into the National Committee structure. The Democrats selected wisely in choosing Charles Manatt as their new national chairman in 1981. Manatt possessed the skills of administration and organization which the wounded Party so badly needed.

The new chairman made it clear that he would not attempt to be a "spokesman" for the Party but would serve as a coordinator and catalyst in attempting to bring the various segments and factions of the Party together. He moved quickly and decisively to set up a commission to review the presidential nomination process and to convene an intraparty policy council. He was determined to involve more elected officials in the affairs of the Party, thus returning some of the control and direction of the Party to "professionals," who had a larger stake in the Party's welfare than might the single-issue "amateurs" who had come to dominate the Party in recent years. Manatt devised a program of "services" to potential candidates and campaign workers. These services were evidenced by the training workshops offered throughout the country and by the installation of a direct mail fund-raising system supported by automated data-processing equipment.

Perhaps the best evidence of Manatt's organizational abilities was the midterm party conference that was held in Philadelphia in June 1982. This conference lacked any of the acrimony and divisiveness that had been present in the two previous such conferences. However, for all of Manatt's skill as an administrator and pacifier, he could not control or effectively channel the individualized, highly proprietary attitudes of the various actors within the Party. The most difficult individuals were to be found in the state party leadership and especially in the Congress—the very ones who had the most to offer and the most to gain by a revitalized Party.

Searching for Policy and Unity

The members of the Congress, particularly the leadership of both the Senate and the House, were determined that policy decisions and any subsequent public pronouncements regarding the course of the Party would be theirs and theirs alone. This stance could have been beneficial to the Party and to the American political system if the members had done more than mere posturing. They refused to participate in the policy council proposed by Chairman Manatt. They ignored the recommendations made by the task forces and study groups of the midterm party conference. The House leadership was even wary of the rather moderate centrist recommendations put forward by the House Committee on Party Effectiveness. When the Democrats attempted to find a voice or a spokesman for the Party, they all spoke at once. Schattschneider has said that "the party in Congress is like a Mexican army; everyone in it takes care of himself."[3]

The accuracy of that observation was never more evident than it was in the 97th and 98th Congresses. Having been a majority for a long period of time, the Congressional Democrats did not know how to form a concerted opposition party. Each member seemed to see the world from the perspective of his own district or constituency. The Democratic members of Congress appeared to have taken the Reagan landslide to mean that the "people have spoken," especially on economic issues, and in the interest of their own electoral imperative, they gave the administration practically everything it asked for in the 1982 budget. The House leadership could not even agree on a strategy, much less hold the individual party members in line. The Senate leadership faded into ineffectual oblivion. Although the cry for "new ideas" had gone up almost immediately after the November 1980 defeat, no really innovative approaches were forthcoming from the Democrats in the Congress, either collectively or individually. The best they could come up with were suggestions for an economic program with an emphasis on productivity, which strongly resembled Reagan's supply-side economic policies. The most highly random of an abundance of random party activity was to be found in the Congress. They were singularly lacking in organizational skills, yet they refused the offices of Manatt and the National Committee. They said *they* would fulfill the role of spokesman, yet they not only all spoke at once, but also did not have anything much to say. On the positive side of the activity of the Congressional Party was the revitalization of the House Congressional Campaign Committee. This committee made some real capital investments in the setting up of television studios and data-processing equipment for direct mail fundraising. Although it was able to disperse only a small amount of money to selected candidates, it had established a routine and a staff that could be useful to the Party in the future.

Searching for Policy Alternatives

The activity of the "extra-legal" party was energetic and, for the most part, highly idealistic. Composed mostly of "amateurs" who are intrinsically interested in politics, the extra-legal groups that sprang up in 1981–82 and attempted to attach themselves to the Party were dedicated to seeking "new ideas" and policy formation or to seeking funding for the support of Democratic candidates—one such group combined both activities in one organization.

For all of their lofty goals, the members of the extra-legal party really had more to gain than they had to give, and much of their activity was done in their own self-interest. The most effective of the groups, that is, the one that had the most concrete services and recommendations to offer the Party as a whole, was the one that appeared to have the least to gain from its efforts. For those groups involved in fund-raising, achievement of their goals was more readily realized. They could send money and support directly to individual candidates. The groups involved with policy and program development did not fare so well. They had no avenue or channel for conveying their findings or recommendations to the Party, even if they had been able to determine just who was in charge.

Searching for Funding and Support

Fund-raising and policy development, especially the search for "new ideas," was engaged in by all three segments of the Party. It is natural for a defeated party to look at the ledger and see where they went wrong. It is also indigenous to Democrats to think that more money sent in a direction of a problem will be the solution. Money for campaigns has been a problem for Democrats for a long time and in recent years has been exacerbated by the change in campaign funding laws. There was a small increase in monies distributed to candidates for Congress by the Congressional Campaign Committee, the National Committee, and the independent political action committees. There was a gain of twenty-six Democratic House seats in the 1982 midterm election and no gain but no loss in the Senate. The twenty-six seat gain in the House, some sixteen more than the average gain for an out-party in an off-year election, probably was due more to the electorates' dissatisfaction with the economy, which was in a recession in November 1982, than it was to increased campaign funds for Democratic candidates.

Searching for Direction

It is reasonable that the Democrats would have felt compelled to seek new ideas. If they perceived that the 1980 election was the beginning of a true realignment, or the threat of one, they realized that they must in some way readjust their ideology, since realignments take place along highly emotional or ideological lines. It was this perception, no doubt, that led them to place so much emphasis on policy development. However, they were ill-equipped to determine a new direction, since many could not agree on where they came from, much less where they were going. Their collective institutional memory seems to go back only as far as the New Deal. They interpreted their defeat as a repudiation of the New Deal and Great Society policies. They perceived that these old solutions did not work. What actually had happened was that they had worked very well . . . they had accomplished much of what they had set out to do. Samuel Beer sums it up succinctly: "The kind of redistribution that took priority in the public philosophy of the New Deal was not a redistribution of wealth, but a redistribution of power."[4]

The programs of the Democrats had redistributed the power in the electorate, and the internal reforms of the Party had redistributed the power within the Party. One of the unintended consequences of this redistribution was the loss of control by an elite corps of amateurs and professionals in steering the Party's direction.

There is ample evidence in this case study that the Democrats lacked a clear sense of direction. Most of all they lacked a leadership willing to put away individual proprietary interests for the sake of the Party as a whole. A very young and idealistic Woodrow Wilson observed: "Eight words contain the sums of the present degradation of our political parties: *No leaders, no principles; no principles, no party.*"[5] Notice here that Wilson refers to leaders in the plural, not just a mythical "titular" leader or a presidential leader. A party can have, and should have, more than one leader, but those leaders must be leading on the same course, not going off in all directions or around in circles as the Democrats were in 1981.

Some Modest Proposals

The Democrats could begin to build a strong group of elite leaders both in and out of the Party without disturbing their ideological posture as the party of the masses. The electoral process, with its built-in accountability, allows for the creation of just such a leadership group which could lend some continuity and stability to the Party. Elected officials who continue to be reelected have the opportunity to gain in stature within their particular milieu. The recent reforms in the Congressional committee and caucus system should prevent a tendency for abuse of such an oligarchical system of leadership. It is most important for an out-of-power party to speak to the electorate with one voice. Of course, this ideal state must be preceded by the sound of many voices as positions and principles are aired for selection by the aggregate party. It will be more difficult for a mass party, such as the Democrats, to find the desired unity and harmony of tone. However, a party such as the Democrats, which is far more nationalized than the Republican Party, has the mechanism for bringing about that unity. If the Democrats had used the machinery they had created in the continuing National Party offices, their efforts in 1981 as an inexperienced out-party would have been more effective and less random. Their problem is more attitudinal than it is ideological or institutional. We can liken what happened to the Democrats in 1980 to a man who has survived a rather severe heart attack and who, upon finding that he is still alive and can get up and totter on, goes right out and celebrates with three double-bourbons and a large high-cholesterol steak, followed by brandy and a cigar. All of their thrashing about, their wallowing in self-pity and self-recrimination, and their random search activity, in which they have indulged themselves since November 5, 1980, could be salutary and beneficial if they

would do it in the true spirit of debate, putting aside acrimonious individual self-interest. They could then have the opportunity to learn
something about themselves and to center on a corporate identity. Of
course, this may be asking too much of the political professionals, but
the more idealistic amateurs could have an elevating influence on the
process.

For the life and health of the Democratic Party, the Democrats must
change their well-established way of one for one and all against all. They
do not need to change their rules; they need to change their attitudes.
They suffer more from want of will than they do from want of power.
For the Democrats, rebuilding will begin when, by a sheer act of concerted will, the Congressional leadership assumes a clear "opposition
party" stance, debating policy alternatives both in committee and on
the floor of the Senate and the House. Although I do not hold with
Wilson that members of the President's cabinet should be admitted to
the floor of the Congress for the purpose of debate, I agree that the
Congress is the appropriate arena for the testing of acceptable principles
and for the emergence of new leaders. The potential for the momentum
of two of the vital centripetal forces, ideology and leadership, lies within
the purview of the Congress. Other elected party leaders in the states
and municipalities must push members of the Congress and officials of
the National Party to listen to and heed local perceptions and concerns.
There must be forums for debate from the provinces. These could be
provided by the National Policy Council and the midterm conference.
Leaders of the extra-legal party could also find a channel for their ideas
and concerns through these formal party mechanisms. There is no doubt
that this process of searching for principles and leaders will be time-
consuming and lacking in immediate gratification.

The role of the out-of-power party is an essential one, and certainly
a requisite of a healthy two-party system. As painful as it may be for
the Democrats, the longer their period as an out-party, the better will
be their chances of producing a clear ideological political alternative to
the Republican Party and the better their chances for discovering and
nurturing a corps of talented and politically acceptable leaders. Of
course, there is an optimum time for this process—too long can mean
extinction. Given the Democratic Party's proven durability, this possibility seems unlikely.

Back in the Senate Again—1986 and Beyond

Just after the Democrats won back the Senate in 1986 with a 55–to–
45 majority, David Broder warned the Party against assuming an attitude
of smugness and self-satisfaction: "The biggest mistake that Democrats
can make is to believe that the 1986 election confirmed them as the

majority party in the country. The biggest mistake the Republicans can make is to resume thinking of themselves as the minority."[6]

Broder's admonition is well taken, but the Party may be forgiven a degree of exultation, having also increased their holdings in the House to 258, as compared to 243 in 1981.[7] By the end of 1987, with the presidential primary campaigns well under way, the Democratic Party was far from the confused, moribund conglomerate of fractious factions it had been in the fall of 1980. The National Party, under the low-key direction of Chairman Paul Kirk, had money in the bank and a Policy Commission that actually produced a report, "New Choices in a Changing America," which, according to the commission chairman, Scott Matheson, "gives us a credible claim as being the party of the future."[8] Once considered to be devoid of both well-defined principles and principled leaders, the Party had *seven* serious candidates for the office of the presidency who were articulating their ideas and policies in a series of nationwide debates. Although Polsby has remarked upon "the demise . . . of presidential primaries as repertory theatre,"[9] the touring road show of the Democratic candidates did much to return the art of oratory and showmanship to the presidential selection process. Not that the speeches and debates always reached the heights of dramatic statesmanship, but they did give the candidates a chance to present themselves and their ideas to a large number of voters.

Of the group of candidates that were in the running prior to the first 1988 caucus in Iowa, four are or were from the Congress (Richard Gephardt, Paul Simon, Gary Hart, and Albert Gore), two are or were state governors (Michael Dukakis of Massachusetts, Bruce Babbit of Arizona), and one, Jesse Jackson, had not held elective office, although he had sought the presidency once before. This group of candidates was criticized for looking and sounding alike and became known in the press as "The Seven Dwarfs." This characterization and chastisement for sounding the same must come as a novelty to Democratic Party observers. In the past, the Democrats have been criticized for being a noisy group of factional infighters. Now that they were coming out with commonality, they were blamed for being boring. Greater differentiation would inevitably emerge as the primaries progressed.

The "New" National Party

The apparent change in attitude and appearance was certainly influenced by National Party Chairman Paul Kirk, who "has tried to broaden the party's appeal by moderating its image."[10] With strong support from organized labor, Kirk, a former member of Sen. Edward Kennedy's staff, was elected chairman of the National Party in February 1985 in what was a typical Democratic Party bloodletting. "From angry blacks to estranged southern conservatives and West coast fund-raisers, Kirk has a lot of fence mending to do."[11] In his efforts to moderate the Party's image as a captive of the special-interest groups and proliferating party caucuses, Kirk joined in a party movement to abolish the special status of the black and Hispanic caucuses. Although Kirk has not demonstrated the colorful partisan activism of Manatt, apparently he has done a good job of working out compromises and "keeping the knives under the table." As a part of his effort to keep the Democrats from killing each other, at least in public, he has appointed a party Unity Task Force "to monitor 'the tone and tenor of the debate between the Democratic [presidential] candidates' and to bring private or, if necessary, public pressures on the candidates."[12] Kirk even went so far as to state that the 1988 party platform would be "off limits for intraparty ideological warfare."[13] Whether it was Kirk's influence or good political sense or a real sense of what the Party stands for or a combination of all three, the Seven Dwarfs set off to their work of defeating the Republicans singing "High Ho" in unison.

However, Paul Taylor sees evidence that the Democrats are working at the same old stand: "Yet it's plain from the early stump speeches of the Democratic Class of '88 that while the vocabulary may be trimmed back a bit, the party is very much back to its old self. Its candidates all are running on a two-decade-old center-left formula that proposes more government activism at home and less abroad."[14]

Changes in the Extra-Legal Party

Although the groups in the extra-legal party have changed, this segment of the Party is a highly visible and vocal component. The Democratic Leadership Council—founded by former Virginia Governor Charles S. Robb and "created early last year [1985] as a kind of political safehouse for moderate and conservative Democrats, mainly from the South and West, to pull their party toward what they consider the mainstream"[15]—has provided a forum for issue consolidation and debate.[16] This group was also instrumental in bringing about the "Super Tuesday" primaries and caucuses held March 8, 1988, in twenty states, many of them southern and considered to be in the moderate, centrist camp.[17] Although it was opposed by Kirk and the National Party leadership when it was first formed, the Democratic Leadership Council has done much to bring state party leaders into the debate on where the Party stands and on where it should go. The director of the DLC, Alvin From, who had served as director of the Democratic Caucus Committee on Party Effectiveness under Gillis Long in 1982, has said that the DLC is "trying to provide a counterpoint to pressures arising out of Iowa [presidential selection caucuses] that if unchecked, will create a leftward tilt in the democratic defense agenda."[18] Robb, From, and the DLC are trying to develop an agenda for the Party so that it will be selling

> a strong but lean defense; the courage to raise taxes and restrain entitlements if necessary; a change in workplace culture to link pay to performance and raise workers' stake in their companies' success; a voluntary program of national service for young adults, and "international competitiveness" proposals that range from increased investment in research and education to policies on trade designed to avoid the label of protectionism while guarding industries against unfairness.[19]

This component of the extra-legal party varies slightly from those observed in the principal portion of this study. The Democratic Leadership Council, like the other groups studied, is largely concerned with ideological issues and is made up of leaders who are among the elite in Democratic politics, *but* these leaders are by no means a group of amateurs. And it is apparent from their stance and the issue papers developed by them that they hope that both their members and their ideology will have permeability in the organized Party.

Business as Usual in the Senate

Yet, for all the positive signs of health, the Democrats are still not absolutely secure in their identity.They retreated to the old and familiar in organizing themselves as the majority in the Senate of the 100th Congress. They reelected Sen. Robert Byrd as majority leader. In my opinion, this was not wise, based on Byrd's ineffectual performance as a leader of the minority. As Byrd himself said, "We never developed a minority mindset. We Democrats have always felt that this was kind of a holding operation."[20] Byrd never seemed to understand that formulating strong opposition policy around the issues is a major function of a political party. Byrd was never able to get the Senate Democrats organized into an effective opposition which not only could *oppose* by sheer obstinacy but also could *propose* alternatives. However, Michael Barone and Grant Ujifusa do not agree with this view of Byrd:

> Byrd was a relatively passive Majority Leader in the 1970's. . . . But in 1987 he seemed to be operating in a different manner. He seemed to have learned from Howard Baker and Robert Dole the need to set a posture for his party in which it can be seen to govern and from which it can advantageously fight the next election. And he added to this his own ability to hone in on important details and get them right.[21]

Critical in the reorganization of the Senate was Edward Kennedy's decision to become the chairman of the Labor and Human Resources Committee, leaving the chairmanship of the Judiciary to Joseph Biden, who at that time had already made it known that he was interested in testing the presidential waters.[22] (As it turned out, Biden's turn as an announced candidate was cut short when he removed himself from the running after questions arose about his educational background and his use of unattributed quotations in stump speeches.)

Changes in the House

In the 100th Congress, there was a more dramatic change in leadership in the House, initiated by Tip O'Neill's retirement in December 1986. Jim Wright of Texas was elected Speaker and proceeded to appoint eight members of the Democratic Steering and Policy Committee who were deemed to be Wright "loyalists."[23] The six major House committees reelected their respective chairmen. Tom Foley moved up to majority leader and was replaced by Tony Coelho as majority whip. Speaker Wright named Beryl Anthony of Arkansas to chair the Democratic Congressional Campaign Committee. Coelho had left the committee in excellent shape. He "did a brilliant job of raising money, erasing the Democrats' debt, building a new party headquarters and media center, and of electing new members and returning old ones."[24] Barone and Ujifusa believe that the Democrats' sustained control of the House rests not on their ability to manipulate the system, but "because the voters want them to." They explain it this way:

> There is a strong and sensible desire in an era when presidential nominating processes give an advantage to extremists or enthusiasts of both parties, to dividing the control of government, for having Tip O'Neill's or Jim Wright's Democrats there to check and balance Ronald Reagan's Republicans. Proof: many more serious Democratic House candidates argue check-and-balances than serious Republican candidates argue support-your-President.[25]

For all of their reputation for capitulating to the whims and whines of special interests and for internal strife made public, the Democrats do seem to be finding an understanding among themselves of what the Party is and what it stands for in the last decades of the century. They are now being accused of being boring and bland, of "collapsing toward a muddy center."[26] At the end of 1987, the Democratic donkey might be sliding toward a muddy center, but he is definitely not still stuck in the ditch. He should be able to move on down the "road to opportunity" if he takes care not to sling that mud on a fellow Democrat. *And* he may also find that the muddy center is where the voters are.

Summary

The Democrats, studied in the particular with the constraints of a limited case study, can reveal a good bit about Democrats, but extrapolation is not only risky but also likely to be intellectually dishonest. As Seymour Martin Lipset observes, "None of the social sciences can predict worth a damn."[27] Probably the principal contribution here lies in the historical account of a rare political phenomenon—that of a long-term party of power which found itself suddenly out of power and threatened by the possibility of a major realignment. From this account, certain generalizations, if not predictions, may be made.

During the time that a party is in power and fulfilling its mission of "holding the line against the centrifugal forces in American society" it may lose sight of the centripetal forces that bind it together as a party. When it has neglected these internal "centering" forces for too long, it will diminish as a party of power and possibly lose that power altogether. In trying to regain its ascendant role, it will engage in highly random search activity. This activity itself can be useful and therapeutic if the party aerates the political soil and ultimately returns to the nurturing of its central concerns of ideology and leadership. Attention must also be given to the other centripetal forces, including a well-articulated message, a unified voice to send the message forth, and a will to create policy and programs accompanied by the means to implement them.

If the Democrats can manage to hitch up the donkey, once he's out of the ditch, and tend their domestic garden, giving especial care to planting a more centrist strain of ideology, then they have a very good chance of reaping a powerful harvest. If they return to their old ways and old methods, they run the risk of remaining out of power for a long time to come.

Notes

1. "That is so," replied Candide, "but we must tend our garden." Voltaire, *Candide, Ou L'Optimisme*, in *Romans et Contes* (Paris: Garnier Freres, 1960), 221.

2. Robert G. Torricelli and Tom Donilon, "Reforming the Democrats' Reforms," *Washington Post*, 24 August 1981, A17; David S. Broder, "Democrats and Unintended Consequences," *Washington Post*, 17 January 1982, A6; Norman Ornstein, "The Democrats' Disease: Reform," *Washington Post*, 1 July 1984, C5.

3. Schattschneider, 196.

4. Samuel H. Beer, "In Search of a New Public Philosophy," in King, ed., *The New American Political System*, 10.

5. Woodrow Wilson, "Cabinet Government in the United States," in Albert

Fried, ed., *A Day of Dedication: The Essential Writings and Speeches of Woodrow Wilson* (New York: Macmillan Co., 1965), 78. This essay first appeared in *International Review* 6 (August 1879): 146–63.

6. David S. Broder, "Democrats Can't Afford to Be Smug," *Washington Post*, 12 November 1986, A19.

7. Paul Taylor, "Senate to Have 55 Democrats," *Washington Post*, 6 November 1986, A1.

8. Paul Taylor, "Democrats Elect Pragmatism Over Ideology," *Washington Post*, 23 September 1986, A4.

9. Polsby, 73.

10. James R. Dickenson, "Democratic Chairman Asks End to Infighting for '88," *Washington Post*, 12 March 1987, A1.

11. Dan Balz, "Kirk Elected Democratic Chairman," *Washington Post*, 2 February 1985, A5.

12. Ibid., A7.

13. David Broder, "A Sudden Outbreak of Democratic Harmony," *Washington Post*, 9 December 1987, A21.

14. Paul Taylor, "Democrats Revive Old Tune As GOP Gropes to Write One," *Washington Post*, 1 May 1987, A1.

15. Paul Taylor, "Robb Keeps Foot in Door To an '88 Campaign," *Washington Post*, 17 October 1986, A10.

16. Paul Taylor, "New Optimism for Democrats," *Washington Post*, 12 December 1986, A3.

17. "And They're Off!" *Washington Post*, 8 September 1987, A10.

18. Paul Taylor, "Robb Warns Against Catering to Interests," *Washington Post*, 23 June 1987, A9.

19. Taylor, 12 December 1986, A3.

20 David Ignatius, "But Do the Democrats Deserve a Senate Win?" *Washington Post*, 2 November 1986, C1.

21. Michael Barone and Grant Ujifusa, eds., *The Almanac of American Politics, 1988* (Washington, D.C.: National Journal, 1987), 1xiv.

22. Howard Kurtz, "Weighing Presidential Campaign, Biden Urged Kennedy to Chair Judiciary," *Washington Post*, 12 November 1986, A4.

23. Edward Walsh, "House Democrats Reelect Six Committee Chairmen," *Washington Post*, 10 December 1986, A8.

24. Barone and Ujifusa, 65.

25. Ibid., 1xii.

26. Paul Taylor, "Politics Collapsing Into Blurry Center," *Washington Post*, 9 November 1986, A1.

27. As quoted in Karen J. Winkler, "Questioning the Science in Social Science, Scholars Signal a 'Turn to Interpretation,' " *Chronicle of Higher Education*, 26 June 1985, 6.

Selected Bibliography

Monographs, Collections, Reports, and Journal Articles

Acheson, Dean. *A Democrat Looks at His Party*, New York: Harper & Brothers, 1955.

Bailey, Stephen K. *The New Congress*. New York: St. Martin's Press, 1966.

Banfield, Edward C. "Party 'Reform' in Retrospect." In *Political Parties in the Eighties*, edited by Robert A. Goldwin, 133–49. Washington, D.C.: American Enterprise Institute for Public Policy Research, 1980.

Barone, Michael, and Ujifusa, Grant, eds. *The Almanac of American Politics, 1988*. Washington, D.C.: National Journal, 1987.

Beard, Edmund, and Horn, Stephen. *Congressional Ethics: The View from the House*. Washington, D.C.: Brookings Institution, 1975.

Beer, Samuel H. "In Search of a New Public Philosophy." In *The New American Political System*, edited by Anthony King, 5–44. Washington, D.C.: American Enterprise Institute for Public Policy Research, 1978.

Bibby, John F. "Party Renewal in the National Republican Party." In *Party Renewal in America: Theory and Practice*, edited by Gerald M. Pomper, 102–15. New York: Praeger, 1981.

Bibby, John F., and Huckshorn, Robert J. "Out-Party Strategy: Republican National Committee Rebuilding Politics, 1964–66." In *Republican Politics: The 1964 Campaign and Its Aftermath for the Party*, edited by Bernard Cosman and Robert J. Huckshorn, 205–33. New York: Frederick A. Praeger, 1968.

Bibby, John F.; Mann, Thomas E.; and Ornstein, Norman J. *Vital Statistics on Congress, 1980*. Washington, D.C.: American Enterprise Institute for Public Policy Research, 1980.

Bonafede, Dom. "For the Democratic Party, It's a Time for Rebuilding and Seeking New Ideas." *National Journal*, 21 February 1981, 317–20.

Bone, Hugh A. *Party Committees and National Politics*. Seattle: University of Washington Press, 1958.

———. "Political Parties and Pressure Group Politics." In *The American Party*

Process, edited by Norman L. Zucker, 351–64. New York: Dodd, Mead & Co., 1968.

Burns, James MacGregor. *Deadlock of Democracy: Four-Party Politics in America.* Englewood Cliffs, N.J.: Prentice-Hall, 1967.

Campaign Funds—A Widening Gap. Special Report, no. 98–1. Washington, D.C.: Democratic Study Group, U.S. House of Representatives, 1983.

Campbell, Angus. "Interpreting the Presidential Victory." In *The National Election of 1964*, edited by Milton C. Cummings, Jr., 256–81. Washington, D.C.: Brookings Institution, 1966.

Carr, Robert K.; Bernstein, Marver H.; Morrison, Donald H.; and McLean, Joseph E. *American Democracy in Theory Practice.* 3d ed. New York: Holt, Rinehart & Winston, 1961.

Ceaser, James W. *Reforming the Reforms: A Critical Analysis of the Presidential Selection Process.* Cambridge, Mass.: Ballinger Publishing Co., 1982.

Clapp, Charles L. *The Congressman: His Work As He Sees It.* Garden City, N.Y.: Doubleday & Co., Anchor Books, 1963.

Clausen, Aage. *How Congressmen Decide: A Policy Focus.* New York: St. Martin's Press, 1973.

Commission on Delegate Selection and Party Structure. *Democrats All.* Washington, D.C.: Democratic National Committee, 1973.

Committee on Party Effectiveness, Democratic Caucus, U.S. House of Representatives. *Rebuilding the Road to Opportunity.* Washington, D.C.: Democratic Caucus, 1982.

Commission on Party Structure and Delegate Selection. *Mandate for Reform.* Washington, D.C.: Democratic National Committee, 1970.

Committee on Political Parties of the American Political Science Association. "We Need a Stronger, More Responsible Two-Party System." In *Problems of American Government*, edited by Neal Riemer, 151–58. New York: McGraw-Hill Book Co., 1952.

Cook, Rhodes, "Learning from GOP Success: Chorus of Democratic Voices Urges New Policies, Methods." *Congressional Quarterly*, 17 January 1981, 139.

Cotter, Cornelius P.; Gibson, James L.; Bibby, John F.; and Huckshorn, Robert J. *Party Organizations in American Politics.* New York: Praeger, 1984.

Cotter, Cornelius P., and Hennessy, Bernard C. *Politics Without Power: The National Party Committees.* New York: Atherton Press, 1964.

Crotty, William J. *Political Reform and the American Experiment.* New York: Thomas Y. Crowell Co., 1977.

Delegate Selection Rules for the 1984 Democratic National Convention. Adopted by the Democratic National Committee, 26 March 1982. Washington, D.C.: Democratic National Committee, n.d.

Democratic Charter Commission. *Charter for the Democratic Party of the United States.* Washington, D.C.: Democratic National Committee, 1974.

Democratic National Committee. *Official Proceedings of the 1982 Democratic National Party Conference.* Washington, D.C.: Democratic National Committee, n.d.

Democratic Study Group. "Special Report: Democratic Campaign Committee and Democratic Steering and Policy Committee," no. 97–63. Washington, D.C.: Democratic Steering Group, 1982.

Democrats for the '80s. *Democratic Fact Book: Issues for 1982*. Washington, D.C.:
    Democrats for the '80s, 1982.
Dodd, Lawrence C. "Congress and the Quest for Power." In *Congress Reconsi-
    dered*, edited by Lawrence C. Dodd and Bruce I. Oppenheimer, 269–307.
    New York: Praeger Publishers, 1977.
Drew, Elizabeth. "A Political Journal." *New Yorker*, 28 March 1983, 64–103.
————. *Portrait of an Election: The 1980 Presidential Campaign*. New York: Simon
    & Schuster, 1981.
————. "A Reporter at Large: Politics and Money—I." *New Yorker*, 6 December
    1982, 54–149.
————. "Reporter at Large: The Democratic Party," *New Yorker*, 19 July 1982,
    77.
————. "Reporter at Large: The Democrats." *New Yorker*, 22 March 1982, 130–
    45.
Duverger, Maurice. *Political Parties: Their Organization and Activity in the Modern
    State*. Translation by Barbara and Robert North. New York: John Wiley
    & Sons, Science Editions, 1966.
Dye, Thomas R. "Oligarchic Tendencies in National Policy-Making: The Role of
    the Private Policy-Making Organizations." *Journal of Politics* 40 (May 1978):
    309–31.
Dye, Thomas R., and Zeigler, L. Harmon. *The Irony of Democracy: An Uncommon
    Introduction to American Politics*. Belmont, Calif.: Wadsworth Publishing
    Co., 1970.
Eldersveld, Samuel J. *Political Parties: A Behavioral Analysis*. Chicago: Rand
    McNally, 1964.
Germond, Jack W. and Witcover, Jules. *Blue Smoke and Mirrors: How Reagan Won
    and Why Carter Lost the Election of 1980*. New York: Viking Press, 1981.
Gurwitt, Rob. "Democratic Campaign Panel: New Strategy and New Friends."
    Congressional Quarterly, 2 July 1983, 1346–48.
Harrington, Michael. "A Path for America: Proposals from the Democratic Left."
    Dissent (Fall 1982): 405–24.
Hart, Gary. *A New Democracy*. New York: William Morrow & Co., Quill Edition,
    1983.
Huckshorn, Robert J. *Political Parties in America*. North Scituate, Mass.: Duxbury
    Press, 1980.
Jones, Charles O. "House Leadership in an Age of Reform." In *Understanding
    Congressional Leadership*, edited by Frank H. Mackaman, 117–34. Wash-
    ington, D.C.: Congressional Quarterly Press, 1981.
Jordon, Hamilton. *Crisis: The Last Year of the Carter Presidency*. New York: G. P.
    Putman's Sons, 1982.
Kaus, Robert M. "Reaganism With a Human Face." *New Republic*, 25 November
    1981, 29–36.
Keefe, William J. *Parties, Politics, and Public Policy in America*. 2d ed. Hinsdale,
    Ill.: Dryden Press, 1976.
King, Anthony, ed. *The New American Political System*. Washington, D.C.: Amer-
    ican Enterprise Institute for Public Policy Research, 1978.
Kingdon, John W. *Congressmen's Voting Decisions*. New York: Harper & Row,
    Publishers, 1973.

Ladd, Everett Carll. "The Brittle Mandate: Electoral Dealignment and the 1980 Presidential Election." *Political Science Quarterly* 96 (Spring 1981): 1–25.

Lasswell, Harold, and Kaplan, Abraham. *Power and Society*. New Haven: Yale University Press, 1950.

Longley, Charles H. "National Party Renewal." In *Party Renewal in America: Theory and Practice*, edited by Gerald M. Pomper, 69–86. New York: Praeger, 1981.

MacNeil, Neil. "The Struggle for the House of Representatives." In *A Tide of Discontent: The 1980 Elections and Their Meaning*, edited by Ellis Sandoz and Cecil Crabb, Jr., 65–87. Washington, D.C.: Congressional Quarterly Press, 1981.

Mann, Thomas E. "Elections and Change in Congress." In *The New Congress*, edited by Thomas E. Mann and Norman J. Ornstein, 32–54. Washington, D.C.: American Enterprise Institute for Public Policy Research, 1981.

Mann, Thomas E., and Ornstein, Norman J. "The Republican Surge in Congress." In *American Elections of 1980*, edited by Austin Ranney, 236–302. Washington, D.C.: American Enterprise Institute for Public Policy Research, 1981.

Mayhew, David R. *Congress: The Electoral Connection*. New Haven: Yale University Press, 1974.

Merriam, Charles Edward, and Gosnell, Harold Foote. *The American Party System: An Introduction to the Study of Political Parties in the United States*. New York: Macmillan Co., 1946.

Nimmo, Dan, and Combs, James E. *Subliminal Politics: Myths and Mythmakers in America*. Englewood Cliffs, N.J.: Prentice-Hall, 1980.

O'Neill, Thomas P., with Novak, Michael. *Man of the House: The Life and Political Memoirs of Speaker Tip O'Neill*. New York: Random House, 1987.

Ornstein, Norman J.; Peabody, Robert L.; and Rohde, David W. "The Changing Senate: From the 1950s to the 1970s." In *Congress Reconsidered*, edited by Lawrence C. Dodd and Bruce I. Oppenheimer, 3–20. New York: Praeger Publishers, 1977.

Osborne, David. "Can This Party Be Saved?" *Working Papers for a New Society* 9 (July-August 1982): 36–45.

Polsby, Nelson W. *Consequences of Party Reform*. New York: Oxford University Press, 1983.

———. "Tanks but No Tanks." *Public Opinion* 6 (April/May 1983): 14–16, 58–59.

Polsby, Nelson W., and Wildavsky, Aaron. *Presidential Elections: Strategies of American Electoral Politics*. 6th ed. New York: Charles Scribner's Sons, 1984.

Pomper, Gerald M. "The Contribution of Political Parties to American Democracy." In *Party Renewal in America: Theory and Practice*, edited by Gerald M. Pomper, 1–17. New York: Praeger, 1981.

Pressman, Jeffery L., and Sullivan, Dennis G. "Convention Reform and Conventional Wisdom: An Empirical Assessment of Democratic Party Reforms." In *American Political Institutions in the 1970s*, edited by Demetrios Caraley, 99–122. New York: Columbia University Press, 1976.

Price, David E. *Bringing Back the Parties*. Washington, D.C.: Congressional Quarterly Press, 1984.

Ranney, Austin. *The Doctrine of Responsible Party Government*. Urbana: University of Illinois Press, 1954.

———. *The Federalization of Presidential Primaries*. Washington, D.C.: American Enterprise Institute for Public Policy Reserarch, 1978.

———. "Political Parties: Reform and Decline." In *The New American Political System*, edited by Anthony King, 213–47. Washington, D.C.: American Enterprise Institute for Public Policy Research, 1978.

Report of the Commission on Presidential Nomination. By James B. Hunt, Jr., Chairman. Washington, D.C.: Democratic National Committee, 1982.

Ripon Society. *From Disaster to Distinction: A Republican Rebirth*. New York: Pocket Books, 1966.

Rossiter, Clinton. *Parties and Politics in America*. Ithaca, N.Y.: Cornell University Press, 1960.

Rubin, Richard L. *Party Dynamics: The Democratic Coalition and the Politics of Change*. New York: Oxford University Press, 1976.

Sandoz, Ellis, and Crabb, Cecil, Jr., eds. *A Tide of Discontent: The 1980 Elections and Their Meaning*. Washington, D.C.: Congressional Quarterly Press, 1981.

Scammon, Richard M., and Wattenberg, Ben J. *The Real Majority*. New York: Coward, McCann, & Geohegan, 1970.

Scarrow, Harold A. "The Function of Political Parties: A Critique of the Literature and Approach." *Journal of Politics* 29 (November 1967): 770–90.

Schattschneider, E. E. *Party Government*. New York: Holt, Rinehart & Winston, 1942.

Shafer, Byron E. *The Quiet Revolution: Reform Politics in the Democratic Party, 1968–1972*. New York: Russell Sage Foundation, 1984.

Shogan, Robert. "The Gap: Why Presidents and Parties Fail." *Public Opinion* 5 (August/September 1982): 17–19.

Simon, Paul. *The Once and Future Democrats: Strategies for Change*. New York: Continuum Publishing Co., 1982.

Sorauf, Frank J. *Political Parties in the American System*. Boston: Little, Brown & Co., 1964.

Stewart, John G. *One Last Chance: The Democratic Party, 1974–76*. New York: Praeger Publishers, 1974.

Sundquist, James L. *Dynamics of the Party System: Alignment and Realignment of the Political Parties in the United States*. Washington, D.C.: Brookings Institution, 1973.

Truman, David B. *The Congressional Party: A Case Study*. New York: John Wiley & Sons, 1959.

———. "Party Reform, Party Atrophy, and Constitutional Change: Some Reflections" *Political Science Quarterly* 99 (Winter 1984–85): 637–55.

Tsongas, Paul E. *The Road from Here: Liberalism and Realities in the 1980s*. New York: Random House, Vintage Books, 1981.

Turner, Julius. *Party and Constituency: Pressures on Congress*. Revised and edited by Edward V. Schneier, Jr. Baltimore: Johns Hopkins University Press, 1970.

U.S. Congress. House. Representative Barnes Speaking on the State of the Democratic Party. *Congressional Record*. 97th Cong., 1st sess. 6 February 1981, E417.

Vogler, David J. *The Politics of Congress*. Boston: Allyn & Bacon, 1974.

Wekkin, Gary D. "National-State Party Relations: The Democrats' New Federal Structure." *Political Science Quarterly* 99 (Spring 1984): 45–72.

Wilson, James Q. *The Amateur Democrat: Club Politics in Three Cities*. Chicago: University of Chicago Press, 1966.

Wilson, Woodrow. "Cabinet Government in the United States." In *A Day of Dedication: The Essential Writings and Speeches of Woodrow Wilson*, edited by Albert Fried, 67–79. New York: Macmillan Co., 1965.

Wolfinger, Raymond E. "Policy Formation and Interest Groups." In *Readings in American Political Behavior*, 2d ed., edited by Raymond E. Wolfinger, 227–28. Englewood Cliffs, N.J.: Prentice-Hall, 1970.

Newspaper Accounts and Commentary

Ayers, B. Drummond, Jr. "Kennedy Says Democrats Face Difficult Comeback." *New York Times*, 17 December 1980, 28.

Baker, Ross K. "Democrats '84 Play." *New York Times*, 14 November 1980, 31.

Barone, Michael. "The Battle for the Democratic Party." *Washington Post*, 30 November 1982, A23.

Broder, David G. "Democrats and Unintended Consequences." *Washington Post*, 17 January 1982, A6.

————. "Democrats Agree on '82 Philadelphia Parley," *Washington Post*, 18 September 1981, A6.

————. "Democrats Aiming for Maximum Control Over Mini-Convention," *Washington Post*, 6 June 1981, A3.

————. "Democrats Can't Afford to Be Smug." *Washington Post*, 12 November 1986, A19.

————. "Democrats, Gearing Up for '82, Launch National Training Academies." *Washington Post*, 28 September 1981, A9.

————. "Democrats, In Turnabout, Shrink Size of '82 Mid-Term Convention," *Washington Post*, 6 June 1981, A3.

————. "Democrats Launch a New Policy-Making Council." *Washington Post*, 17 October 1981, A7.

————. "Democrats' New Calendar, Rules May Produce Early Winner," *Washington Post*, 22 August 1983, A2.

————. "Democrats' Policy Session a Big Gamble." *Washington Post*, 19 October 1981, A4.

————. "Diary of a Mad Majority Leader." *Washington Post*, 13 December 1981, C5.

————. "Hill Democrats Grant Amnesty to Boll Weevils." *Washington Post*, 17 September 1981, A1.

————. "A Sudden Outbreak of Democratic Harmony." *Washington Post*, 9 December 1987, A21.

————. "Those Wayward Democrats." *Washington Post*, 12 July 1981, C7.

————. "Top Democrats Struggle to Find Fuel for a Political Comeback," *Washington Post*, 18 October 1981, A3.

Bumiller, Elisabeth. "The Happy Days: Politics Aside, The Democrats Had Fun in Philly." *Washington Post*, 28 June 1982, C3.
———. "Pamela Harriman: The Remarkable Life of the Democrats' Improbable Political Whirlwind." *Washington Post*, 12 June 1983, L3.
Bumiller, Elisabeth, and Romano, Lois. "The Ages of Harriman." *Washington Post*, 13 November 1981, B3.
Clymer, Adam. "Academics Debate Changes in Party Loyalty." *New York Times*, 7 September 1981, A7.
———. "Democrats Seek Party Chairman in Bid For Unity." *New York Times*, 12 November 1980, 1.
———. "Democrats Select Manatt as Chairman," *New York Times*, 28 February 1981, 7.
———. "Two Democratic Leaders Seek Aid for Local Candidates," *New York Times*, 22 November 1980, 8.
———. "What Next? Democrats Seek a Way to Rebound." *New York Times*, 1 March 1981, sec. 4, p. 2.
Dewar, Helen. "Democrats Sticking with Byrd While They Seek New Strategies." *Washington Post*, 14 March 1981, A6.
Dewar, Helen, and Lyons, Richard L. "10 Senators Team Up to Nudge Democrats to Right." *Washington Post*, 31 January 1981, A4.
Dickenson, James R. "Democratic Chairman Asks End to Infighting for '88." *Washington Post*, 12 March 1987, A1.
———. "$900 Million to Elect a Government?" *Washington Post*, 1 August 1982, B4.
Edsall, Thomas B. " 'Atari Democrats' Join Party Conflicts Revived by Gains." *Washington Post*, 7 November 1982, K1.
Greenfield, Meg. "A Stirring Among the Democrats." *Washington Post*, 5 March 1981, A9.
Hornblower, Margot. " 'Horatio at the Bridge': O'Neill Fought Back, Feels Like a Winner." *Washington Post*, 10 October 1982, A12.
Ignatius, David. "But Do the Democrats Deserve a Senate Win?" *Washington Post*, 2 November 1986, C1.
Johnson, Haynes. "Party is Trying to Chart Political Realities of '80s." *Washington Post*, 18 May 1981, A19.
Kaplan, Martin. "Elections Aren't Won By 'New Ideas.' " *Washington Post*, 29 November 1981, C3.
Kraft, Joseph. "Democrats, After Defeat." *Washington Post*, 4 August 1981, A15.
———. "The Struggle Inside . . ." *Washington Post*, 16 November 1980, L7.
Long, Gillis. "Shaping Up the Democrats." *Washington Post*, 5 February 1982, A27.
Marcus, Ruth. "Stubborn: DNC and Vermont May Prefer, But New Hampshire Insists." *Washington Post*, 24 January 1983, A4.
Ornstein, Norman J. "The Democrats' Disease: Reform." *Washington Post*, 1 July 1984, C5.
———. "Paul Tsongas: A Liberal for All Seasons." *Washington Post Book World*, 13 September 1981, 6.
Rauh, Joseph L., Jr. "Dear Charles Manatt . . ." *Washington Post*, 3 March 1981, A13.

Sawyer, Kathy. "Byrd Faults Party Panel in Handling of Election." *Washington Post*, 16 November 1980, A5.

Schram, Martin. "Why Can't Democrats Be More Like Republicans? They're Trying." *Washington Post*, 23 March 1982, A2.

Shields, Mark. "The Democrats' Boutique Politics." *Washington Post*, 11 February 1983, A23.

———. "Democrats, Seize the Rules." *Washington Post*, 21 August 1981, A29.

———. "Don't Underestimate Tip O'Neill." *Washington Post*, 7 August 1981, A15.

Smith, Terrance. "Carter Forseeing Only Limited Role in Rebuilding Party." *New York Times*, 13 November 1980, 1.

Squier, Robert D. "Dear Joseph Rauh (Copy to Charles Manatt) . . ." *Washington Post*, 5 March 1981, A19.

Sweeny, Louise. "Democrats' Boss Has No Time for 'Goofiness.' " *Christian Science Monitor*, 8 September 1982, B8–B11.

Taylor, Paul. "Democratic Alternative Not Ready." *Washington Post*, 16 October 1981, A7.

———. "Democrats Revive Old Tune As GOP Gropes to Write One." *Washington Post*, 1 May 1987, A1.

———. "Democrats Elect Pragmatism Over Ideology." *Washington Post*, 23 September 1986, A4.

———. "New Optimism for Democrats." *Washington Post*, 12 December 1986, A3.

———. "Politics Callapsing Into Blurry Center." *Washington Post*, 9 November 1986, A1.

———. "Robb Keeps Foot in Door To an '88 Campaign." *Washington Post*, 17 October 1986, A10.

———. "Robb Warns Against Catering to Interests." *Washington Post*, 23 June 1987, A9.

———. "Senate to Have 55 Democrats." *Washington Post*, 6 November 1986, A1.

Torricelli, Robert G., and Donilon, Tom. "Reforming the Democrats' Reforms." *Washington Post*, 24 August 1981, A17.

Walsh, Edward. "House Democrats Reelect Six Committee Chairmen." *Washington Post*, 10 December 1986, A8.

Will, George F. "Pushing and Pulling the Party Together." *Washington Post*, 5 March 1981, A19.

Index

Nuclear arms freeze, 72–74, 101, 104, 137

Obert, John C., 134
O'Hara James, 8, 140
O'Hara Commission, 3–5
Ohio, 6
O'Neill, Thomas P. ("Tip"), 23, 46, 53, 84–85, 110, 128, 162; criticism and difficulties with Congress, 92–96; party policy, 55–57
"Open convention, " 12, 34
Ornstein, Norman, 84, 103
Osborne, David, 93–94
Overby, Mary–Margaret, 122

Party "regulars," 40. *See also* Professionals; Elites
Pechman, Joseph, 99
Pennsylvania, 6
Pepper, Claude, 52
Peterson, Bill, 122
Pinaire, Richard A., 78–79
Platform Accountability Committee, 78–79
Policy council, 28, 33, 53–59, 65, 98, 110, 159. *See also* Democratic Advisory Committee; Democratic Advisory Council of Elected Officials; Democratic Policy Council; Democratic Strategy Council
Polsby, Nelson, 1, 19, 34–35, 38–39, 49, 126–27, 130, 142, 147, 159
Pomper, Gerald, 47
Price, David, 4, 6–7, 11–12, 54–55, 98, 100
Primaries: Democratic, 10–11; "loophole," 6, 27; "open," 12, 39; proliferation, 40–41; Super Tuesday, 160; timing, 41–42, 64
Professionals, 120, 122, 141, 146, 154. *See also* Party "regulars"

Quotas, 4, 6, 11, 43

Rangel, Charles, 59–60
Ranney, Austin, 12, 21, 43, 47, 64, 140–41

Rattley, Jesse, 79–80
Rauh, Joseph L., Jr., 28
Realignment, 156
Rebuilding the Road to Opportunity. See Committee on Party Effectiveness
Republican Party, 46, 50, 56
"Responsible party," 13, 20–21, 37, 55
Ripon Society, 101, 120
Robb, Charles S., 160–61
Rossiter, Clinton, 85–86
Rostenkowski, Dan, 94
Rubin, Richard, 21

Sanford, Terry, 7, 121, 123
Sanford Commission. *See* Charter: Sanford Commission
Sawyer, Kathy, 89
Scammon, Richard M., 141–42
Schattschneider, E. E., 17, 148, 154
Schlossberg, Stephen, 99, 121
Schneier, Edward, Jr., 98
Senate Democrats, 57, 90–92, 155, 161–62; factionalism among, 91–92
Shafer, Byron, 30
Shields, Mark, 42–43, 92
Shogan, Robert, 117
Simon, Paul, 76, 103–4, 159
"Six Basic Elements," 2, 37, 43
Smith, Will, 134
Special Equal Rights Committee, 2–4
Spirou, Chris, 42
Squier, Robert, 28
State parties, 7, 34, 46–47, 49
Steinbrunner, Maureen, 121–22, 125–26, 128
Stevenson, Adlai E., III, 123
Stewart, John G., 21, 85
"Stratarchy," 19
Strauss, Robert, 10, 21, 49, 52, 55–56, 60, 80, 131
Sundquist, James, 61, 127
Svahn, John, 52

Taylor, Paul, 57, 160
Thomas, Maria H., 142
Titular leader, 87–88, 157
Truman, David, 1, 59

About the Author

CAROLINE ARDEN, formerly an assistant professor of library and information sciences at the Catholic University of America, is an independent consultant to libraries, government, and public policy organizations.